THE SHAME OF REASON IN ORGANIZATIONAL CHANGE

Issues in Business Ethics

VOLUME 32

For further volumes:
http://www.springer.com/series/6077

The Shame of Reason in Organizational Change

A Levinassian Perspective

by

NAUD VAN DER VEN

Nijmegen University, The Netherlands

Translated by

DAVID BEVAN

University of London, Surrey, UK

 Springer

Dr. Naud Van der Ven
Opera 63
1507 VH Zaandam
The Netherlands
aj.vdven@xs4all.nl

Translator

David Bevan
Royal Holloway, University of London
School of Management
Egham Hill
TW20 0EX Egham, Surrey
United Kingdom
David.Bevan@rhul.ac.uk

ISSN 0925-6733
ISBN 978-90-481-9372-1   e-ISBN 978-90-481-9373-8
DOI 10.1007/978-90-481-9373-8
Springer Dordrecht Heidelberg London New York

Library of Congress Control Number: 2011927920

Printed on acid-free paper

Springer is part of Springer Science+Business Media (www.springer.com)

Preface

Shame exists in many shapes and sizes. We can feel shame for our negligence, our appearance, our family, our car or for our inhumanity.[1] Also, we may find the most diverse forms of shame within work organizations: shame for our lack of professionalism, for your (forbidden) emotions or for the boss. In this book I choose one of a multitude of many possible kinds of shame: I focus on the shame that managers, consultants, trainers – in short, all organizers – may experience in their organizing. And then specifically I focus on those moments at which they receive signals of distress or resistance from their employees or clients that arise as direct a consequence of the organizational rationality which they use as organizers.

Chris Argyris describes this shame in a retrospective on his work as a consultant. He tells how at one time in his career he believed in the concept of double-loop learning.[2] In his view, such a conceptualisation would make it possible to link creative thinking and the democratic participation of employees to change projects: in other words to help create an almost utopian situation. However, at one of the first training sessions he led on the basis of this conceptualisation, and which he presented as a joint research project by himself and by the students, he immediately encountered a fierce resistance, and this prompted him to abandon his plan.

He describes the most devastating moment of this confrontation as follows: "One executive said, in effect, he would cooperate with the research if it helped my (the

---

[1] The phenomenon "shame" is so complex that highly divergent views on the phenomenon can be found among authors who write about it. Nonetheless, based on Lynd (1958), Van Veghel (2003) and Nauta (2003) some four aspects of shame can be designated which regularly figure in philosophical and psychological studies. A first aspect is the feeling that one does not master the situation; shame then is something one cannot do about anything but at the mercy of which one is left. A second aspect is that one feels put on show with respect to the group one belongs to or wants to belong to; an intimate part of oneself is being exposed to the gaze of others while it is not appropriate for publicity. A third frequently noted aspect is the existential nature of shame: our basic trust in life is concerned; we *are* our shame and a sense of meaninglessness may therefore strike. Finally, it is often argued that it is difficult or impossible to talk about shame; it does not want to be revealed and conceals itself as best as possible.

[2] Double-loop learning describes a method of learning with a double content. First, the content is related to monitoring and correcting behavior based on given principles; secondly, to changing these principles themselves.

author's) promotion. I will never forget my reaction that I kept private. Is this what I meant by creating liberating alternatives? Is this what I meant by strengthening justice?" (Argyris 2003: 1185). Shame is here the shock of this being rebuked: in spite of all of my beautiful, thoroughly-rationalised plans and ideas, I am put off by the spontaneous, not even well thought-out resistance of my "objects".

Such shame will be a recurring subject of attention in this book. For that reason I will define its specific character again, in a more precise way. Our subject here will be shame in the context of organizations. This arises when an organizer (i.e. manager, supervisor, consultant) acting in good faith, wants to implement rationally justifiable plans and schemes and in this action encounters the – sometimes enigmatic – resistance of those who are supposed to be subordinate to those plans and schemes. The moment of shame does usually not last long. It may be only a matter of seconds, as it seems was the case with Argyris. But in general, the experience of this shame, as all shame experiences, has a severe impact on the individual who goes through this, albeit very short, moment. Because of the prominent part played in the appearance of the shame by the organizer's well-intended rationality, I will refer to this phenomenon as rationality shame.[3]

The centrality of rationality shame to this book is reflected in the subtitle of the Dutch edition: Thinking about organizational change in the light of the philosophy of Emmanuel Levinas. I shall suggest that for Levinas, rationality shame is much more than an embarrassing moment. It is also the inception of a new, qualitatively improved rationality and as such it offers opportunities for change. It is the creative potential of rationality shame that makes it possible to connect such diverse areas as organization studies and the philosophy of Levinas. But why would one wish to make such a connection? I am doubly motivated in suggesting this connection.

Firstly, I am fascinated by the philosophy of Levinas, and in particular by his observation of a fundamental deficit in Western philosophy that manifests itself as a poverty of meaning in many of its principal tenets. Levinas analyzes this deficit of meaning and relates it to the neglect in the Western tradition for a fundamental source of meaning – the Other. The Other – as such – has never been fully theorised in Western philosophy. I find it intriguing that such an analysis seems to provide numerous possibilities for identifying in a concrete way – namely in the interaction between people – matters which hitherto were only discussed in abstract terms.

Secondly, and working as a quality organizer in an organization, I get to read a lot of management literature. It strikes me that, although interaction between people often is raised as a topic, no use is being made of insights in this area that a reading of Levinas' philosophy provides. True, the problems you may run into are not small,

---

[3] It seems that the four often mentioned aspects of shame (see note on p. v) do not all four manifest themselves equally strong with respect to rationality shame. Prominently present in rationality shame are, as we shall see in the sequel, the first aspect (of the broken control) and the third aspect (the basic trust in life is being touched). The second aspect (one feels being exposed to the gaze of others) seems to play a lesser role: one feels particularly put on show for oneself. The fourth aspect (the shame is not or hardly communicable) is partially reflected in rationality shame, but – see, for example the story of Argyris – not to an insurmountable degree.

because even though Levinas has the tendency to be practical or concrete, he tells a story that remains entirely within the language field of philosophy. No sympathizer of Levinas can avoid the fact that intensive translation has to be done for his work to be understood outside the field of philosophy. But that is not to say that his work is unworldly or naïve. And it says nothing about the possible relevance to organization studies of at least some of his thoughts. To bring about the envisaged connection between Levinas and organization studies I select the perspective of organizational change, and again for two reasons.

In the first place it is striking to observe that in management literature organizational change continues to be a recurrent problem that is widely discussed. That is evident from the large number of publications that point to the failure of change projects and from the many management book titles that have change as their subject. This observation reflects the mysterious kind of powerlessness that I discuss in Chapter 1 under the title "the glass ceiling of organizational change". This powerlessness shows a certain affinity with the mysteriousness that Levinas finds around the encounter with the Other and such a parallel suggests possibilities for connection.

In the second place, organizational change may be understood as an enlargement of all forms of management and organization. As long as organizing and managing continue to be associated by many with the development and implementation of strategy and with the application of planning and control in primary and secondary processes, then improvement measures in response to identified deficiencies are implied as a standard part of management. By definition then this implicates the creation of a new situation of change. We must get things done, not least by employees. From such a perspective the difference between ordinary management and change management is gradual, and mainly a matter of intensity and scale. Change is a kind of turbo-management. I am confirmed in this view by the overwhelming number of management books that have change for their subject and that are aimed at managers, not necessarily in their role as change manager, but as ordinary manager. This suggests to me that managing and changing, to some extent, run parallel to each other and that problems that we identify in change management can be understood as problems of management in general. On this basis I can use the enlargement of problems and the enhanced reflection on them which the change literature has to offer. Its results can be used fruitfully for reflection on "normal" management and may even cover a large part of the organization studies field.

So, the intention of this book is to establish a connection between organization studies and philosophy of Levinas through the themes of organizational change and embarrassment. However, before that connection can be established, it is necessary that we follow a trail that takes in completely different subjects that are seemingly far removed from both organizational change and shame.

The starting point of the trail suggested in Chapter 1, is the observation that in organization studies there is a lot of reflection on organizational change. At the same time we find that a number of these approaches, despite their thoughtful nature, are incongruent or dissonant with each other. A kind of glass ceiling seems to hang over the field of change. Some authors suggest that the incongruence is based in problems inherent to rationality while others suggest it is more to do with a radical resistance to be captured by that rationality. The chapter explores – in a necessarily superficial way – whether such a suggestion offers points of contact with Levinas because his philosophy thematizes those same matters. The aim of this study can then be formulated as to examine the contribution that Levinas can provide to clarifying the enigma's that change problems put before us, through his discussion of these two themes.

However, this theme of problematic rationality requires that we first – in the course of Chapters 2 and 3 – take a detour. The reason for this is that Levinas himself is situated in a philosophical tradition that already problematized rationality, and in the course of that problematizing made use of specific terms and concepts. The same applies to the management authors who problematize rationality: they stand in an organization studies scholarly tradition with its own specific terms and concepts. Before the thinking of Levinas can be considered relevant to organization studies, we may have to acknowledge that there are sufficient similarities in the way that both traditions apperceive the problematization. As a result of this exercise, it will turn out that the philosophical tradition in which Levinas finds himself on the one hand, and organization studies on the other hand, reflect on the theme of problematic rationality in a related way. To a great extent we shall see that both sides lead the problem(s) back to reification and to the way in which the human mind functions, summed up in the term "representation". The problems entailed by representation can be summarized under the headings deception and exclusion.

In Chapter 3, I take this view in order to discuss responses to problematic rationality from two other philosophical currents, prior to the presentation of Levinas' treatment of representation and for the sake of comparison. The post-modernist[4] philosophy of Foucault and Derrida and the thinking of Heidegger and Wittgenstein leave a trail through organization studies scholarship. I shall try to determine the extent to which deception and exclusion, as symptoms of problematic rationality, can effectively be countered by these authors.

In Chapter 4, I present Levinas' treatment of the issue of problematic rationality, seen as such a problem of representation. It will appear, from the way he approaches this problem, that at the same time the theme of the enigmatic resistance becomes the subject of attention. The presentation of issues that is ultimately given by Levinas, can be considered as his elaboration of the two original themes from Chapter 1: problematic rationality and radical resistance to encapsulation. He

---

[4]The term "post-modernist" is controversial and has varying interpretations. I use the term because the organization studies literature which I draw on does so as well. Within this literature, and following on that within this book, "postmodernism" refers to positions in the areas of knowledge and ontology. It represents the view that "[w] hat passes for truth or objective knowledge depends not only on the applied research methods, but also on implicit and explicit agreements within the scientific community, on networks of influential scientists and on power and morality" (Boomkens 2003: 84; translation NvdV). "Post-modernist" thus refers to a theoretical positioning and as such should be distinguished from the adjective "postmodern" which refers to a sociological or cultural situation.

brings together these two issues in a vision in which the deficiency of rationality, resistance to that deficiency, rationality shame and a new beginning are all connected. Combined, they constitute a new way of thinking and talking about both rationality and resistance, directly put in terms of change. For the articulation of this vision Levinas takes recourse to idiosyncratic language and some original concepts.

Up to this point, the presentation of Levinas has taken place within the field of philosophy. The challenge for us in this book is whether and how Levinas' presentation of these issues can be expressed also in terms borrowed from the world of organizing and organizations. It is the aim of Chapter 5 to realise this challenge. Primarily I carry out that realisation by examining the extent to which Levinas' thinking resonates within the organization studies literature. This appears partly to be the case, but not for some important aspects of Levinas' themes. Secondarily, therefore, I present some empirical or practice cases in which organizers tell what of my rendering of Levinas' descriptions they recognize. This shows that the presented vision of rationality shame can fully manifest itself in organizations.

Contents

Editing Translator's Introduction

*The translator must translate the meaning to be understood
into the context in which the other speaker lives . . ./. . . thus
every translation is at the same time an interpretation
(Gadamer, 1975: 386)*

In the context of the work that follows, the epigraph from Gadamer's work "Language as the medium of hermeneutic experience" is deliberate and appropriate. Reading Levinas is indeed a laborious and attention-consuming process of translation, or hermeneutic conversation. As the following text will show, Van der Ven's study is also itself a labour of elaborate care and patience that brings to Anglophone readers a number of original insights. These arise not only from the overall purpose of the book – to make clear the relevance of Levinas for organizational managers, academics and students – but in a number of particularities. I shall hope to refer to some of these later in the course of this appreciative introduction.

What Have I Done?

Essentially my contribution to the publication of this work in English has been to take a literal translation of the author's work from Dutch into English, and to translate this into an English that will be readily readable to Anglophone managers, management and organisation studies scholars. I have no doubt that it will have significance also for readers, students and followers of Emmanuel Levinas.

The final text, including the choice of words, is largely unchanged from Van der Ven's first drafts. What has changed substantively is the sequencing of these words. The approach I have taken is simply to attempt to render the work into my native language. This involved transposing Dutch syntax and particularly the sequencing of adjectival clauses and phrases, into the English mode. The process has given me some insights into the possible origin of the archaic English tag "double Dutch" to mean confusing. Nonetheless by changing as few words as possible I trust I have remained true to the author's original work. There were contextual particularities however.

In some cases this would be around a specific word – like "the ratio" – which in my experience is rarely used in contemporary English in the sense it is used in Dutch. After more than one extensive discussion over a period of some months, Naud chose to use "rationality", and in some cases "(R)eason", as the best substitute(s). There was much discussion between us about Levinassian terminology and particularly the use of the other/Other. As Levinas himself seemed to offer no consistent notation, and given that such eminent authorities as Lingis and Spivak appear unable to agree on such refinements – here, with the author's agreement, we perpetuate an inconsistent approach to its precise orthography. Other troublesome words, not to say concepts, included "capture", or Naud's preference for "encapsulation" to propose a verb which equates to the rational activity of reducing an experience to a palatable, or understandable, morsel.

How I Came to Be Doing This . . .

I first came across Naud's work – referenced in contributions – at the University of Leicester in the summer of 2005. The occasion was a Levinas symposium organised by Campbell Jones. The symposium was to discuss potential papers for a Special Issue of "Business Ethics: a European Review" (Volume 16, Issue iii, 2007). At the time, I was undertaking my research training at the Management Department of King's College London with the accounting research group lead by Richard Laughlin and supervised there by Jeffrey Unerman. My research into managers' experience of accountability in publically quoted multinational firms had taken a Levinassian turn as the result of my reading of work by Teri Shearer (2002) and John Roberts (2001). Both these authors – one contributing to critical accounting and the other to organisation studies/business ethics – foreground the phenomenologically informed ethics of Emmanuel Levinas. This discovery and a fuller reading of Levinassian ethics provided a theoretical lens for my research sites and made it possible to problematise the legitimacy of such organisations as fields of totalisation.

I began to follow Naud's practice through his web log communications – which provide regular original insights from his practice: this practice features as an empirical emphasis to the critical relevance of the book in organizational interventions. I finally met Naud in person in Bristol, at the UK European Business Ethics Network conference at the University of the West of England in 2009. After some extensive discussion we agreed that I would assist him with translating the book from Dutch into English. We tried exploring one chapter to begin with and when that seemed to work out, we continued with the rest of the book chapters. The original book in Dutch was taken from Naud's doctoral thesis, supervised by Rene Ten Bos. Now in translation in English, he has added a foreword and a reflective afterword.

Levinas and Management

With the exception of a few papers – such as those I found in Accounting, Organization & Society and Business Ethics Quarterly – Levinas is not by any means a big name in management scholarship or practice by comparison with Michael Porter, nor yet more reasonably compared to Michael Foucault or Jacques Derrida. My own attempts to read Levinas reveal him to be an enigmatic and recondite interest – so, perfect for an innovative doctoral thesis.

The capable administrator of the philosophy department at my university politely listened as I asked for guidance and swiftly directed me to the French department – "it's not actually philosophy you know". Even there, while Foucault and Derrida were well spoken for, I could only find that there were other places I needed to look for interest in scholarship with a Levinassian focus. So the reading group set up by Campbell Jones – taking a small group of avid readers through first "Totality and infinity" and then "Otherwise than being, or beyond essence" in 2004/2005 was a rare find. It is not my role here to provide a bibliography of Levinas, much of which becomes clear in the course of Van der Ven's text.

The point is to begin with acknowledging the scarcity of any explicit appreciation for Levinas's work in the fields of management and organisation studies scholarship and practice on a scale anywhere approaching its potential value. On this basis, the work Van der Ven has done here is of great potential. As I shall review in the next section, this is a work of elaborate scholarship and care which will make clearer to any reader the prospective value of Levinas's impact on a wide area of management and encompassing all organisational relations. Whether you have only just become aware of Levinas in picking up this book, or whether you have read any amount of management literature along with Levinas's original works and commentaries, the taxonomy and content are organised as a revelation of analytic insights into the momentous contribution Levinas can bring to management scholarship and practice.

The Contribution of This Book

In the author's preface which precedes this introduction, Van der Ven explains to you the journey you are about to undertake both overall and chapter by chapter: further rehearsal or anticipation is superfluous. My appreciation here is more of a reflection on the evident contribution of this book for someone who has read neither as widely as the author, nor come to as many thoughtful interpretations as are here presented in an integrated revelation.

In many cases this arises because he finds and presents commentaries on Levinas which have not previously been made available in English. This enriches the reading and the advancement of arguments considerably. The bibliography is scattered with examples of work which focuses on Levinas in particular, and which supports the notion that Levinas is an under-exploited resource in Anglophone management literature by comparison with the work available (principally) in Dutch.

The enigmatic focus in this work is the embarrassment inherent in change as mediated by reason, and the relevance of Levinas' ontological insights to that specific context. Given that almost all organizational behaviour is in some way related to change – and in particular the management (that is to say the opitimizing and/or constraining) of that change – one early and difficult implication for managers and academics alike, is that management is itself a nexus of embarrassment. This is not a particularly easy story to sell in mainstream business practice, or education, as the Western view of management is one which takes itself as highly respectable and unquestionably legitimate (Jackson 2005). It is nonetheless compellingly relevant for those who are bold enough to see the ramifications for managerial practice, organizational change and education.

As for this practice of embarrassment, I experience it personally and daily in almost every single institutional transaction that twenty-first century life impersonally constructs. It is present, indicatively, in the way that tasks are modelled around a rigid work load; how I am managed (abused) from a distance; the imperious, abrupt and whimsical changing of plans; the always increasing demand for greater/faster performance; the surreal inadequacy of all institutional communication; the derisory and careless treatment of the client/employee relation(ship); the extended hours of intrusive access to personal time – all the gifts (or, to be indulgent, the unintended consequences) of technology. Technology, which largely and impartially hastens us to an albeit collateral oblivion.

These multifarious embarrassments resonate with my reading of organizational sociology, successively, in Ulrich Beck's (1992) precarious modernity replete with risk, in Zygmunt Bauman's (1993) theorisation of the structural and morally palliative purposiveness of bureaucracy; with Robert Jackal's (2000) observed tyranny of organizational pragmatism; in Courpasson's (2000, 2006) managerial domimation, and with Claudia Card's (2005) inscription of institutional evil. The embarrassment has been perhaps always present in rationalised relations, but it is exacerbated anecdotally, as well as experientially, by the relentless financialisation of life in the process of commercial globalization and technological advances since the 1980s. Consequently, unhappiness at work is widespread if not endemic (Steiler, Sadowsky, & Roche, 2010).

Van der Ven seeks to explain his insights to a clearly defined audience: management practitioners – managers, trainers and consultants who are dealing with change – and because of their interest in this field, he includes scholars and students of organisational behaviour. Van der Ven seems not to envisage introducing the relevance of the philosophy of Levinas to analytic philosophers – that is perhaps within the scope of a subsequent work. This exclusion is also somewhat predictable as Van der Ven will explain in the course of the text. It is not my place to rehearse the entire book in advance of his carefully arranged arguments. The effective and practical schism between Levinas and the Western philosophical tradition is categorically *unreasonable*, and on that basis Levinas is bracketed among continental philosophers. "Continental" in common usage is simply a polite term for inconvenient: continental philosophy, and in particular as here where it repudiates and dismisses the sovereign orthodox epistemological legitimacy of positivism, is most uncomfortable and inconvenient for the totality of Western thought. This discomfort is cognate with the embarrassment or shame of reason central to the institutional projects in which apparently we are all enmeshed.

The problem of knowledge so radically simplified in Levinas, is central to the work of other writers who also are marginalised as continental philosophers or sociologists. Not least among these Pierre Bourdieu (2002) and Derrida (2001) whose work may be seen to exemplify the crisis suggested by Merleau-Ponty:

> Philosophy and sociology have long lived under a segregated system which has succeeded in concealing their rivalry only by refusing them any meeting-ground, impeding their growth, making them incomprehensible to one another, and thus placing culture in a situation of permanent crisis (1964: 98)

Van der Ven makes it quite clear in the course of his unravelling of Levinas that this incomprehensibility is entirely grounded in the defects of rationalism. This tends to suggest that Merleau-Ponty's adjudication is arbitrary and provisional and that analytic philosophy – in the embrace of rational positivism – is at best unreliable. For Van der Ven however, these defects of rationalism do not implicate a dichotomous relation between rationalism and emotion (for example). Indeed he insists that he does not agree with the playing off – as in Merleau-Ponty – of one against the other. Rather, and employing Levinassian argument, Van der Ven advocates an opposing relation between emotion and rationality as knowing or knowable on one side, and unknowing/unknowable mystery on the other side. In this he imitates or at least borrows from Levinas' formulation of totality as a necessarily incomplete understanding of irreducible infinity.

An original deconstruction of mainly postmodern writing traces the origins of Van der Ven's insights into the defects of rationalism. These are largely constructed from an intricate and meticulously insightful re-reading of Chia (1996) along with previously un-translated work of Ten Bos (2000) to articulate a formidable critique of functionalism and representationalism. Against this background, Van der Ven then turns to rationality and rationalism in Western philosophy and its basis in Descartes. Employing Weber's characterisation of instrumental rationalism, he locates the totalizing project of rationality which along with its inherent power to deceive, leads to the highly problematic issues of representationalism and scientism. This problematic formulation of occidental interests opens up the structural potential for the organizational dystopia with which we all live, organized around the preposterous managerialist fallacy of certainty. I leave to Van der Ven the elaboration of why Levinas is relevant to this context.

It is not plausible to suggest that we could live better enitrely without reason; nor even without institutions of some kind. Van der Ven however shows that Levinas has an explicit contribution to make to improving organization studies and management education and practice.

Acknowledgements I would like to conclude this appreciation with an acknowledgement for their helpful comments to Campbell Jones, Mollie Painter Moreland and Rene Ten Bos, and finally to express my thanks to Naud Van der Ven for his patience and forbearance in working with me to bring this edition to the attention of English speaking readers.

Grenoble, France   David Bevan
February 2011

References

Bauman, Z. 1993. *Postmodern ethics*. Oxford: Blackwell.

Beck, U. 1992. *Risk society: Towards a new modernity* (trans: Ritter, M.). London: Sage.

Bourdieu, P. 2002. *Outline of a theory of practice* (trans: Nice, R.). Cambridge: Cambridge University Press.

Card, C. 2005. *The atrocity paradigm: A theory of evil*. Oxford: Oxford University Press.

Chia, R. 1996. *Organizational analysis as deconstructive practice*. Berlin: Walter de Gruyter & Co.

Courpasson, D. 2000, 2006. *Soft constraint: Liberal organizations and domination*. Copenhagen: Liber and Copenhagen Business School Press.

Derrida, J. 2001. Structure, sign and play in the discourse of the human sciences. In *Writing and difference*, ed. A. Bass, 351–370. London: Routledge.

Gadamer, H.-G. 1975. *Truth and method* (trans: Weinsheimer, J., and Marshall, D.G.). London: Continuum.

Jackall, R. 2000. *Moral mazes: The world of corporate managers*. Oxford: Oxford University Press.

Jackson, I. 2005. The corporation: Transcripts. In eds. M. Achbar, J. Abbott, and J. Bakan. Canada: Metrodome.

Merleau-Ponty, M. 1964. *Signs*. Evanston, IL: Northwestern University Press.

Roberts, J. 2001. Corporate governance and the ethics of narcissus. *Business Ethics Quarterly* 11 (1): 109–127.

Shearer, T. 2002. Ethics and accountability: From the for-itself to the for-the-other. *Accounting, Organizations and Society* 27: 541–573.

Steiler, D., J. Sadowsky, and L. Roche. 2010. *Eloge du bien être au travail*. Grenoble, FR: Presses universitaires de Grenoble.

Ten Bos, R. 2000. *Fashion and utopia in management thinking*. Tilburg, NL: Proefschrift Katholieke Universiteit Brabant.

David Bevan PhD (King's College London); Professor of Applied Ethics and Management, Grenoble Graduate Business School; Academic Director of the Academy of Business in Society (EABIS); Senior Wicklander Fellow at the Institute for Professional and Business Ethics (DePaul); member of the Editorial Board at the Professional and Business Ethics Journal. He has designed and delivered courses in Applied Ethics and Sustainability in numerous universities and business schools including King's College London; Royal Holloway, University of London; and, HEC Paris.

Chapter 1
Introduction

In this first chapter I touch upon a number of themes with the intention of giving an impression of the field to be covered. These themes are successively: organizational change and related issues; points of contact between the organization studies literature and Levinas that point forward to topics that will be developed further in this book; and finally, the formulation of a central question that will guide these elaborations.

This book reflects on organizational behaviour. In this reflection it relies on the thinking about organizational behaviour presented by many other authors. I will present those authors without systematically making distinctions between them, whether they are practitioners or theorists, management gurus or academics. It appears that critical and refreshing ideas are not the monopoly of one of these groups, but are distributed among them. Equally, problematic conceptualisations, naïvete and dogmatic thinking are not confined to one group, but found among all of them. My motivation in referring to such author(s), is that he or she reflects on organizational behaviour and change, and puts forward ideas which are interesting in relation to my theme.

I make no sharp distinction between the literatures of "management", "organizational behaviour" and "change". The primary reason for this is that I approach the field of basic assumptions regarding rationality, knowledge and science, which I hold to be valid throughout the realm of the social sciences. Knowledge about change and organizational behaviour are based on these assumptions.

The second reason is that I conceive of "change" in a specific sense. As I have indicated in the Preface, in an organizational context both "management" and "change management" become unified to some extent in each other's continuation. Change in organizations, within the framework of this book, will be associated with the following type of issues: how to initiate and maintain momentum? how to motivate people? The justification for choosing such an approach comes from the observation later in this chapter in which I find that in cases where the failure or success of change initiatives cannot be explained (entirely), the human factor and the extent to which that factor can be influenced plays a leading part. By relating the potential for change to opportunities to influence organization members, any dividing line between changing and managing becomes indistinct. In both activities

N. Van der Ven, *The Shame of Reason in Organizational Change*, Issues in Business Ethics 32, DOI 10.1007/978-90-481-9373-8_1, © Springer Science+Business Media B.V. 2011

people wrestle with the above questions, so the difference is only gradual: similar problems get a more pregnant character to the extent that change is more explicitly formulated as a goal.

Therefore, the change-*work* that I have in mind in the context of organizations includes such diverse matters as: the efforts of a team leader, in streamlining work processes, to get his team members to do their registrations in a spreadsheet rather than on paper; the actions of a Quality Director to improve the alertness of his workers when they undertake quality checks; the launching of a plan by a CEO to tilt the organization to better respond to the requirements of the market. According to conventional classifications, the first two actions would be likely to be classified as "management" because they can be regarded as improvement measures resulting from the planning and control routines. The third action – the intervention by a CEO – would be more likely to be interpreted as a form of change management. When, however, the influencing of organizational fellow members is considered as a crucial aspect of change – and that is my position, – all three actions can be considered a form of change.

A consequence of this view of change in organizations is that the role of change agent can be played by various officials within and outside the organization. I shall consider anyone as change agent if he or she tries to bring organization members to new behaviour with a view to the interest of the organization. Such a role may be played by (for example) a team leader, a consultant, a coach, or a supervisor. Here and for the sake of simplicity I will refer to them as "managers", because they are frequently in the role of change agents.

Organizational Change and the Glass Ceiling

Organizational Change: A Much Discussed Topic

How do you bring about change in an organization? This question is raised in many books on management and organization. The question may relate to various aspects of the organization, such as cooperation, the product range, the capacity for learning or the design of work processes. It is a theme in popular management literature, as shown by the volume of new titles each successive year dealing with the art of change: Total Quality Management (TQM); Business Process Redesign (BPR); product innovation; motivating employees; corporate social responsibility (CSR); and sustainability/sustainable development. Organizational academics, both those within that group who analyze concrete organization problems, and those who study organizations from a philosophical perspective, are also occupied by this question.

The way in which the question of change potential in organizations is treated in the management literature differs according to each author. Examples from popular literature can be found in the work of Senge, Kotter and De Caluwe. Senge, in *The Dance of Change* (2000), relates change to the learning capacity of an organization.

Kotter, in cooperation with Cohen in *The heart of change* (2002) presents a plan of eight steps or phases for the successful completion of a change plan. De Caluwe and Vermaak in *Leren veranderen* (1999) distinguish different situations for which appropriate change models are offered.

To illustrate the diversity of treatment of the change management issue in the academic literature, authors such as Lewin, Kanter, Stein, Jick, Gagliardi and Chia can be mentioned. In the 1950s Lewin presented his model of change as a cycle of unfreezing, change and refreezing. Kanter, Stein and Jick protest in *The Challenge of Organizational Change* (1992) about the over-simplification of such an approach. They suggest that organizational change is a complex, layered process. Gagliardi (1986) approaches change issues from the perspective of organizational culture and then distinguishes apparent change, revolutionary change and changes that are culturally anchored. Chia in his book *Organizational analysis as deconstructive practice* (1996) offers a post-modernist perspective for augmenting possibilities of change in organizations.

It is remarkable, amidst this multiplicity of themes and perspectives, that many authors have one thing in common: a high degree of attention for motivating employees and, in conjunction therewith, for leadership. Jacques suggests in his book *Manufacturing the Employee*: "At the center of the present knowledge management universe are the interrelated topics of motivation and leadership" (1996: 159). The motivation and leadership issues are often raised because authors consider them as non-negligible part of, or condition for the specific organizational change which their book envisages. The importance of those issues is also reflected in those book titles which focus on them as their main theme as in *How do I get them there?* (Van Luijk 2003) or *The 7 characteristics of effective leadership* (Covey 1997).

Desirability of Change

It is striking that a certain prestige seems to be linked to change, which suggests that managers like to identify with change. The presupposition is that change is good. The question whether change in organizations is desirable is answered positively by almost all authors. But they do not all have the same kind of changes in mind, and on the basis of those differences, also the motives why they want to change vary widely. A review of selected literature reveals the following possible positions.

First there is the so-called managerial position: to stay ahead of the competition in a rapidly changing, globalizing world, change is good and necessary. This position is dominant, i.e. taken by far the largest part of the authors, as evidenced by surveys of Armenakis and Bedeian (1999), Pettigrew et al. (2001) and Van de Ven and Poole (1995). Then there is the view of many advocates of the Critical Management Studies. This group of authors, including, for example, Hugh Willmott (1993), Mats Alvesson and Hugh Willmott (1992) and Campbell Jones (2003b), emphatically takes the promoting in a structural way of the emancipation and participation of employees in the organization, as its goal. Such a goal requires major changes in the way organizations function, so change (provided it goes in the right direction) is also good and desirable for them. The author Björn Gustavsen, who will be referred to later in this book, is a supporter of this position, even if he has little connection to the current which presents itself under the name Critical Management Studies, and of which an account is to be found in the article *In de naam van kritiek* by Spoelstra (2004). A third position, the post-modernist one, is more explicitly philosophical in nature. It departs from the idea that there is any such thing as a stable reality and that everything is in a constant state of construction and, therewith, of change. So the main issue here is not so much to bring about change (because there is already and always change), but to lift any blockages to change and thus to do more justice to reality. Allowing change is desirable and worthy to strive after. Gergen (1992) and Chia (1996) are exponents of this view to which a special edition of the journal *Organization* (2000, 7 (3)) is dedicated. A fourth position focuses on people in organizations. Authors within this current such as Chris Argyris (1957, 1982) and Jacques Roy (1996, 1999), stress the value of personal growth. Transformation that people can experience is regarded as an intrinsic good. Change here is above all a matter of personal and collective learning. This position is reflected in the HRM-special of *Organization* (1999, 6 (2)).

The views reviewed above may occur, overlap and conflate with one another. Their supporters have in common an appreciation of change as something positive and rational. They interpret resistance to change as irrational or, for instance in the case of a number of critical management authors, as politically objectionable, or both. Together they cover almost the entire field of management literature. Only a few authors venture to question the obvious desirability of change in organizations. So for example Sturdy and Gray speak about the change totalitarianism that tends to demonize and pathologize any resistance to change (2003: 655). But these are not representative. The vast majority of authors is open to change. This may explain why there are so many reflections and publications on the subject of change. In what follows I will take the desirability of change as a starting point.

Current Approaches to Organizational Change

What are the main approaches that are applied to achieve desired change in organizations? In his introduction to *Dynamics of Organizational Change and Learning* (Boonstra 2004a), a handbook on organizational change, Boonstra indicates that roughly two common approaches can be distinguished with respect to organizational change. One is the Planned Change approach (also called first-order change), the second is the Organizational Development approach (also called second-order change).

Boonstra (2004a: 5–7) describes Planned Change as a conscious and deliberate attempt to adjust and improve the functioning of a human system by making use of scientific knowledge. The approach is based on the assumption that an organization should be in a state of balance, both internally and in relation to the outside world. If the environment changes, the organization must move from equilibrium-stage A to equilibrium-state B. This change process can be planned in a rational way, controlled by such means as environmental analysis, goal formulation, strategy development and strategy implementation. Feedback mechanisms and interventions ensure control during this change process. Because of the importance attached to scientific justification, well-defined methodologies themselves play an important role. They should be applied by change agents, i.e. experts who initiate and lead change by using socio-psychological theories and behavioural knowledge.

> The approach is solution-oriented and decision-making is mostly highly structured and formalized and greatly influenced by top management. Decisions are made based largely on economic and technical arguments. The method of change is based on formal models in order to reduce the complexity of the organization. Generally valid uniform work rules and procedures are adhered to. The change process usually has a linear structure with a clear beginning and end and with strict standards and planning (...) Little attention is given to increasing the learning capacity within the organization. It is difficult to enlist the participation of the people in the organization because existing work procedures are consciously pushed aside. (Boonstra 2004a: 6)

Planned Change is also called "first-order change". This means that both the problem which is to be solved and the solution are known at the start of the change process and can be formulated in technical terms. Examples of the Planned Change approach are Business Process Redesign, Management by Objectives, Total Quality Management, ISO Certification and the Balanced Scorecard.

Organizational Development is linked by Boonstra (2004a) to second-order change, i.e. to situations where the problems to be solved are known but vague, and where the way to solve them is not yet clear.

> Second-order changes focus on renewal and innovation. Once the organization's leaders and change agents have assessed the existing needs and opportunities, they develop a more desirable future state. To achieve this new state, the old way of working must be set aside and the organization must pass through a period of transition when it is not yet out of the old and not yet fully in the new. During the course of the change process, the aspects that inhibit this transition are examined, and the change agents and consultants try to eliminate these obstacles by means of interventions. (Boonstra 2004a: 9)

For these interventions systematic use, on a larger scale than for Planned Change, of principles from the behavioural sciences and social psychology is made. This has led to a range of methods and techniques that purport to increase individual and organizational effectiveness like Conflict Management, Team Development, Cultural Change, Empowerment and Personal Effectiveness. Human Resource Management (HRM) is connected closely to Organizational Development.

> In general, a process of organizational development starts with an analysis by all parties concerned of problems and possible solutions. The changes are realized gradually, and the members of the organization are involved in all phases of the change process. Experts provide support by contributing their experience of change processes and by facilitating the change process. The procedures and methods are highly dependent on the course of the change process. A coordinating and guiding framework and guidance of the process by managers and process experts are often necessary to accomplish the changes. (Boonstra 2004a: 9)

Glass Ceiling

The methodical approach and the striving for scientific justification that characterize both Planned Change and Organizational Development might suggest that both approaches are successful and produce good results. I suggest this is a false rationalisation. On page 1 of his manual Boonstra (2004a: 1) writes:

> More than 70 per cent of the change programs in organizations either stall prematurely or fail to achieve their intended result. Goals are not achieved, policies are not implemented, customers do not experience improvement in service and quality, and employees, supervisory staff, and middle management are confused by all the change efforts. In the USA, by far the majority of the attempts to redesign business processes turn out to be in vain (Bashein et al., 1994). The development of new strategies also runs aground in 75 per cent of cases (Beer et al., 1990). A study by Pettigrew (1987, 1988) in the UK showed that many change programs, such as total quality management, business process redesign, and empowerment, are unsuccessful. A study of change processes in the Netherlands showed that more than 70 per cent of the change programs lead to poor results (Boonstra, 2000). (Boonstra 2004a: 1)

Such an observation, also made by many others,[1] has of course a provocative effect on the change-minded popular and academic management literature. The failure of so many change projects surely calls for further reflection and research into the causes of failure and for proposals for improvement. This impulse may be one explanation for the continuous flow of publications that deal with change. Boonstra offers starting-points for reflection on the high failure rate in the manner in which he evaluates the two common approaches. Regarding Planned Change he says: "This is a useful approach in the case of readily definable problems that are not too complex and do not involve too many people. However, many changes do not satisfy these conditions" (Boonstra 2004a: 7). If one nevertheless makes the choice for Planned Change and it fails, then soon the blame – according to Boonstra – is assigned to rigid structures and cultures. That is: to exactly those aspects of organization that are neglected. This self-deception probably explains why the majority still opts for Planned Change, while it is known that in three quarters of the cases this leads to problems. As to Organizational Development, Boonstra (2004a: 9) believes that this approach is certainly effective, but that the risk of paternalism is lurking and with it the potential for manipulation and social engineering. Apparently these dangers cooked the goose of many a change process of this type, given their disappointing results in the end.

Impotence

This state of affairs may easily arouse feelings of powerlessness. Indeed, the usual interventions wear themselves out: by pursuing methodical approaches to change, they work hard to justify their approaches scientifically and yet it does not seem to get anywhere. There seems to be a glass ceiling above the field which prevents the change-minded with all their good behaviour achieving the desired results. "Anyone

---

[1] For example Sichtman (2005), Ten Have and Ten Have (2003), Scott-Morgan et al. (2001).

for *real* change?" Böhm and Jones (2003: 165) exclaim. And Blaug notes that "For some reason, organizationally, we do not learn".

In his reflection on the impotence he observed, Boonstra (2004a: 11) suggests that most problems may not be of the first or second order anymore, so Planned Change and Organizational Development may be the wrong answers. There are actually, by globalization and growing complexity, increasingly more third-order problems which he describes as "ambiguous questions and poorly defined problems, where situations are unstable, and interaction patterns are unpredictable" (2004: 11). According to Boonstra, the answer to these problems should no longer be sought in improvement projects or change processes *within* organizations, but in innovation processes in which employees *from several organizations* are involved. This is third-order, or transformational, change. That this suggestion does not lead us straight away to an operational formulation may be explained by Weick and Quinn's (2004) presentation of third-order change: "Recently, it has been proposed that there exists a third order of change that basically questions the adequacy or schemas themselves and argues for direct exposure to the "ground for conceptual understanding" in the form of music, painting, dance, poetry or mystical experience. Organizational change thus gains intellectual power through alignment with aesthetics (. . .)" (2004: 181, 182).

But Weick and Quinn (2004) goes beyond these rather vague-looking proposals for third-order change. It presents an approach for third-order problems under the heading Continuous Change (2004: 186), which perhaps can be regarded as a valuable addition to Planned Change and Organizational Development.

> The phrase 'continuous change' is used to group together organizational changes that tend to be ongoing, evolving, and cumulative. A common presumption is that change is emergent, meaning that it is 'the realization of a new pattern of organizing in the absence of explicit a priori intentions' (Orlikowski, 1996: 65). Change is described as situated and grounded in continuing updates of work processes (Brown & Duguid, 1991) and social practices (Tsoukas, 1996). Researchers focus on 'accommodations to and experiments with the everyday contingencies, breakdowns, exceptions, opportunities, and unintended consequences' (Orlikowski, 1996: 65). As these accommodations 'are repeated, shared, amplified, and sustained, they can, over time, produce perceptible and striking organizational changes' (p.89). (Weick and Quinn 2004: 186)

A characteristic difference of Continuous Change in relation to traditional approaches to change is that thinking no longer departs from the sequence, derived from Lewin, of unfreeze, transition, refreeze, but – taking change as normal – from the sequence freeze, rebalance, unfreeze. Schedules and plans are still being made, but they have no longer the important function of indicator of the right direction. They are just temporary snapshots. "To freeze is to capture sequences by means of cognitive maps (. . .), schemas (. . .), or war stories (. . .) To rebalance is to reinterpret, relabel, and resequence the patterns so that they unfold with fewer blockages" (Weick and Quinn 2004: 189).

Many authors argue in their response to such glass ceilings in change, that too little attention is paid to the human factor in organization studies. De Caluwe and

Vermaak (2004: 203) put this as follows: "The tendency to forget the human factor and to pay a lot of attention to decisions about the outcomes of change, but little to the change process and implementation just creates new problems, such as a lack of support, unnecessary resistance, and so on." And on p. 205: "When an organization is extremely dynamic or in flux, then structures, systems, strategies provide fewer footholds to a change agent than the people who create them." And then it appears, according to some authors, that, despite so much HRM and similar approaches, this human factor has never seriously been taken into account. Take for example, say Sturdy and Grey (2003: 656), the resistance of workers against change proposals. This resistance is probably so much greater than we always have thought it to be, that taking it seriously could possibly lead us to question the whole concept of managerial leadership. The sting is in the idea that change can be led. "Indeed, although recognizing the "fears" and "irrationality" of employees, the task of "leading change" entails leading those employees to an eventual acceptance of that which they initially resisted."

Jacques follows the same track when he says (1996: 187) "[T]he question 'what motivates the worker?' has been treated as an adequate formulation for research. A more appropriate question if social reality is treated as quasi-real might be 'what motivates the worker to do task work structured by *others*?'" Besides Jacques points to the increasing, but not adequately treated, importance of the relational factor. "[R]elational skills are increasingly critical for effectively organizing and these skills can not currently be found in the norms of the industrial workplace" (1996: 178). This is about relationships with customers, but also about internal relationships within the organization between bosses and employees.

Cynicism

If the failure of many change efforts is recognized, it can cause the above feelings of impotence and reflection thereon. But the many failures, if they are not acknowledged, may have another effect that, in my view, plays an important role in contemporary organizations. This effect is the occurrence of a widespread feeling among employees that there is a lot of hypocrisy around organizational change.

This may apply to managers in relation to professional change agents. Scarbrough (2002: 180) for instance reports research showing that the implementation in many BPR projects, which had been promised to the managers, lagged behind compared to the rhetoric of professional change agents. This is particularly true for subordinate employees in relation to their managers, who in cooperation with change professionals, run their change programs. The experience of hypocrisy arises especially, and paradoxically, in a change project when the human factor has not been neglected, but has been explicitly addressed, making use of behavioural theory or other methods of social psychology. As we saw, to a small extent this is the case for Planned Change and to an important extent for Organizational Development. Boonstra (2004a: 4) points out that strategies that explicitly aim at motivating people run a high risk of becoming manipulative and (apparently because of that) may lose their effectiveness.

Examples of strategies and tactics that are strongly oriented to social and psychological sciences are HRM, cultural management, socio-technics and empowerment. These approaches to change are characterized by a heavy emphasis on motivating people and on their identification with the organization. According to a number of authors, exactly because improvement of labour satisfaction or of labour conditions are explicitly being promised to employees, there appears a harsh discrepancy with everyday reality as it is experienced after unsuccessful change attempts. This may lead to "[t]he widespread cynicism among workforces who have been told they are being 'empowered' reflects the contradictions deployed in everyday life between the discourse of 'rights' and the practice of humiliation" (Smith 2001: 542). Willmott (1993: 531) points out that gurus, while relying on a soft form of HRM, may well create the appearance that worker's interests run parallel to business interests. But this lasts only as long as the economy allows, or as long as employees let themselves be talked into it. Armstrong (2000: 356) states that the combination of the term "learning organization" and increasing job insecurity for employees borders on deception. That is why, in an insecure atmosphere, the concept will be quickly unmasked as fraud and eventually disappear. Knights and Willmott (2000) point to the untrue character of empowerment where employees are supposed "to devote themselves unreservedly to goals that have been determined by others" (2000: 11, cited in Scarbrough (2002: 179)).

Some writers wonder how cynicism and experiences of hypocrisy acquired such prominence in organizations. The more benevolent amongst them do not immediately question the good faith of managers and consultants. They take their attitude as a form of successful self-deception by organizers. Thus O'Connor (1999: 240) presents an anecdote from the work of Mcgregor. It speaks of a boss (Evans) who succeeds in convincing his employee that he (Evans) is fully at his service and does not talk to him as a boss. O'Connor shows how McGregor appears to believe firmly in the effectiveness of hierarchically driven HRM: "McGregor points out that Evans has taken a 'helping role rather than an authoritative one'."

Jacques (1999) also does not doubt the organizers' good will, but he does state that the era of self-deception for managers is over indeed. "Because worker attitude becomes a critical element of effective functioning, the need for top management to convince *themselves* that they have a mutually satisfying relationship with employees is being replaced by a need for top managers to convince the *employees*, creating a need for greater authenticity and mutuality in managerial dealings. In this context, one can not be "strategic" about HRM in the sense propagated by the managerialist HRM literature." (1999: 217)

A number of authors interpret the difference between rhetoric and practice as a conscious managerial strategy. For instance Bendix and Fisher reproach Elton Mayo who can be seen as a precursor to HRM: "[T]he implicit denial of the inevitably authoritarian aspects of a factory system plays a strategic role in Mr. Mayo's philosophy" (cited in Landsberger 1968: 32). Braverman (1974) assigns a role to humanistic approaches in the class struggle. Bourgeois humanism rationalises job enrichment and job humanizing to bridge the opposition between capital and labour, but actually it leaves the oppressive structure intact (Knights and Willmott 1989:

537). Räisänen and Linde (2004: 102, 103) believes that the humanistic function-alism links new values such as flat organization and empowerment to traditional control and to new institutions for implementing control.

Such ambivalence, not to say cunning, on the part of the organizers is still under-standable, according to Jacques (1996: 166, 168). Indeed, self-management, when taken seriously, and TQM/BPR, which are necessary to motivate employees, proba-bly reduce the need for managers to a significant extent. So, as a manager you may easily lose your job. In such a truly transformed organization it may be that "what constitutes authority and who will hold it will have changed."

Some authors note that the problem of hypocrisy does not have to be similar for all levels within the organization. For example, Weick and Quinn remark that "Beer et al. raise the interesting subtlety, based on their data, that inconsistency between word and action at the corporate level does not affect change effectiveness, but it does have a negative effect for leaders at the unit level. Their explanation is that inconsistency at the top is seen as necessary to cope with diverse pressures from stock holders and the board but is seen as insincerity and hypocrisy at other levels." (2004: 190)

We must conclude that something special seems to be implicated in the "human factor". As change problems accumulate, this element is identified increasingly as one, if not the decisive, factor for the success or failure of change efforts. This "human turn" from the 1920s has led to a range of people-oriented approaches to change, nowadays usually grouped under the title Organizational Development. But so far this turn seems to have promoted only to a modest extent the success of change attempts. Instead, this approach appears to produce a number of neg-ative effects, which give rise to forms of cynicism about hypocritical organizers. Apparently, with the interest in the human factor, a field full of unpredictable and contradictory possibilities is laid open.

Reactions to the Glass Ceiling

Such an observation can deject us and make us want to return to the clear predictabil-ities of Planned Change. This is what happens for instance in the blueprint thinking that De Caluwe and Vermaak (2004) describe and in books like *The McKinsey Way* by Ethan Rasiel. For simple[2] change projects that is likely to remain a viable option. But, for the many more complex change projects, in line with authors such as Ten Bos, Ten Have, Quinn, De Caluwe and Vermaak, I think that we have no choice but to further explore that people-oriented field. I believe we must acknowledge that while the human factor gets attention, it is not adequate, nor sufficiently well

---

[2]Given my focus on the human factor "simplicity" or "complexity" of change projects in this book are mainly related to the extent to which the human factor plays a role and possibly creates resis-tance and unpredictable situations. Simplicity and complexity are therefore not primarily derived from the scale or technical aspects of the proposed changes.

thought-out. Apparently, there is still a large field to explore when it comes to the situation of people, and their unpredictability, in organizations.

There are authors, especially from Critical Management Studies, who in response to the above described impotence and hypocrisy develop a critical disdain towards all things (change) management. Among these, striving for control or desire for order often appear to be presented as though immoral. This is the case in the exemplary plea for disorganization by Blaug (1999: e.g. 38) or for joining the organizational fringe areas (Steyaert and Janssens 1999: 194). These authors tend, according to Alvesson and Willmott (1992: 442, 443), to do away with the managers' conventional insights and fashionable trends as worthless, and tend to assume an attitude of moral superiority. Such a superior critical attitude, even if inspired by engagement with the victims of management in organizations, is disapproved of by Alvesson and Willmott. Such attitudes lead to nothing because they are not communicative for managers, nor for the victims of management. Indeed, a kind of utopian negativism places one at about the same distance from the victims as the managers and change agents who rely on their utopian reasoning. Furthermore, such an attitude is unrealistic, given the overwhelming success (Ten Bos 2004b: 5) of the Western, high level of being organized. Alvesson and Deetz rightly argue that "critical management research should be sensitive to the economic and organizational constraints within which management operates, whilst seeking to unveil and combat 'unnecessary' forms of domination and control that 'distort organizational decisions and lead to less satisfactory fulfilment of the full variety of human needs and desires'" (Fournier 2002: 176). They believe that (a form of) appreciation for the managerial position leads to better opportunities to reflect on management.

In this regard it may help that we do not need to be impressed by the failure rates with respect to changes. As mentioned above, the boundary between organization and change is gradual, and a lot of ordinary organization and improvement work, which is missing in the statistics, may well be handled through Planned Change. Indeed, do we not all organize our birthday party or alteration on the basis of plans and checklists? So that is to a great extent also the fairly well-functioning practice of managers. A lot goes well, but – we apparently want more than that.

Another reason not to lapse into negativity is that the focus on people of Planned Change and particularly of Organizational Development, is not to be regarded as just rhetoric. Alvesson and Willmott (1992: 458, 459) say in this respect that, even if for example corporate culture has an encapsulating effect, the rhetoric itself offers an invitation to human growth which employees can also exploit. And in the same vein, Jacques (1999) notes that although HRM is to be regarded as something which predominantly promotes the interests of top management, it is nevertheless true that "[t]hose interested in mere effectiveness must now engage with questions of power in order to be effective. Those interested in emancipatory action must engage with representation of the worker as technical resource as well as a human being" (1999: 206). Managerialistic as well as critical thinkers thus get opportunities. One may hope that also the critical current will seize them through engagement with the situation of employees in organizations.

But, as mentioned already, to make the most of those opportunities, a fallow field of research may be explored. This exploration will focus on the glass ceiling: the unruliness and unpredictability that people show in change processes, even with regard to well-meaning "human" approaches to change. New perspectives on what it means for a human being to work in organizations will be welcome.

A Remarkable Combination: Levinas and Organizations

Broad Survey of Points of Contact

For such a new perspective in this book, I will look at the philosophy of Emmanuel Levinas. This will be a remarkable manoeuvre because so far, within the organizational behaviour literature, the work of Levinas has been the object of attention only to a limited extent. And as far as attention was granted, it took in general a specific perspective, namely that of the ethical aspects of management and organization. Authors in this area who have been inspired by Levinas include Bauman (1993, 1998), Jones (2003a) and Roberts (2003).

Bauman, particularly in his book *Postmodern Ethics* (1993), objects to the application of rule-led ethics in organizations.[3] In support of his objections, he takes what he calls the "moral impulse" of individuals for his starting-point. For the characterization of the moral impulse he uses descriptions of Levinas, from whom he derives the terms "proximity" and "face". Proximity, namely to someone else, he conceives of as indicating the area of intimacy and morality. The face stands for the eyes that look at me from the closeness, and thus trigger in me a moral impulse and prevent me doing violence to the other. This moral impulse is considered by Bauman as valuable, but he notes that business ethics, being a rational affair, does not know what to do with the emotional nature of the impulse. Regulation and professionalization, guided by reason, are incompatible with this impulse.

There are reasons (see Van der Ven 2001) to argue that Levinas in the work of Bauman is represented in a somewhat distorted way. This comes to the fore in the dualism he applies, for example in the contrast he makes between reason and emotion, and between rules and morality. In Levinas we do not find such a schema. What remains however, is that Bauman in his books, which are frequently cited within organization studies, was one of the first to link Levinas' work to the world of organizations.

Jones (2003a), relying on Levinas and Derrida, wonders whether business ethics as articulated nowadays in codes and regulations, is possible at all. He thinks it is not and subsequently he offers on the basis of the work of Levinas and Derrida a number of proposals for a more credible business ethics. Jones' criticism, partly inspired by Levinas, on the current conception of business ethics is also a theme in the book *For Business Ethics* (2005) by Jones, Parker and Ten Bos. Roberts (2003) discusses the

---

[3]For a critical discussion see Ten Bos (1997) and Ten Bos and Willmott (2001).

trend, observable in particular in large companies, to exhibit their social responsibility. He notes that this trend runs the risk to be no more than window dressing and a new, profitable form of calculative acting. He examines in his article if it is possible to build upon the work of Levinas to achieve a more substantial form of Corporate Social Responsibility.

The above makes it clear that Levinas is not unknown within organization studies, but that his name there is associated with ethical issues. My interest in this book, as may be clear by now, is directed primarily to another aspect of management, namely to bring about change in organizations. Regarding this aspect, I note that in the existing management literature possible connections between Levinas and organization studies are not, or hardly, the object of any attention.

A first indication however that there may be interesting links is to be found in the central question that resounds from the change literature, namely: "How is real change possible?" Indeed, that question has a lot of similarity to a question which Levinas poses regularly, dispersed across his writings, namely: "How can something really new come into being?" (e.g. 1998a: 157–159; 1987: 57, 255). The congeniality between these two questions suggests that Levinas on the one hand, and organizational change science studies on the other hand, have something to tell to each other. However, more indications of possibly interesting links exist. These can be found in the reflections of a number of management authors as a response to experienced change problems, and to the cynicism and dullness involved. These reactions manifest themselves in the thematizing of two issues: problematic aspects of rationality and resistance to capture.

It is my intention to show below and broadly for each of these two topics, on the one hand how they are treated in organization studies out of reflection on the change problems; and on the other hand how they constitute important themes within the work of Levinas. My presentation will be brief and exploratory in nature. It is meant to show merely that the said subjects have interfaces and that the organizational scientific studies literature and Levinas have those interfaces in common. A more detailed and substantive discussion of how the issues are understood by respectively the organizational scientific studies literature and Levinas will take place in subsequent chapters. It is also there that we consider the important question of whether those ideas show enough congeniality so as to be able to connect Levinas to organization studies in a fruitful way.

Problematic Rationality

The Management Literature

A number of authors relate the change problematics of organizations to the rational tradition that prevails in organizations. That there is such prevalence is no question for many an author.

In the literature, as in the general perception, management is to a large extent linked to rationality. According to Alasdaire MacIntyre, in the West, the manager stands for instrumentality, efficiency and rationality. Others stress how in the current imaging the manager is seen as the thinker of the organization, i.e. the one who uses reason par excellence. As Berglund and Werr state: "The myth of rationality is deeply institutionalized, and one of the central myths in the business domain" (2000: 640).

According to some authors, such rationality has properties that can be associated with the observed change problems. These properties are a certain rigidity of thinking and a tendency to totalitarianism. These symptoms are the subject of widespread attention in both popular and academic literature. Rigidity of thinking by managers, for example, is identified by Mintzberg, in his book *Managers, not MBAs* (2004). He notes that too many of them are trapped in a regime of rational tunnel-thinking, schematic planning and calculating management. For an explanation he points to an excessive focus in management training programs on scientific analysis and theoretical linearity. Björn Gustavsen, who is much involved in participatory research in organizations in Scandinavia, observes that "the core problem in using research in work places is the linear nature of theory when compared to the participative, interactive nature of real workplace processes" (1998: 108). This is a handicap, not only for his research work, but just as much for the practical daily functioning of these organizations when their managers let themselves be guided by those theories.

This rigidity may take the shape of unworldly-ness, or as Gustavsen formulates it: "[T]he issue is rather that implementation of theory presupposes that action takes place in a form and for reasons which are alien to the ways in which workplace practices generally emerge, particularly when experienced from a worker / union perspective." What happens when you depart systematically from reason and the world of ideas, is expressed by Ten Bos as follows: "The difference of orientation between people who move towards an idea *and* organizations that move from an idea, explains why people are always the central problem in organizations" (2004b: 4; translation NvdV). Starbuck shows the tragi-comic results of the persistence with which managers continue to believe in rational plans: "Managers keep forgetting that it is what they do, not what they plan, that explains their success. They keep giving credit to the wrong thing – namely, the plan – and having made this error, they spend more time planning and less time acting. They are astonished when more planning improves nothing" (quoted in Koene 2001: 92).

Townley et al. (2003: 1062) discuss an improvement project for the provincial government of the Canadian state of Alberta. The starting point for the project was a model of Osborne and Gaebler from their book *Reinventing Government* (1993). This book is also known as the "bible" for change because the authors share the view that when it comes to government organizations, in many cases old, traditional practices no longer work and a radical new beginning must be made. Their model promises control over the change process by defining the main ingredients in advance: the basic mission, organizational goals, the road to achieve them, a timetable, the method of measuring progress and evaluating results and feedback. All this presupposes the existence of linear progress through causal relationships which can easily be determined. "The possibility that the links between measures and outcomes, inputs and outputs, expenditure and monetary accomplishments, may not be explicit, is not considered" (Townley et al. 2003: 1062). The project ran aground because the officials concerned were excessively obsessed with the measurement and achievement of targets that no longer had any relationship with good governance.

The totalizing effect of rationality is reflected in the finding that a line of thinking, once elected, creates its own logic from which it is then difficult to escape. One example at the macro level is the choice for the logic of shareholder value as a management objective. Jacques (1996: 153) shows that, once such a choice has been made, there is sometimes nothing to stop it. You can end up in a spiral in which enlargement of production and demand creation keep whipping up each other and subordinate all other organizational interests.[4]

But also at the level of the internal ordering of organizations, the blind domination of applied rationality manifests itself. Jacques (1996: 73) explains how, as the scale and complexity increase as a result of industrialization, rationality takes flight and therewith it the homogenizing of all employees concerned. "In order for the organization of scale to operate, hundreds or thousands of people had to participate in a single plan of action." Ten Bos (2004b: 3; translation NvdV) is inspired by a statement of Ben Okri to compare this rational way of organizing to a road, built to lead to a certain destination. And that road is, in the words of Ben Okri, devastating totalitarian indeed: "The road devours people and at night you can sometimes hear them scream for help; they beg to be redeemed from the inside of his stomach."

Levinas

To what extent is rationality a problem for Levinas? Rationality is an important issue in the work of Levinas, and he considers the rationality of the Western tradition to be on the one hand a great achievement and on the other hand something problematic. Levinas' work has been characterized, both by himself and by others (see Levinas 1978: 29 ff, Peperzak 1978: 7, 8) as a large discussion with Western thinking, especially with what he sees as the dominant current therein: the rationalistic philosophy of consciousness. In his eyes this tradition ignores important parts of reality by stating that all human ordering and sense-making activity ultimately has its origin in the rational necessity of those activities for life. Reason, in its turn, is supposed to be its own origin, to be self-sufficient, and not to need any nourishing force outside itself. Levinas protests about this and argues that reason can not be its own foundation: reason, which incites us to ordering and sense-making, must have been preceded by a more original meaning. And he situates that meaning in the appeal that comes from the Other, that is, in the fact that man, through the confrontation with the Other, can be pushed from his centre and can be brought to disinterested servitude. That is where rationality comes into being.

---

[4]For another, more positive evaluation of shareholder value with respect to the interests of all stakeholders see Cools et al. (1992).

The importance of this reasoning for my argument is that rationality, as it is typically understood in the West, is a problem. What this prevailing conception of rationality exactly looks like, in philosophy and in organization studies, and what precisely are possible objections against it, is addressed in Chapter 2. At this point the most important is to establish that rationality in the West, according to Levinas, often functions as a kind of undisputable deepest ground that can justify or condemn our actions. The problem with this way of dealing with rationality is, says Levinas, that we forget that rationality itself is grounded in something else. This forgetting has unpleasant consequences: it leads to rigidity of thinking and tends to totalitarianism.

Radical Resistance Against Capture

The Management Literature

Above we noted already that indicative management literature, in response to change problems, struggles with motivation problems and resistance from employees. Also, that in many cases resistance has a slightly mysterious character, especially when it is directed against well-meaning, rationally-sound plans that have the intention to respect the human factor. But then (p. 8) it was discussed in terms of "unnecessary resistance" (De Caluwe and Vermaak 2004: 203) and furthermore the somewhat vague conclusion was drawn that the human factor is something complex and unpredictable to which further research should be applied.

This vagueness potentially conceals the possibility that further elaborations of the conclusion may fundamentally oppose one another. On the one hand, we may infer that still more research should be carried out than has been done in the course of the last eighty years to find out how we can *really* seduce and effectively motivate the human factor. That would mean that social psychology and behavioural sciences devote even more attention to the human phenomenon. In this case the resistance is not seen as radical, but as basically compatible with the organizational order, provided we get enough time to arrange the organization and the employee on the same single line. On the other hand, the above conclusion may mean: no longer think in terms of temptation, accept that resistance can not be encapsulated, take resistance one hundred percent seriously at the risk that the employee's wishes are not or only partially compatible with organizational objectives. This second approach, which views resistance as radical, could prove to have something in common with the philosophy of Levinas.

There are management authors who advocate the second approach. They infer from change as a problem, and from observed resistance to such change, that it may be necessary to concentrate on the unruly subject as the origin of the resistance. However, not in order to seduce it, but in a way that takes the resistance fully seriously. With all the, maybe risky, implications thereof: that you let the other win, you let yourself be addressed, and you are willing to actually listen. The above quotation from Jacques points in that direction. "Because worker attitude becomes a critical element of effective functioning, the need for top management to convince *themselves* that they have a mutually satisfying relationship with employees is being replaced by a need for top managers to convince the *employees*, creating a need for greater authenticity and mutuality in managerial dealings. In this context, one can not be "strategic" about HRM in the sense propagated by the managerialist HRM literature" (1999: 217). One can read this quote as an encouragement of preparedness to be addressed by employees and their resistance and to refrain from temptation tactics.

Knights and Willmott deals with the following question: "[I]s it possible to take subjectivity seriously without degenerating into a "subjectivist" analysis of the social world?" (1989: 535) In the possible answer to that question, apart from a somewhat romanticized picture of the self and personal identity, resounds that willingness to take employee resistance completely seriously: "In every testimony to the dehumanising experience of the pressure of modern industrial society, there is also a testimony to a contrary sense of self, of personal identity, of being human; of what it is or might be like to be in control of our own lives, to act in and upon the world, to be active human agents. So, in the name of our personal identities, our personal hopes and projects and longings, in the name of our selves, we resist" (Dawe 1978: 364–365, cited in Knights and Willmott 1989: 537).

Ten Bos, building on the metaphor of the road as a name for the compelling nature of organizational rationality, even suggests that man falls by definition victim to that rationality: "Man in an organization is always a ghost driver" (2004b: 5; translation NvdV). And he leaves no doubt as to what he must do: "I will, against all organizational rationality, take the ghost driver's part." Janssens and Steyaert (1999) is aware of the precarious nature of a choice for the second approach which is seriously sensitive to resistance: "Sensibility may mean *accepting* the irrational and emotional, and designing organizations that do not drive the other person crazy (. . .)" (1999: 380)

Levinas

This focus on radical resistance resonates in Levinas. In his descriptions, the human being who with his sovereign rationality orders the world according to his own categories, takes a prominent place. Crucially, for Levinas, this ordering movement sometimes encounters an absolute resistance. Namely, from the defenceless other who threatens to fall victim but does not let himself be reduced to rational categories. This is "the defenseless resistance in the eyes of the Other, in which is inscribed: You shalt not kill. This resistance can not be appropriated" (De Boer 1997: 13), and it is radical in this sense. Through its appearance, the Face, it embarrasses the raging rationality. The equalizing power of reason is at that moment halted by the confrontation with the grief of a victim and allows itself to be addressed by it. The most concise way Levinas expresses this is: autonomy (i.e. being in your own power) gives way to heteronomy (i.e. letting yourself be addressed by someone else). This confrontation and reversal of relationships may last just a short while.

But, according to Levinas, that does not affect the impact of such a moment: it has, even in its transience, the force of an absolute resistance.

Evaluation: There Are Connecting Points

Searching for an entrance by which to introduce Levinas' thinking into organization studies, I have looked amongst the above for connections from his thoughts to issues which, in response to the problems of organizational change, are the subject of attention in organization studies. These topics are: the problematic nature of rationality, and the radical resistance which is associated with the totalising impact of that rationality and that manifests itself as Face. The discussion of these issues so far seems to suggest some relationship between the organization studies scholars presented, and Levinas. There are some evident interconnections. This finding encourages me to consider, in the following chapters, in a more detailed way the treatment of these themes: on the one hand in the management literature; and on the other hand in the work of Levinas. This research will reveal whether these two sources of reflection can be connected in a convincing and fruitful way. The associated meta-question will be: what contribution has Levinas to offer, through his discussion of the issues of problematic rationality and resistance to capture, to the thinking in organization studies about change problems?

Chapter 2
Rationality: A Problem?

Introduction

Two Different Disciplines

In Chapter 1, two themes were presented that, at least at first sight, constitute interfaces between the work of Levinas and parts of the management literature. Those themes were the possibly problematic character of rationality and the issue of radical resistance, in the shape of the Face, against the totalising effect of rationality. Traces of both these themes were indicated from management literature as well as in the work of Levinas.

For the argument of this book this is important because, as announced in the Preface, it is my intention to shed light from the philosophy of Levinas on problems of organizational change science. The finding in Chapter 1, that we can identify interfaces between these two areas with respect to some relevant topics, is a necessary first step. The interfaces provide connecting – points to link those areas. In Chapter 1, however, the precise content of rationality issues and of resistance to capture has been only barely approached. Such an approach is an essential preliminary step which will now be developed.

The authors cited in Chapter 1 belong to two different intellectual disciplines: on one side, management authors from organization studies and on the other side, Levinas from philosophy. This observation raises the question whether the interfaces that one observes superficially, are also real interfaces under closer scrutiny. How are these indicated themes understood by each of the two disciplines? While they may use the same vocabulary, they may mean very different things.

The answer to that question determines whether it is appropriate to project light from philosophy, where Levinas is located, onto questions in the field of organization studies. The next necessary step therefore must be to establish that the issues which organization studies finds around the themes of problematic rationality and resistance to capture are treated *in a comparable way* within philosophy. To determine whether the superficially observable interfaces are real, we must establish that Levinas and organization studies speak about the same things.

However, such reasoning is only partially valid. This applies to our first theme, that of problematic rationality. This topic has been extensively thematized in philosophy and, importantly for us here, Levinas situates himself within that tradition and he refers to it. Indeed, the commonality between Levinas and a particular philosophical tradition (that of phenomenology) with respect to the rationality problematic serves, as we shall see in Chapter 4, as a starting point for the development of Levinas' own ideas.

Levinas' ideas are certainly original but they coincide to a large extent to the problematizing of rationality which was already under way within the philosophical tradition in which he was trained.

For an understanding of Levinas, and also for testing the congruency between Levinas' treatment of the subject, and the treatment of the subject in organization studies, it is important, prior to the presentation of Levinas' view on problematic rationality, to take a detour. We need to compare the way organization studies deals with rationality with the way philosophy deals with it. If we can establish that what organization studies means by problematic rationality is similar to what philosophy says about it, then we may also safely speak of an interface between Levinas and organization studies. Only then it will be justified and possible, in the search for new light on the problematic nature of rationality, to look from organization studies for authors who find themselves within the philosophical discipline, including Levinas.

The link between Levinas and organization studies through philosophy does not apply to our second theme, that of the radical resistance against rationality. This interface that – at least at first sight – seems to exist between organization studies and Levinas bypasses philosophy. While the theme of the Face (heteronomy) as resistance to rationality hardly resonates at all within the philosophical tradition – interestingly enough in apparent distinction to its resonance within organization studies, given the management authors we could cite about that resistance.

Resistance against rationality is indeed thematized philosophically, but the conception of that resistance as Face (i.e.: heteronomy, in the sense of a break with autonomy) is absent. That conceptualization itself should be regarded as Levinas' most original contribution to philosophy. It is the culmination of the task that Levinas sets himself and which De Boer defines as follows: "An experience has to be brought out or translated which has never been put into the words of philosophy before" (1997: 84).

This implies that any treatment of the questions, what exactly is meant by the Face as resistance, and whether that can be related to themes in organization studies, will have to take place in a direct comparison with Levinas and without any necessary mediation by philosophy. Such treatment is addressed in the central Chapters 4 and 5. Chapter 4 sets out the views of Levinas, Chapter 5 presents a translation of his views to organization studies. An affirmative answer, if there is to be any, to the question of whether the theme of the Face is more than just a superficial interface between Levinas and organization studies will have to wait for those chapters before it can develop. And, in the case of any affirmation the next question will be in what way can Levinas' contribution help to elucidate that topic.

The detour through philosophy, which we just found is needed for the theme of problematic rationality, is the focus of this chapter. Therefore below, in reply of the question to what extent philosophy and organization studies talk about the same things, two issues are dealt with. First of all the question of what problems are associated with rationality, on the one hand by organizational scientists and on the other hand by philosophers. And secondly, the question of how precisely the relation between those problems and rationality is conceptualized respectively in organization studies, and in philosophy. The conclusion of the comparison will be that organizational scientists and philosophers discuss rationality and its problematic nature in very similar terms, which carry similar meanings for both groups. This creates a justification, as far as clarifying the problematic nature of rationality in organization studies is concerned, for consulting philosophers. As indicated, I will then use that justification to examine in Chapters 4 and 5 the extent to which Levinas' own philosophical contributions shed light on the issue of problematic rationality.

But the justification for consulting philosophy in general also provides the opportunity to investigate other answers from philosophy on these topics than those of Levinas. I want to use that opportunity, with the intention to be able to show more clearly the specific nature of Levinas' answer. Therefore, Chapter 3 will be devoted to two alternatives: on the one hand some answers which depart from postmodernism and on the other hand some answers that are inspired by Heidegger and Wittgenstein.

So attention in this chapter will focus on problematic aspects of rationality. As to the above questions, I will first discuss them with respect to organization studies and then with respect to philosophy. In the conclusion of the chapter, an answer will be formulated to the question as to whether the treatment within the two disciplines shows enough congruence that it may be judged justifiable and meaningful to shed light in this way from one discipline onto the other.

Rationality

At this point, and prior to that elaboration, I would like to briefly consider the concept of rationality. Rationality in this book will be understood as: the use by man of his reasoning ability (reason) to know and control his environment and to account for his actions and thoughts. Additionally, I will speak regularly of Rationalism, by which I mean the ideology that assigns great, sometimes exclusive, value to rationality and reason.

Two notes are important in this regard. The first concerns the width of rationality. How many aspects of life can be affected by it? There are authors, both within organization studies and within philosophy, who associate rationality and Rationalism primarily or exclusively with the hard, measurable aspects of life. The most extreme expression of this view in the management literature is the theory of the Highest Expected Benefit. According to this theory, rational action is action which, in comparison with other actions, produces the highest expected utility value (Hampton

2000: 742). This value can be measured and the chance to achieve it can be determined statistically. This approach to rationality leads to the caricature of a rationalist as someone who does not care for anything else than for business and the technical aspects of life. This is for an example the view of Scott when he defines his criterion for calling an organizational perspective rational or not rational: "Whether the organization's purview should incorporate more or fewer facets of the lives of its participants is a basic philosophical difference separating the two perspectives" (1981: 101). He then designates as rational that perspective that incorporates fewer facets of life into the organization's purview. In the realm of philosophy there is a comparable tradition that wants to strictly limit the content of the concept of rationality. In particular under the influence of Descartes and other seventeenth century philosophers that tradition reduces rationality to theoretical arguments which, at some considerable distance from real life practices, pretend to offer eternal truths and logical necessities (Toulmin 1990: 20).

That is not my position. I see rationality as a concept that can be associated with almost all aspects of life. I recognize this view in what De Caluwe and Vermaak say about a number of organizational change theories which they discuss: "They emphasize the irrationality of change processes or, put more precisely, they emphasize the existence of other sorts of rationality that we might not be aware of, or familiar with in organizational life" (2004: 212). This means that something which from a narrow perspective may seem to be irrational, can be seen – from a broad perspective – as being also a form of rationality. Conversely in my conception, this view implies that what is in the strict sense designated as rational, in some cases is not rational at all. There, accountability and control fail because too many aspects of life are ignored. Another implication of this view is that, from a broad perspective, multiple rationalities simultaneously can coexist.

The second note is motivated by what I have formulated as my conception of Rationalism: an ideology that attributes great, sometimes exclusive, value to rationality. Such a formulation raises the question: exclusive in relation to what? What is it that can be regarded as "the other" of rationality and to which rationality stands possibly in opposition? This question is not easy to answer. Some authors (e.g. Bauman 1993: 114 and Abrahamson 1996, cited in Berglund and Werr 2000: 647) suggest that emotionality is the "other" or the opposite of rationality. As Ten Bos and Willmott (2001: 785 ff) point out with respect to Bauman, this can lead to an entangledness in a hierarchizing dualism, in which the traditional dominance of reason over emotion is simply reversed.

But I disagree with such a play off of reason and emotion against one another, on the basis of my aforementioned broad conception of rationality. Indeed, a broad conception of rationality implies good intercourse with emotionality. Fineman (1996: 547) and Vetlesen (1994: 162) indicate that it is perfectly possible to view emotions not only as support for rationality. Emotions and cognition can, according to them, be seen as intertwined issues. It is as Sturdy says: "being rational is also being emotional" (2003: 94). On this basis I do not find it strange when Albrow states that "[t]he new recovery of emotionality may indeed prove only to be the next phase of the rationalisation process" (1997: 113). But this implies that emotionality is not the opposite of rationality. Similarly it is valid to say that the taking seriously of matters such as "the human factor", communication and organizational culture can be acknowledged as rational. They are not the "other" of rationality. To say positively what indeed this "other" of rationality actually is, is more difficult to determine. If an opposite is to be designated, it seems that, almost by definition, this can only be done in rather mysterious terms. In my view it is one of the merits of Levinas that he brought in this mysteriousness into philosophy.

Section 1: Problematic Rationality in Organization Studies

Rationality in Organization Studies

In Chapter 1 we found to a large extent that management is identified with rationality. Such identification may appear from the description of basic mechanisms in the world of organizations such as the market or the bureaucracy in terms of systems for getting things done rationally (Smith 2001: 549). Further, management and managers themselves are often presented in the usual imagery as icons of rationality. With respect to management, "[t]he myth of rationality is deeply institutionalized (...), and one of the central myths in the business domain" (Berglund & Werr 2000: 640).

According to Schneider "[o]rganizations and managers are considered rational, almost by definition. The irrational is considered dysfunctional" (1999: 283). At the same time there is another myth about managers in circulation with an opposite tendency. This myth fosters the normative and pragmatic nature of management and likes to present managers as men of action who are not distracted by academic discussions and theoretical reflections. Managers as doers, not thinkers (Berglund and Werr 2000: 639).

My search for the problematic aspects of rationality therefore implicates only partially the management literature in so far as that management literature identifies with rationality. However, there is widespread consensus that such identification is extensive and strong. Jacques shows in his study *Manufacturing the Employee* (1996) how for nearly the entire last century management thinking has sought confirmation by the so-called "value-free science" and academic experts. In his book *Managers, Not MBA's* (2004), Mintzberg discusses the prestige that a scientific label, such as an MBA degree, enjoys in contemporary – management circles. This close identification with rationality, therefore, despite the existence of an opposing myth, suffices for me to consider my proposed quest as relevant.

As mentioned in the introduction to this chapter, I conceive of rationality, also organizational rationality, in a broad sense. That rationality does not need to be equated with a caricature of an inanimate way of thinking that for example addresses only technical and organizational structure issues, and fails to give attention to the functioning of people in organizations. Jacques says that "[h]aving dealt with the basic problems of rationalizing *material* inputs, business attention turned to the rationalization of *human* inputs" (1996: 98). And, within the organizational scientific developments of the twentieth century, that has led to profound investigation to such things as motivation and participation of employees, teamwork and communication. Elton Mayo for instance demonstrates extensively an eye for the human factor. And although he himself designates many of its aspects as "irrational", I call his dealings with those issues a rational undertaking, because of the fact that Mayo considers it possible and desirable for employees to learn to separate the irrational from the rational so as to keep matters manageable (Schneider 1999: 283).

For me to designate organizational scientific views as "rational" it is essential that a desire for accountability and control is manifest in those views. There is the wish to create controllability, also with respect to those elements in the situation that are acknowledged as irrational, and to account for actions on the basis of arguments. In this regard, it is of only secondary importance as to whether managers indeed behave rationally, if such a behaviour could exist at all. The importance of the finding that managers and rationality are linked, is that it says something about the way managers want to account for their actions towards each other and others. This should be done through a rational argument by the managers that can suggest thoughtful promotion of the interests they are supposed to serve. So, the connection between management and rationality is primarily situated in the *claim* by managers themselves of being rational, not so much in their *actual behaviour*: they take for their ultimate goal to be rational. In reality, says Abrahamson (cited in Berglund and Werr 2000: 647), management discourses often mix up accounted-for and not-accounted-for arguments (which actually he refers to as emotional), but the final image must be one of rationality, that is to say, of accountability and control.

Problems with Rationality

Is Not Irrationality the Real Problem?

Is there something wrong with accountability and control? As the objective of this chapter I stated that I want to provide an overview of the problematic nature of rationality. But to assume that there is anything wrong with that is not so obvious. Quite the contrary. If someone accounts for his actions, that may be appropriate. To mutually account for one's actions may be considered as a basis for coordination and reliable cooperation, both within organizations and beyond. And the promise of control is perhaps a bit naive, while the aim may be nonetheless respectable. The release of these efforts will give free rein to all forms of irrationality, which is a real problem indeed.

We may conclude, therefore, that the claims of rationality, namely the possibility of accountability and control, whether or not recorded in scientific theories, are almost as a matter of course considered as valuable and inspiring. In regard of the history of management thinking this is shown through a long line of management thinkers who, starting with Frederick Taylor, took that view as point of departure for making management more rational. Among other means, Taylor did so by time studies which were aimed at eliminating "unreasonable" fluctuations in the amounts of time workers used to perform their jobs.

Another example. Elton Mayo feared the irrationality and the power of sentiments of employees and sought to control them through an external force (O'Connor 1999: 224). The movement of Human Resource Management (HRM) builds on Mayo's ideas and it is still directed towards the disciplining of employees to increase their self-management and self-responsibility, i.e. to teach them more rationality (Steyaert and Janssens 1999: 189, 190). Any lack thereof is interpreted within HRM as a worrying form of immaturity that should be turned into maturity by using various techniques if the organization is to perform better.

For now, the obvious attractiveness of manager/managerial rationality is also validated by the fact that the possibility of rational control of organizations – if necessary, simply top down – and the elimination of unpredictabilities, remain dominant themes for many management thinkers. The best illustration of this is that the vast majority of current management books still offer exactly that: models; a systematic approach for "seamless" change; roadmaps; and, above all the promise not to be surprised anymore. The obvious attractiveness and merits of such rationality seem almost undeniable.

Nevertheless, there is a growing group of management authors who question this orthodoxy. In most cases the problematic aspects of rationality they identify are not isolated, and often they show a certain coherence with one another. To give an idea of how those critics make an idiot of managerial rationality, I will highlight two clusters of these inter-linked, problematic aspects of rationality present in their writings.

The first cluster arises from the observation that many organizational scientific theories have an unworldly character and simplify reality in an unacceptable way through their descriptions. This connects with the rigidity of thinking which in Chapter 1 was associated with rationality. Authors who address this issue link those phenomena to the linear and structure-oriented nature of organizational theory. I designate this cluster of problems by the term Deception, because of the problematic distortion of reality which finds place.

The other cluster of problematic aspects is being formed around the observation that organizational thinking produces a hierarchical, and therefore a constraining, effect. This corresponds to what was referred to in Chapter 1 as the encapsulating, totalizing tendency of rationality. A number of authors connect this hierarchizing effect with the pretension of objectivity which is inherent to all rationality. I bring this cluster of problems under the heading Exclusion.

Deception

The unworldliness of many organization studies theories becomes apparent when one hears the optimistic, if not euphoric tone of some management maxims and compares these with the lack of effectiveness in practice. In Chapter 1 we saw that the highly elaborated organizational change theories of Planned Change and Organizational Development in many cases fail to meet expectations.

The finding that so much theory does not match up with experienced reality is associated with the linear structure-oriented nature of rationality by a number of authors. Linear suggests that the coherence exhibited by associated phenomena is supposed to be both unequivocal and stable, showing itself in reliable chronological or causal patterns. An orientation towards structure is implied, as it is assumed that there are independently existing patterns of ordering. These authors consider linearity and structure-orientation to be inherent characteristics of the rationality of accountability and control. In Chapter 1, I presented quotes of, among others, Mintzberg, Gustavsen and Starbuck who decry the rigidity of management rationality. The importance of structures in rational thinking is confirmed by Scott. He calls an organization rational only if there is that attention to structure:

> In a larger sense, however, rationality resides in the structure itself, not in the individual participants – in rules that assure participants will behave in ways calculated to achieve desired objectives, in control arrangements that evaluate performance and detect deviance, in reward systems that motivate participants to carry out prescribed tasks, and in the set of criteria by which participants are selected, replaced, or promoted. (1981: 77)

The reality-reducing impact of linearity is produced, according to a number of authors, because rationally manageable categories from the study-room are taken as a starting point. When, thereupon, those are considered to represent the real world, unworldliness enters the scene. Referring to the classic book by Mintzberg *The Nature of Managerial Work* (1973) Winograd and Flores formulate this objection as follows: "Careful observers of what successful managers do (. . .) have remarked that their activities are not well represented by reflecting the stereotype of a solitary mind studying complex alternatives" (1986: 151). And that, therefore, managers are not helped by theorists who brood on their theories in that classic solitary way.

Weick (2003: 463) understands the emphasis of those theories on structure, oversight and control that leads to reductionism and, through that, to unworldliness. Paradoxically, this emphasis stems precisely from the desire to join the practice of management. Manageability for practitioners is a crucial issue indeed. Unfortunately, correspondence with and relevance to practise is not so easily achieved by reference to those theories. This emerges from research by John Miner (1984), presented by Weick, to the validity and usefulness of the 32 theories Miner at that time could identify within organization studies. The theories that focused on structure, strategy and governance of the organization proved to offer the least guidance to practitioners. "The four theories judged most useful and most valid were all motivational and included theories of job characteristics (Hackman), goal-setting (Locke), achievement (McCelland), and role motivation (Miner)" (Weick 2003: 464). These four are inherently psychological theories, i.e. of a type of rationality that is generally considered "soft" or diluted. Namely, as softer than the rationality which does not have people, but only plans and structures for its content.

But even if one, theorizing, enters the field of psychology, reductionism and therewith unworldliness may strike. Linstead (2002: 97) presents as an example of reductionism the way in which the concept of "work motivation" is made rationally manageable. Motivation is then imagined as satisfaction of needs and desires that become more or less intense depending on the extent to which they are satisfied. Here needs and desires are considered isolated, measurable data and disconnected from the context. Whereas it could very well be maintained that that context (culture, moods, environment, psychic factors) determines at least as much the intensity of those needs and desires as does the extent of achieved satisfaction.

Reason and Torbert note that the prevailing rationality is completely alienated from practice and therefore is misleading. "Put simply, it does not even address, much less provide guidance for the question each of us can potentially ask at any time we are acting, namely: 'How can *I act* in a timely fashion now?' " (2001: 3, 4). They link this finding to the nature of that rationality which hopes to find controllability in "hard", objective, measurable and necessary relationships.

Exclusion

This brings us to the second cluster of problematic aspects of rationality. This cluster shows up around the claim of the prevailing rationality that the thought-products it produces (management theories, organizational scientific causal relationships), have a necessary and objective nature. This is considered objectionable because this conception of necessity and objectivity produces an exclusive effect. Matters that do not fit into these said theories and causal relationships are simply denied existence. Which has a colonizing impact on the people for whom these matters are important. Thus Ten Bos speaks of the "dictatorship of the timeless form" (2004a: 87; translation NvdV) that places work in the realm of objectivity and necessity and leaves no room for people to act themselves. Hierarchy in the domain of knowledge ("a timeless, objective truth on organizations exists") appears to have its counterpart in hierarchy and exclusion in the social domain.

Those with the largest overview, senior management and organization scientific experts, are supposed to be closer to those timeless truths than ordinary employees. And owing to that circumstance they have, as a matter of course, more right to define and shape reality. To power then: Jacques makes it clear that in the case of a conflict between the view of the experts and that of the employees "it is the workers' opinions which are not supported. Within a discourse of objectivity, their opinions are reduced to *data*; beneath what they *think* they experience, the expert measures what they *really* experience" (1996: 141). And Jacques' own contribution as a consultant was valued by managers as "a far more 'real' object in terms of managerial influence than the often perceptive written comments of employees" (idem). That mechanisms of social exclusion play a role is pointed out by Lee and Hassard:

> Expertise, sustained by well-organized research, has been so good at discriminating what/ who really matters from what / who does not matter, that it has long been able to portray the undesirable effects of its interventions as 'side' effects (...). Of course, whether an effect is a 'side' effect depends on whether one is experiencing it or not. (1999: 397)

The totalizing impact of rationality is not confined to rationality in the strict sense, which is mainly concerned with technical and business control. This is shown by Willmott (1993) on the basis of a discussion of the bestseller *In Search of Excellence*

(1982) by Peters and Waterman. These authors argue in response to the Japanese economic threat of that time, for attention in management to culture and emotions. This in fact means a broadening of rationality, as evidenced by the following quote from Peters and Waterman that Willmott (1993: 525) cites:

> [W]hat our framework has done is to remind the world of professional managers that 'soft is hard'. (...) It has enabled us to say, in effect, 'All that stuff you have been dismissing for so long as the intractable, irrational, intuitive, informal organization can be managed" (Peters and Waterman 1982: 11).

Willmott agrees with the authors to designate this approach as rational, with the difference that he is much less enthusiastic about it than Peters and Waterman. He fears the concomitant totalizing impact which comes forth from the broader conception of rationality: "Its central element is that, in the name of expanded practical autonomy, it aspires to extend management control by colonizing the affective domain. It does this by promoting employee commitment to a monolithic structure of feeling and thought, a development that is seen to be incipiently totalitarian" (1993: 517). Indeed, Peters himself does not mince matters: "These devices – vision, symbolic action, recognition – are a control system, in the truest sense of the term. The manager's task is to conceive of them as such, and to consciously use them" (Peters 1988: 486).

Reification

After the observation of the rational nature attributed to management by many and of the problems that rationality entails, we cannot but find that the whole field of organization studies is marked by difficulties with organizational scientific rationality. In the immediately preceding sections I have brought these together under the headings "deception" and "exclusion".

But is there more to say about the connection between rationality and the problems we observed? Is it sufficient to note, as most authors quoted until now, that management discourse is marked by rationality and that at the same time a set of recurring problems presents itself? That connection is not precise and convincing enough. It can only become convincing through a further development in the form of a possible intrinsic link between the nature of rationality and the unwanted phenomena occurring in management practice. In the following I try to make plausible that such an intrinsic link exists. I will refer to it as the "deficiency of rationality".

I find starting points for describing the deficiency of rationality within the more reflectively minded management literature. The problems that I designate as deception and exclusion are derived by some authors in that literature from the occurrence of illusions, which are related to rationality. These illusions cause phenomena (mostly social phenomena) to be misinterpreted (deception) or not to be seen at all (exclusion, blindness).

But what exactly is that illusory character of rationality? Judging from a number of reflective management authors, the illusion appears to be an illusion that the world consists of stable, well-definable entities that can be known as such. And the motive – which does not have to be deliberate – for the establishment of that illusion according to those authors stems from the pursuit of control which is inherent to rationality.

Blaug considers this mechanism to work across the entire width of the established social sciences that wish to start from "an institutionalized illusion of surprising stability" (1999: 34, 35). This pursuit of stability manifests itself in *reification*, i.e. the granting of a thingly character to concepts such as "individual", "society", "organization". Further, Marx already understood that reification is misleading because that mechanism creates its own reality which it is difficult to escape from: "[H]e knew that reification resists empirical falsification. He understood that this kind of illusion was almost inescapable" (Blaug 1999: 40).

Knights and Willmott speak of "sociology's unreflective adoption of common sense understandings about 'the individual', 'society', and their relationship" (1989: 536). Especially with respect to organization studies, De Caluwe and Vermaak describe this way of presenting matters as follows: "This explicit order is often equated with steady states, structures and systems, predictability, and controllability. Organizations are orderly constructions consisting of clear-cut elements (objects) that behave in an understandable manner" (2004: 204). Hernes and Bakken (2003: 1516, 1517) also note a connection between the search for stability and deception. They show how the desire to control, inherent to rationality, requires stable elements. In their turn stable elements inhibit people's capacity for acting and changing.

Exclusion, that is to say a blindness to aspects of social reality, is also linked to the illusion of stability. The inability to observe particular social phenomena is according to Winograd and Flores directly connected with reification, the mechanism that they describe as the analyzing of reality in terms of objects and their properties. If we do that "we thereby create a blindness" (1986: 97). The social phenomena that disappear from sight are those phenomena that are difficult to reconcile with a reified universe, such as interaction or communication. The focus on steady states assigns to the fixed entities a kind of determined nature. Interaction between these entities loses its naturalness and becomes suddenly problematic: what can communication look like between entities the boundaries of which are preferably defined as sharp as possible? It is hard to imagine opportunities for change arising in that circumstance.

When it comes to attempts to innovate products Deuten and Rip (2000: 90) give insight into how the mechanism of reification acts to defend the status quo. Within the prevailing rationality stereotypes are created such as: "the user", "the ally", "the product-to-be", "the adversary", as if these are isolated actors who each have their own pre-programmed course. Subsequently the managers involved come to wonder why matters are so tightly wedged. Hosking shows the negative relationship between reification and interaction (and therewith the potential for movement and change) by a reverse approach. She tries to imagine that reification is done away with and then she sees change potential grow.

By shifting from entities and individual acts, the locus of change shifts to interaction processes and how they co-construct, reproduce, and change social realities and relationships.
This has a major implication for change work in that interactions become both the 'unit of
analysis' and the locus of transformation. (2004: 266)

Knights and Willmott search in the same direction: "An alternative is to take
social practices as the focus of analysis, and to explore how these practices are
simultaneously mediated by subjectivity and by relations of power" (1989: 536).

To summarize, we can say that a connection can be made between the observed
deception and exclusion on the one hand, and organizational rationality on the other
hand, namely: through the occurrence of illusions as a result of reification. These
illusions and reification are regarded as intrinsic to rationality and designated as
the deficiency of rationality because reason has to perform its controlling work by
means of those hampering devices.

By drawing this conclusion, we end up in the field of epistemology. It is now
all about organizational scientific knowledge and about how reliable and complete
that can be. This has implications for the continuation of our investigation into the
problematic nature of change rationality. The problems that arise appear to originate from certain views on cognition that link to that rationality. We have to further
investigate those views.

Representation

Thematizing of the problematic nature of rational cognition within organizational
scholarship is, again, only found in its more reflective currents. Blaug expresses
the sentiments that live there with the statement that mainstream political science,
towards which those scholars are orientated, is seriously hampered by persistent
forms of perceptual and cognitive failure (1999: 34).

It should be noted that within organizational scholars' circles, especially in the
mainstream, there are also ardent supporters of rational cognition, who believe that
organization studies fails seriously in its perceptual and cognitive achievements.
Their diagnosis is exactly the reverse: for them there is nothing wrong with reification. Jeffrey Pfeffer for instance defends the thing-oriented approach of traditional
organization studies when, in disgust, he notes that the contemporary organizational
scientific literature "has moved too far from the basic properties of organizations.
Organizations are material entities with physical characteristics, characterized by
social relations and demographic processes" (quoted in Chia 1996: 62).

So these mainstream organizational scientists, also known as functionalists, make
a different diagnosis of the causes of organizational scientific failure than the more
reflective authors do, and consequently suggest also a different solution. In their
eyes, rational cognition is not applied consistently to the precise context. If it were to
be so applied, in their view, the situation would be a lot better. Given my conclusion
from the previous paragraph, that the rational approach has a number of problematic
properties, such as deception and blindness in respect of certain social phenomena,

I do not agree with their view. I therefore will not comment on the suggestions for improvement from this group of traditionalists.

Within the group of authors that acknowledge the "deficiency of rationality", a key role is assigned to a certain philosophical-technical concept from the rationality tradition in cognitive failure, which is connected with rationality. That is the concept of *representation*. "A representation" – taken as a noun –, or "representation" – taken as an action – can be described as something mental which within the human mind gives a reliable reflection of an entity from outside the human mind. (The) representation may be expressed in signs or words. The concept of representation presupposes a certain arrangement of the world. Namely, in the words of Chia (1996: 70), "that a fundamental split exists between the world and the word and that the world is made up of discrete and identifiable material and social entities which can be faithfully documented using precise literal concepts and categories." From this perspective, in this world-view, four presuppositions can be distinguished which are essential to arrive at the concept of representation:

a. A representation is separated from that which it reflects ("the thing itself").
b. Notwithstanding any separation, the reflection is reliable and usable for cognition, thinking and speaking: there is correspondence between the representation and that which it reflects.
c. The things themselves have a clearly identifiable, stable identity; they are separated from one another by clear boundaries.
d. Combining (b) and (c): also representations, being reflections of those things, are thus separated from one another by clear boundaries.

In assumption (c) we recognize what in the previous paragraph we called reification: the idea that entities have a thing-like nature and are separated from one another. The approach to the world that starts from the thing-like nature of entities is referred to by Chia (1996: 21, 68) as "being-realist ontology" and by De Boer (1976: 125) as "thing-ontology".[1] In this approach things are characterized by their stability, amidst the changes of their properties. In the way in which Descartes in his *Meditations* assigns a stable identity to the piece of wax, despite the fact that now it is hard and then it is soft, and that, in soft condition it can take many different forms. Through assumption (d), this stability is also claimed for the representation as a reflection of the thing. So, the outlines of identities repeat themselves in their representations.

Winograd and Flores (1986: 20) explain the function of representation within the rational tradition. Representation, according to that tradition enables language

---

[1] I understand thing-ontology, based on the writings of De Boer (1976 and 1989), as follows. Thing-ontology assumes that material and immaterial things have a definable identity. In this point of departure reification (i.e. the attributing of a thing-like character to what exists) is linked to the postulate of a reality outside us which can be known by us. That connection is triggered by the finding that things are not always empirically distinct, so that for defining of the assumed identities recourse has to be taken to a knowable order which exists independently of us (and therefore is reliable) in which those identities are established.

because it mediates between the objects and the corresponding words. For thinking and knowing, representation is important because representations, easier than the things they reflect, can be manipulated. Questions can be addressed to them, and on paper and through computers they can be processed and communicated in the form of schedules and structures, with the pretence that such manipulation does not affect their correspondence with the "real" things. Thus, the concept of representation proves to be linked to a cognitive view which for knowing assigns a crucial role to representation. This cognitive view is called *representationalism*. Representationalism therefore is supported by the same set of above mentioned presuppositions, (including (c): reification) as is representation.

It may seem unlikely for such a philosophical-technical concept as representation to be problematized in management literature. But actually, representation is under attack there indeed, and by some authors it is regarded as a problematic part of the rationality tradition.

That is, for instance, the view of De Caluwe and Vermaak (2004: 204). Referring to the theoretical physicist Bohm (1992), they discuss a number of conventions of thinking in the rationalist management literature. These conventions consist in a tendency to consider neatly separate representations in the mind as reliable reflections of reality. The organizational reality is then supposed to be built out of the same categories as we work with in our heads. The authors argue however that it is very much the question whether those conventions are justified.

Shotter turns against the concept of representation. His objection is that representations like they are in the head, are stripped of any context, while organizational phenomena are always embedded in a set of relationships and practices:

> Instead of a decontextualized theoretical-representational understanding of how things should be, ideally, we want a continually updated, ongoing, contextualized practical-relational understanding of how they actually are for us, in relation to our involvement in a practice. (1998: 137)

Linstead (2002: 98) shows what that means, for example, when it comes to motivating employees. Motivation can not be considered as an isolated psychological variable. Whether someone is demotivated by certain factors proves to be dependent on an unimaginable multitude of other things, like someone's character, the relative power in the organization, the informal relationships within and outside the organization. The impact of these matters, which often is physical and emotional in nature, provides more insight into reality than the "symbolic representations through which the intellect works."

Weiskopf and Willmott make the connection with the control- and accountability-oriented character of the rationality tradition. "Representations are, in this sense, always self-referential: they refer back to the attempt of the representer to impose order on a changing and unrepresentable "real". The knowledge generated by this effort reflects our "will to order" (. . .) rather than some pre-existing state of reality" (1999: 564). Pålshaugen (1998: 32, 33) can understand the attraction of representation. It is often the pressure of organizational issues and dilemmas that brings us to create a picture of the situation in the form of diagrams, matrices and blueprints. But those images imprison us in one-dimensionality and biases.

Also Ten Bos talks about the oppressive force of organizational rationality and the function of the image therein. He is looking for a way out through breaking the images – that is to say – the representations.

> It always comes to making fade the hierarchy and consistency of the image that you see – foreground versus background. Only in this way the finite image opens up with respect to infinity. Only thus infinity can enter the image. But the entrance of the infinite is not organizable (...) All this is about 'border' as a principle of organization. (2004b: 5; translation NvdV)

Summarizing, we find that many of the problematic features of the rationality tradition within organizational studies can be traced back to the concept of representation, in close conjunction with the concept of reification, and coming together in the view of cognition which is named representationalism. The fact that this complex of reification and representation is being problematized has important consequences. For representationalism can be considered as an essential part of the prevailing view within the social sciences on what science is or should be. Chia (1996: 34) points to the wide impact of representationalism on the formation of views on social science:

> Thus, a singular belief in the idea of an ideally isolated system (based upon a being-realist ontology) has propagated a whole chain of epistemological commitments, intellectual priorities and research rationales that include the correspondence theory of truth, the persistent emphasis on theory–building in human inquiry, the insistence on a causal explanation in accounting for material and social phenomena, and the often obsessive pre-occupation with designing research methodologies that are believed to help minimize the effects of theory on observation. (1996: 34)

Apparently, by formulating the deficiency of rationality as a problem of representation, a complete social and thereby organizational scientific tradition comes into question.

Functionalism

The prevailing conception of science within the social sciences, of which representationalism is such an essential element, is referred to as functionalism.

Functionalism is inspired by ideas about social science of, among others, Comte, Spencer and Durkheim. The latter saw social phenomena as "social facts" that must be considered as things which can be objectively defined (Durkheim 1969: 41). Study of those phenomena should search for their origins and explain their function within the whole of society as a social order. As to the method of research the exact sciences should serve as a model.

The most important functionalist schools and their most famous representatives within organization studies include the Scientific Management school (e.g. Taylor, Fayol), the Socio-technical systems theory (e.g. Argyris), the Equilibrium Theory (e.g. Barnard, Simon), the Structural Functionalist approach (e.g. Selznick) and the Contingency Theory (e.g. Lawrence and Lorsch). Acclaimed contemporary exponents of functionalism are Pfeffer, Hilmer and Donaldson. Ten Bos calls them "the new rationalists" (2000: 187), and presents, among others, the following characteristics of the assumptions in respect of scientific knowledge that the latter two depart from in their book *Management Redeemed* (1997):

- The knowledge management theory produces should be universally applicable, regardless of different geographical locations of organizations.
- This knowledge comes from organizations that for that reason should be regarded as laboratories. However, in those laboratories, the senses cannot be considered reliable because they generate primitive forms of knowledge. Experiments should therefore be conducted in an objective and reproducible way.
- Precise terminology is of utmost importance. Knowledge must be defined in unambiguous definitions and rules.
- This knowledge should be accessible to all practitioners, but without simplification.
- This knowledge should be useful.

If we combine the characteristics mentioned by Ten Bos with those of Chia from the quote presented slightly earlier, then the following four principles can be considered as important characteristics of functionalism:

1. Knowledge of universal truths is possible; therefore, generalizations and theories are desirable.
2. There are objective, value-free methods for those truths to be reached.
3. Explanation of social phenomena is possible by identifying unambiguous causal relationships.
4. Social theories can be applied in practice.

It is not difficult to recognize in these characteristics the influence of representationalism. To elucidate that influence I want to indicate for these four characteristics of functionalism the extent to which they follow logically from the four assumptions of the representationalism we earlier came across. These four assumptions were:

a. A representation is separated from that which it reflects ("the thing itself").
b. Notwithstanding any separation the reflection is reliable and usable for cognition, thinking and speaking: there is correspondence between the representation and that which it reflects.
c. The things themselves have a clearly identifiable, stable identity; they are separated from one another by clear boundaries.
d. Combining (b) and (c): also representations, being reflections of those things, are thus separated from one another by clear boundaries.

With respect to the first mentioned principle of functionalism (about universal truth, generalizations, theorizing) applies that it may be associated with assumption (a) in combination with assumption (c). Indeed, precisely the separation (formulated in (a)) is, within representationalism, the guarantee for the purity of that reflection. That reflection is not affected by the random appearance of the thing in the world, but shares in an ideal, essential, perennial truth. And that ties back to the argument of (c) that things, notwithstanding their changing properties, are stable, like Descartes' piece of wax. Chia (1996: 41, 42) explains that, precisely because representation and reality represent two different orders the purity of the representations is guaranteed.

This manifests itself for example in the convention to describe social concepts as precisely as possible. The order of representation expressed in words and concepts, is considered to contain truth. This also means that the knowledge we derive from a word is wider than just the knowledge of one concretely appearing thing: it is knowledge about the genera and species of which the appearing thing is only a sample. In this way, representation is indispensable for generalization and theorizing.

The second principle: the possibility of value free, objective methods leads back to the same premise (a), now in combination with premise (b). The latter is reflected in the belief that the representations and patterns of thought that we use in performing experiments correspond in a unambiguous and reliable way with the things which they reflect. Simultaneously, the belief in the separation (a) ensures that our manipulations do not affect the behaviour of our research object. In this way non-distorting manipulations are being thought of as a serious possibility.

The possibility of univocal, causal explanation is the third premise. This assumption can be linked to assumption (c). Indeed, because things in the world are regarded as stable entities, it is possible to assume that also the interactions between those entities will have a stable character. Starting from that assumption, you can choose modes of explanation of interactions based on repetitive patterns. These patterns suggest the existence of fixed and necessary chains of causes and consequences, whereby any cause has necessarily one or more associated consequences. Explaining phenomena then boils down to discovering these causal relationships between the entities studied. De Boer (1976: 125) in his explanation of the thing-ontology points to Husserl's statement that a thing can only be understood from the forces that are being brought to bear upon it and by varying those forces. What does not fit into this overall consistency, we can not call "real": it is ghost-like.

The fourth principle is that social theories are applicable in practice. This starting point connects with principle (b): the reflection of a thing in its representation is to be regarded as reliable. So that reflection contains, notwithstanding the completely-disconnected-from-the-world, mental nature of representation, information on which actions in the world-as-it-is can be performed in the way that was projected by the representation.

The above exposition makes clear the extent to which functionalism is based on representationalist assumptions. This means, however, that the problems of reification (i.e. deception and exclusion), through representation, are reproduced within functionalism. Thus the deficiency of rationality, led back to representationalism, makes problematic a whole scientific tradition which is based on that representationalism. Jacques defines that science or tradition as the "discourse of objectivity" and leaves no ambiguity about his position on this:

> To blindly insist on the superiority of the scientific discourse of objectivity, in the absence of compelling evidence of its success, is to enact the dynamics of dysfunctional family abuse at a societal level. (1996: 175)

In the circles in which the above diagnosis takes place, dissatisfaction with functionalism looms large. For this reason, and since this dissatisfaction became manifest, the discontents looked for alternative approaches that are not affected by the deception and exclusion of representationalism.

Social constructivism provides such an alternative to functionalism. Its principles were to a large extent defined in the book *The Social Construction of Reality* (1966) by Berger and Luckmann. Social constructivism counters the view of social phenomena as entities through the awareness that they – i.e. "organization", "society" and "individual" – are to a large extent of our own creation. These concepts have been socially constructed and are, according to the view of social constructivism, a tissue woven from interaction and symbols. In this view the social reality of organizations, therefore, has no objective, independent character. That reality is fluid in nature and is largely determined by how the organization members on a daily basis deal with each other and talk about it.

Interim Balance

It is time for making up an interim balance. What is the significance of the actions that we performed in the first half of this Chapter 2, and which began with concrete problems and ended with abstract epistemology?

First of all, for the field of organization studies we identified problems that are associated with rationality by reference to management authors that relate those problems to rationality. Then we considered the intrinsic connection between rationality and those problems by demonstrating how reification and representation, as functions of the control-oriented rationality, cause those problems to arise. We have called this the "deficiency of rationality". Finally, we have suggested that functionalism, being the dominant social science tradition, through its embracing of representation and reification, is contaminated by the same deficiency of rationality.

At the beginning of this chapter I made it clear that to associate Levinas with organization studies, it would be important to establish parallels between the field of organization studies and Western philosophy. For that reason it must be shown that within philosophy a parallel link of rationality to certain problems can be found. I need to show that problems with rationality are identified by Western philosophers, and also that these philosophers associate those problems with reification and representation, which thereby render questionable an entire scientific tradition. The second part of this chapter will therefore discuss how philosophy identifies and deals with problematic aspects of rationality.

Section 2: Problematic Rationality in Philosophy

Rationality in Philosophy

As indicated in the introduction to this chapter, I understand rationality as the use of the human reasoning ability (reason) to know and control the environment and to account for one's actions and thoughts. By Rationalism I mean the ideology that assigns great, sometimes exclusive, value to rationality.

For a good understanding of these concepts in a (cultural-)philosophical sense, it is appropriate to say something about the emergence and development of rationality in Western society.

Rationality has already for millennia been a feature of Western civilization. At least since the days when Parmenides, relying on reason, defined reality as one and immutable, Plato marked sensorial knowledge as inferior and Aristotle regarded rationality as the property through which human beings are distinguished from animals. The appreciation of reason was taken over by the Romans, had a temporary setback in the early Middle Ages, but played an important role again from the rediscovery of the classical writers in the thirteenth century, up to our time.

The intensity of the appreciation and the belief in the power of reason could vary a lot during those 2,500 years. Parmenides, for example, but to a lesser extent Plato as well, assign to reason a superior if not exclusive, position as a gateway to absolute Truth, that means as a source of knowledge and control. All this at the expense of the senses which they consider to be misleading and therefore unreliable. For Aristotle, however, the senses play a major role. He sees them as part of the reasonable capabilities of human beings and as such they contribute to knowledge and to control of the environment. So his conception of rationality is broader than that of Parmenides and Plato.

A strong narrowing of the conceptualisation of rationality took place in the seventeenth century. Particularly under the influence of Descartes the view was established that rationality primarily relates to ideas. And that that is good, because true knowledge can only be found in the sphere of ideas, for example in mathematics and logic. Thus, true knowledge and thereby mastery of the world are achievable for us only through reason. If sensorial impressions can contribute to our knowledge, control and accountability at all, that is only after they have been screened by reason as to misconceptions, presuppositions and blind faith. Scientific work, under the influence of Descartes, becomes above all working methodically under the guidance of reason. It is not difficult to recognize in this Enlightenment rationality a philosophical and scientific tradition that has perpetuated in Western society through the twentieth century.

A number of cultural philosophers (Guthrie 1978, Toulmin 1990, 2001) wonder why conceptions of rationality change in the course of Western history and are understood in a broad sense at one time, and in a narrow sense at another time. They point to a likely connection with the socio-political situation of the periods in which those changes occur. Narrowing of the conception of rationality takes place in situations of great social unrest. Plato lived in Athens during a period when great confusion took hold of the city after losing a series of wars against the Persians and Spartans. He was, in the footsteps of Socrates, most concerned about the sceptical and amoral climate that prevailed in the city under the influence of the Sophists.

In response to that atmosphere he stressed, says Guthrie (1978: 75), the possibility of solid knowledge, even in the moral field. He found his answer in the conception of eternal ideas that are accessible for reason and which offer more certainty than the false information provided according to him by the senses. Toulmin (1990: 35ff, 2001: 97) notes that the religious wars in the early seventeenth century across Western Europe caused a defeatist mood. The physical violence and the devastating theological doctrines caused thinkers to look for certainties convincing enough to bring fighters of different camps together. They dreamed of restoring social order and sought guidance for that in thought. Descartes found an unquestionable principle in his own reasoning.

Whatever may be the links between changing conceptions of rationality and socio-political history, the fact remains that during some periods in Western cultural history rationality has been conceived of in a narrow, sometimes very narrow sense. Actually, true knowledge and control according to that narrow view is to be found only through reason, and the experience of the senses is to be mistrusted. Sensory experiences may be accepted as a source of knowledge, but only after they have passed the formal screening procedures designated by reason.

I see this conception of rationality as another caricature, related to the earlier caricature of rationality which focuses on the highest expected utility. My own conception of rationality is, as noted above, broader. I conceive of rationality to be the use of our intellectual capabilities in general, including the capacity for sensory experience. That means rationality is the use of our individual capabilities to distinguish sense from nonsense and to offer resistance to blind faith and thoughtlessness.

The important role played by rationality in the Western cultural history has been extensively exposed by Max Weber. This historian, economist, philosopher and sociologist observed in European history a trend of rationalization: human behaviour was according to him increasingly determined by rational considerations rather than by affective motives or by tradition. Weber also found within this historical increase of rationality a distinction that helped him to characterize better the modern societies of Europe and America.

This distinction is one between "instrumental rationality" (also known as: formal, functional, technical or objective-related rationality) and "value rationality" (also known as: substantive rationality). De Jong identifies those two forms of rationality as follows: behaviour is instrumentally rational if "it focuses on the successful achievement of a particular objective, and both means and objective are deliberately chosen" (1997: 116; translation NvdV), whereas value rationality stems from the conviction "that a particular act possesses an intrinsic value (*Eigenwert*), regardless its benefit or result. The execution of the act itself is the goal. Behaviour is value rational if the objective has not been chosen deliberately, but the means to achieving that objective are based on rational considerations. A person acts according to value rationality, for instance, when he attunes his behaviour to cultural, religious, ethical or aesthetic values" (idem).

Weber believed that the modernizing societies of his time were characterized by an increase of *instrumental* rational action at the expense of *value* rational action. This manifested itself in an increasing focus on the collection and efficient use of resources, which was coupled to capitalism, well-organized states and bureaucracies. In opposition to this there was, according to Weber, a decline in the attention given to values which cannot directly be expressed in terms of efficiency, economy and self-interest. Weber saw in these trends a threat. He was afraid that man would become the prisoner of bureaucracy and standardization, that were called forth by his own instrumental rationality. Modern man was engaged in imprisoning himself in a self-made iron cage.

In addition to Weber, there are many other historians and philosophers who discovered problematic aspects to the way in which rationality came to function in the West. Below I will give some fuller detail.

Problems with Rationality

Totalitarianism

One of the first things to catch the eye when it comes to problematic aspects of rationality in our culture is the fact that some cultural historians relate the Holocaust to the Western rational tradition and mainly with regard to rationality as it is manifest in bureaucracies in the manner described by Max Weber.

Zygmunt Bauman (1989: 14) believes that the Holocaust is essential to our understanding of the modern bureaucratic method of rationalization, among other reasons because it shows how the bureaucratic aspiration for efficiency is both terribly formal and ethically blind. And later he says: "This is not to suggest that the incidence of the Holocaust was *determined* by modern bureaucracy or the culture of instrumental rationality it epitomizes; much less still that modern bureaucracy *must* result in Holocaust-style phenomena. I do suggest, however, that the rules of instrumental rationality are singularly incapable of preventing such phenomena" (ibid.: 17). Apparently a kind of blindness is at work here that plays into the hands of totalitarianism.

This can be related to a shortcoming of Enlightenment thinking that Critchley points out, namely the distancing from the daily lives of people. "The values of modernity – the Enlightenment – have no connection with the fabric of moral and social relationships: so, with daily life" (2003: 101; translation NvdV). They miss, as he summarizes, a purposefulness, which should come from experienced problems within living social practices. Instead, they offer rational instrumentality which, in the absence of goals, is a form of nihilism and can create a serious sense of emptiness in society. Alvesson and Willmott seem to point to the same issue in their reference to the *Dialektik der Aufklärung*, (Horkheimer and Adorno, 1987) that qualifies as a classic diagnosis of the mutilations that reason inflicted upon nature and upon (Western) culture: "Horkheimer and Adorno (. . .) and Marcuse (. . .) were very conscious of the limitations of human reason but had no way of dealing with this problem" (Alvesson and Willmott 1992: 439). Actually it made them desperate. Apparently, we are confined by rationality in our capacity to discuss moral, social and perhaps other questions in a satisfactory way.

According to Lyotard the tendency to totalitarianism is not limited to political-bureaucratic rationality. Indeed, the very urge-to-control, a feature of all Rationalism, is totalitarian. "[Lyotard] further argues that, although totalitarian regimes may be disappearing, the 'spirit' of totalitarianism is not at all extinguished. This spirit lies according to Lyotard in the attempt to forget or exclude the 'unmanageable'" (quoted by Janssens and Steyaert 1999: 376).

Putnam sees a danger in the generalizing tendency of reason, especially if the latter is related to ethics. "The danger in grounding ethics in the idea that we are all 'fundamentally the same' is that a door is opened for a Holocaust. One only has to believe that some people are not 'really' the same to destroy all the force of such a grounding" (2002: 35). Apparently, rationality is inseparable from the exclusion it entails: exclusion follows rationality like a shadow.

Deception

Obvious disasters such as the Holocaust and wholesale moral inadequacy contribute to a problematisation of rationality at the level of our present culture as a whole, because of the primacy we afford to rationality. But there are much vaguer forms of dissatisfaction with, and outright opposition to the dominance of rationality which arose in advance of this.

These were expressed in philosophical and literary writings starting with the Romantic movement of the early nineteenth century. They continued during the nineteenth and twentieth centuries in a broad European cultural-philosophical movement that saw itself as a cultural revolt against the traditional belief in reason of the eighteenth and nineteenth centuries. Amongst others Schopenhauer, Nietzsche, Kierkegaard and Bergson (Mann 2003: 106) are included in this movement.

Schopenhauer's complaint is directed mainly at the misleading effect which is produced by reason.

> This (Schopenhauer's, NvdV) insight: the observation, contrary to as classical humanism would have it, that the function of the human intellect is to serve and justify the will, to provide it with deceptive motives and to rationalize the impulses, contains a skeptical and pessimistic psychology, unrelentingly pervasive, that not only prepared, but already is what we call psycho-analysis. (Mann 2003: 57; translation NvdV)

Others, like Bergson and in a sense also Husserl, emphasize the impoverishment of the experience of reality that the dominance of reason entails. Bergson elaborates on this theme especially with respect to the experience of time. This latter has lost, under the influence of rationality, its original flow character that, according to Bergson, is typical of true experience of time. Linstead relates that to the operations of the intellect, "which too often get entangled in the factitious – the artificial world of false problems rather than the apprehension of pure process" (2002: 102).

We may conclude that, over the entire field of Western culture, from politics to philosophy, there is an awareness that rationality has a deficiency. For example: rationality does not know how to address itself to moral questions; rationality entails exclusion; rationality distorts perceptions of reality and is thus misleading. These aspects of rationality, experienced as problematic, may explain why in contemporary cultural-philosophical debates rationality is a much discussed topic. Critchley believes that the question of the status of reason and rationality has become, because of the experience of irrationality in human existence, a predominant theme. In the words of Beiser (quoted by Critchley; translation NvdV): "It is no exaggeration to say that (. . .) the problem of the authority of reason has become one of the key issues throughout the continental tradition" (2003: 40).

Representationalism

The above-identified problems with rationality have been arranged on the one hand under the heading of blindness especially to moral phenomena, which leads to exclusion; and on the other hand of blindness to reality, which has a misleading effect. Winograd and Flores summarize this succinctly: "Reflective thought is impossible without the kind of abstraction that produces blindness" (1986: 97). From the moment, around the end of the eighteenth century, that these deficiencies have been recognized, thinkers in the West tried hard to determine more precisely what exactly is the connection between the use of the reasoning and the ostensible signs of blindness. Since blindness can be understood as a failure of cognition, possible relations between the functioning of reason and the occurring problems should be looked for in the two areas which together enable cognition: ontology, i.e. the set of views about the nature of reality; and epistemology, i.e. the views on the way the process of knowing proceeds. The contribution to this reflection of Nietzsche, building on that of Schopenhauer, has been very important.

Nietzsche noted that, for the dominant Western ontology, properties of reason play an important role. Our thinking proceeds through concepts and, as Groot quotes from *Die fröhliche Wissenschaft*, we can only perform thinking "under the illusion 'that durable things exist, that similar things exists, that things, substances, bodies exist' " (2003: 32; translation NvdV): i.e. by reification and by equalizing the unequal within specified categories (31). On that basis we assume that the world is a whole of defined entities. But that illusion then takes us in because the definitions, which at first are only emergency constructs for performing reflection, take the place of the real world: "With these concepts the human genius creates its own world, no longer on the basis of the world as it is, but based on the concepts and schemes that he has made himself of it. That is an illusory world which however is being assented to for so long as to make its artificial character no longer noticed" (31).

The reason that we need those concepts and schemes has much to do with the way in which rationality performs in the process of cognition. This process is considered to proceed through representation; that we have described above as something mental that within the human mind gives a reliable reflection of an entity from outside the human mind and that can be expressed in signs or words. Thus, the concept of representation presupposes a certain arrangement of the world. This interdependence between the functioning of representation and its associated assumptions, can be described now more precisely as follows, with the benefit of Nietzsche's analysis: the mechanism of representation creates its own conception of the arrangement of the world, while the latter simultaneously is assumed to be an independent, a priori given.

In the above, it is clear how blindness can strike: rationality (including the capacity for cognition) imposes its condition "to know" upon the world before it starts the process of cognition, because otherwise it (rationality) does not *know* how to deal with that world. The world must be composed of separate entities. But, at the same time, we must believe in the fact that the world, regardless of our cognitive apparatus, is really reified. If at least we want to conceive of representation as something that provides us with true knowledge, and not with something that we have put into it ourselves.

Through his diagnosis, Nietzsche made it clear how blindness and illusory thinking are – as it were – concomitant with reason. This diagnosis was the starting point for further reflection on reification and representation by a series of late nineteenth and twentieth century writers such as Bergson, Heidegger and the post-structuralists. In their works above all language, as a means of expressing concepts, came to be the centre of attention, again departing from the observation that deception plays a part here. "As Bergson was aware, 'language, as the instrument of the intellect, is a great deceiver' " (Moore quoted in Linstead 2002: 106). Emancipation from the tyrannies of representation is therefore needed, according to Linstead (103). And Toulmin (2001: 87) says:

> Looking back to the twentieth century historians will talk about it as the 'age of representation': a time when people in all areas of art, thought, literature and science reflected on, or returned to, the place of language in human life and the basis on which our confidence in it relies. (Idem)

In Nietzsche's diagnosis it is not difficult to recognize representationalism – or to put it in other words: the cognitive philosophical complex in which reification and representation are interlinked – that we already came across in discussing organizational studies' problems with rationality. Indeed, those authors who see this mechanism at work within organizational studies, rely for their analyses on the philosophical tradition which problematizes reification and representation and stems from Nietzsche.

Scientism

Some of his analyses on cognition Nietzsche presented in the already mentioned book titled *Die fröhliche Wissenschaft*. His choice for this booktitle suggests that, over the entire field of the sciences, a relation can be observed between what I am summarizing here as representationalism, and the prevailing way in which science operates. And thus that the shortcomings of rationality that we find in representationalism are reproduced in the established sciences. How should we imagine this reproduction?

The dominant Western scientific view is that of scientism, which developed from the seventeenth century under the influence of the Enlightenment. Scientism says that there is only one type of science that may be called the "true" science and that may pretend to lead to "true" knowledge. This form of science is characterized by its compliance with certain strict criteria of objective and method. In their book *Beyond Theory* Toulmin and Gustavsen (1996: 205) present a list of requirements with which "true" science – called High Science by the authors – should comply.

"To summarize its main features:

1. The aim of scientific inquiries is to extend our theoretical knowledge of Physical Nature, or of Human Mind and Society.
2. The results of scientific inquiries are universal statements of theory, which describe the Order of Nature (or Humanity) in general, timeless, abstract terms and are ideally related together in axiomatic systems.
3. The empirical bases of scientific theory comprise, either, carefully designed experiments – not random unanalyzed experiences – or detached observations – unaffected by the observer's own interventions.
4. Experimental or observational reports can be stated in historical terms, but the universal principles of a theory must be a-temporal.
5. Practical disciplines comprise applications of theoretical knowledge."
(Toulmin and Gustavsen 1996: 205)

This scientific ideal was used primarily in the natural sciences. Application quickly led to great and revolutionary discoveries and the expansion of knowledge. But since scientism assumes the existence of one, stable, all-encompassing order, it can not allow the applicability of "true" science to be limited to the sphere of natural objects. The first of the above features of High Science therefore mentions society as a research field. Indeed, scientism is inclined to consider the High Science approach as the only appropriate method of research, also with respect to the social sciences. The latter's scientistic manifestation is functionalism which we already came across as the dominant approach within organization studies.

Some of the important features of functionalism we noted there, return in the characterizations of scientism by Toulmin and Gustavsen we have just read. These are: the belief in the possibility of generalizations and theories, the confidence in careful scientific methods, the confidence in causal relationships based on non-distorting manipulations and the view that theoretical knowledge is applicable in practice.

This similarity helps us to answer the question about the way in which the shortcomings of representationalism affect established science. Indeed, as for functionalism: we have seen already, through a comparison of the characteristics of representationalism and those of functionalism, that the problematic nature of rationality is reproduced in functionalism through the representationalism it embraces.

Since functionalism is nothing else than scientism for the realm of the social sciences, the characteristics that apply to functionalism apply to scientism as a whole. This means that scientism is affected by the shortcomings of rationality in the same way as functionalism.

Of the many works that focus on the connection between scientism, representationalism and rationality and its consequences, I will cite three to clarify the above. Each of them formulates its own answer to the problem of rationalist science and the answers are quite different.

In the beginning of the twentieth century Husserl intensively worked on what he regarded as *Die Krisis der Europäischen Wissenschaften*. In his diagnoses, Husserl links the crisis of the sciences with the role played by representationalism in scientism. He asserts that the shortcomings of prevailing science, which he describes as naturalistic, need to be overcome by a profound philosophical reflection on the process of cognition. New, more reliable forms of science can only arise, according to Husserl, if we become more aware of the origin and functioning of our representations.

So Husserl's suggestion does not imply that we distance ourselves from representation and side-line it. On the contrary, he indeed focuses on representation, extensively discusses the way it operates and assigns it an important role in the cognition process. However, he simultaneously problematizes its traditional pretensions, particularly the key claim of a reliable connection with the outside world. The world as-it-is is put between brackets in the so-called phenomenological reduction. Instead, Husserl tightly focuses his phenomenological research on the way representation works. He is committed to describing as precisely as possible how (sensory or imaginary) objects and situations are being "made concrete or 'constituted' " (Van Nispen 1996: 12; translation NvdV) in series of acts of consciousness.

Contemporary social scientists Shotter and Lannamann (2002: 589ff) speak about the imprisonment of scientists in the head, leading to a unilateral approach to the world and a deficient discourse. They indicate that this inadequate way of talking can directly be traced back to Descartes' conceptions of representational thought and the role that thinking plays in cognition.

There are two Cartesian beliefs which are still deeply rooted in our minds: (1) the idea that we can get to know an independent reality through representation and (2) the idea that a method exists to do that in a totally reliable way. So that thereupon the representations in your head suffice for the world to be investigated. About the first belief the authors say, quoting Charles Taylor, that one of Descartes' fundamental assumptions was that "knowledge is seen as *correct* (my emphasis, NvdV) representation of an independent reality" (Taylor 1995: 2–3 cited in Shotter and Lannamann 2002: 590). About the second belief that the certainty about the correctness is to be achieved by a method that derives its power precisely from the distance to the object (Shotter and Lannamann 2002: 591). This, according to the authors, must end up in "aboutness-talk": speaking in terms of principles, categories, generalizations, the results of observations at a distance. And thus in inadequacy to reality.

This deficiency of scientism, stemming from rationality, is also Bauman's target of criticism in his book *Modernity and the Holocaust* (1989: 19). That deficiency would imply blindness to fundamental social phenomena such as moral responsibility. Bauman points out that, in sociological terms, Eichmann and other perpetrators do not belong to a problematic category. "We know already that the institutions responsible for the Holocaust, even if found criminal, were in no legitimate sociological sense pathological or abnormal." For Bauman, this makes the common and thoroughly rationalistic sociological discourse highly problematic.

The Search for Alternatives

The dissatisfaction with scientism is reflected in the fact that – across the board within science – people seek alternative conceptualisations of science. Indeed especially those which are non-representationalistic since they should serve to get rid of the problems that are associated with representationalism such as linearity, reification, causality and, ultimately, deception and exclusion.

With regard to the natural sciences, this tendency manifests itself for example in the designing by Bohr and Heisenberg of another mathematics and physics. Plotnitsky indicates that they do not perceive of reality in a linear way anymore. For them there are no "knowable" objects because these are often the result of the experimental set-up (Ten Bos 2002).

Another approach that breaks with stability thinking is the chaos theory which invades a multitude of sciences. Chaos theory suggests (Baets 2004: 75) that our hierarchically structured and organized thinking is unable to fully understand planning and change processes. Biological and social systems can be regarded as networks of largely autonomous components which interact with each other. These interactions make the networks to develop and reproduce themselves into continuously different functional patterns. This continuous self-creation and self-organization is a very complex event that human ordering attempts can only disrupt. As far as people can contribute to these spontaneous processes, it is by creating the right conditions: to determine a simple objective and simple interaction rules, to give a lot of freedom and above all: the opportunity to learn and adapt.

Specifically with respect to the social sciences, I indicated in the previous section how social scientists are looking for an alternative to functionalism. A number of authors in that area consider social constructivism as an opportunity to break with representationalism.

Evaluation: There Is Congruence

In the previous two sections we examined, first with respect to organization studies and then to philosophy, how the problematic nature of rationality manifests itself. This was undertaken to determine for both areas whether rationality is experienced as a problem and, if so, whether the problematic aspects of both areas have similarities. The answers to those questions are important in considering whether Levinas can be related to organization studies.

The conclusions we draw with regard to both questions are in the affirmative: both in organization studies and in philosophy people identify and talk about problematic aspects of rationality. And there is much congruence between the two areas with respect to the way these issues are discussed.

In the first place, there is affinity as to the manifestation of such problems. In organization studies we could bring these under the headings deception and exclusion. In philosophy we ran up against a blindness which entails deception and totalitarianism, the latter of which can be associated with exclusion.

Secondly, it appeared with respect to organization studies that those phenomena can be traced back to views on the world and about cognition that are intrinsically connected with rationality. At an ontological level, rationality leads to reification and on to the assumption of a man-independent order of identities, together called thing-ontology; and on the epistemological level to the concept of representation. Reification, order-thinking and representation are linked to one another in representationalism. The same applies to philosophy, and the discussion of this element revealed that the parallel is not accidental but logical. The organizational studies authors who trace back the rationality problems to representationalism with regard to this subject, have been influenced by the philosophical reflection that for a large part goes back to Nietzsche.

Finally, with regard to the prevailing scientific view in organization studies, namely functionalism, we established that it is stamped by representationalism and that, because of that, it reproduces the shortcomings of Rationalism. Functionalism is a name for the social science version of scientism, which can be regarded as the dominant view on science of Western culture. Since functionalism and scientism share similar main characteristics we conclude that also scientism reproduces the shortcomings of Rationalism. The congruence between the two disciplines in attributing a crucial role to the mechanism of representation was confirmed by the finding that within both disciplines people seek for concepts of science which are freed from representationalism.

On the basis of these parallels, the conclusion is justifiable that the problems with rationality that we identified (in the first instance in Chapter 1) in the field of organization studies may apply over a broader area. These are also problems of Western science as a whole and thus a cultural-philosophical problem. But if this is the case, we are justified in consulting philosophers in any discussion of organizational studies issues which relate to rationality.

In this respect I have Levinas in mind; but not only him. Indeed, Levinas is not the only philosopher to whom we can turn to shed light on problems in organization studies. In the course of time, other philosophers have been explicitly seized upon to help clarify organizational scientific issues. To be able to value Levinas' unique approach, it is important to compare his with some of the other alternative approaches. I have chosen to present two of them. First approaches that are guided by postmodernism and then approaches which are inspired directly by the works of Heidegger and Wittgenstein.

With regard to the mode of presenting both these approaches and that of Levinas, another conclusion is important that can be drawn from this chapter. Namely, the conclusion here that representation and representationalism play a crucial role as causes of the problems themselves. The significance of this conclusion is that I will examine the works of these philosophers to the extent to which they too problematize representation, and that our attention will focus on the question of what credible alternative(s) to representation they offer.

Chapter 3
Two Alternatives to Representationalism

Introduction

The conclusions I draw in the previous chapter constitute the starting point for discussions in this and the following chapters. One of these conclusions was that the problems associated with rationality must be regarded as problems that are intrinsically linked to representationalism. The other conclusion was that the problems of organization studies with rationality are very similar to the problems that philosophy identifies around rationality.

From these observations I derive a justification to consult philosophers for my discussion of problematic rationality in organization studies. In doing so I am primarily interested in Emmanuel Levinas, who will be the subject of Chapters 4 and 5. In this chapter I will first present two strands of organization studies literature each of which, in its own way, searches for an alternative to representationalism. One strand does so by orientating itself towards the postmodernism of Foucault and Derrida; the other does so by turning directly to Heidegger and Wittgenstein. It should be clear that I do not set out to offer a complete account of the thinking of these four great philosophers. This chapter will simply map the way in which that thinking has been conceptualised by a number of management authors linked to organization studies themes.

The fact that I choose those two organization studies streams for discussion means that the thinking of Foucault and Derrida on the one hand, and that of Heidegger and Wittgenstein on the other, have something in common. Indeed they are both located, along with the philosophers towards whom they orient themselves, in a tradition of criticising representationalism that started with Schopenhauer and Nietzsche. But the affinity is in some ways even more direct within that critical tradition, as Heidegger and Wittgenstein chronologically precede the postmodernists. These affinities, among other influences, are direct sources of inspiration for postmodernism. Among other things, this can be seen from the views that both movements share with one another on the relationship between language and reality.

In spite of this chronologically logical sequencing, I will start with the presentation of the orientation of organization studies towards postmodernism. The

N. Van der Ven, *The Shame of Reason in Organizational Change*, Issues in Business Ethics 32, DOI 10.1007/978-90-481-9373-8_3, © Springer Science+Business Media B.V. 2011

reason for this is that in this book, in line with the countering of representation-alism, I seek a schema which runs from more-, to less intellectualism: or, in other words, from less- to more pragmatism. Within that scheme, it is appropriate to position Heidegger and Wittgenstein after postmodernism, as their contribution to more pragmatist views within organization studies – on the relation between theory and practice – has been significant.

Orientation Towards the Postmodernism of Foucault and Derrida

Representationalism: No, Representation: Yes

To overcome the inherent problems of representationalism, a number of organization studies authors seek to connect with the thinking of postmodern philosophers. These include Cooper (1989), Law (Cooper and Law 1995), Gergen (1992, 2003), Townley (1993), Parker (1993, 1997), Linstead (2002) and Hassard (1993). Why they do so, and what that connection can look like, has been described by Robert Chia in his book *Organizational Analysis as Deconstructive Practice* (1996). This book can be understood as a plea for the orientation towards postmodernism, in its Foucauldian and Derridian variants. Because Chia pays much attention to the confrontation with representationalism, in my presentation of the significance of postmodernism for organization studies, I will allow myself be guided by Chia's view on the developments that led to that orientation.[1] This means that my presentation will also focus on versions of postmodernism from Foucault and Derrida.

As a point of departure for his book, Chia takes the problematic nature of the views of dominant, functionalist, organization studies analyses towards knowledge and reality. He assembles these views under the heading of representationalism. By the term representationalism, in agreement with what I said in the previous chapter, Chia means the conception of cognition which views representation as being the reflection, in words or signs, of an independent, knowable reality (1996: 33, 34). The problem of representationalism for him lies in the imprisonment through reification and thinking in terms of mental pictures, which results in the inadequacy of organization studies to understand organizations really, and the inability to deal with change issues in a fruitful way. Chia points emphatically to the two components which make up representationalism: an epistemological component which

---

[1] The choice for Chia's book therefore is not based on the idea that he would be representative for the group of mentioned authors who are orientated towards postmodernism. Indeed, this group is too diverse and there is too much mutual criticism within that group (see for example, Organization 7 (3)) to allow anybody to be representative. The fact that Chia takes representationalism and its problems as a starting point for his argument determines the importance of his book within the context of my book.

states that representation can be an exact image of something else; and an onto-logical component, namely the view that such "something different" actually exists, i.e. that an unambiguous external and observation-independent reality exists. The latter view is called the being-realist ontology by Chia (1996: 26).

At this point it is important to stress the distinction between representation and representationalism. According to Chia, only representationalism is problematic among these two. Indeed, this latter is a constructed composition of speculations that is based on dubious presuppositions of which their supporters are unaware says Chia (1996: 49). Chia is therefore inclined to consider representationalism as an "ideology", whereas there is not much wrong with representation itself. As Chia says: "It has to be remembered that the postmodern critique of representationalism does not entail an outright rejection of the activity of representing (...)" (1996: 121). Indeed, such a rejection would be absurd, as imagining things (as happens in representation) is an intrinsic human characteristic (37). Because of the inherently human nature of representation, any conception of science – including those of organization studies – will have to assign to it a place within the process of cognition. But representation, for yet another reason, should get a (new) place in an organization studies that wants to put representationalism behind it. According to Chia, the very subject of organization studies – i.e. organizing – has everything to do with representing things. For representation has a major economic and pragmatic signification, he says. In his view representation is about making the world manageable; about bringing under control of what initially is beyond our grasp. That connection is situated in the process of thickening, summarizing and giving overview that is characteristic of representation: "[T]he act of representing needs to be understood as a form of economic, advantage-gaining strategy which mirrors the concerns and preoccupations of the representer in his/her engagement with his/her own experiences rather than as an attempt to accurately mirror an already-constituted and external reality" (Chia 1996: 102). From this perspective representation is motivated by the "will to order", and is even synonymous with organizing: "'Organizations' are formed by cumulative acts of representational abstraction in which the remote, the obdurate and the intractable are rendered more easily accessible and manipulable for the purpose of mastery and control" (1996: 119).

How should we imagine such a conceptualisation of representation? For his account of the pragmatic meaning of representation, Chia harks back to Robert Cooper's elaboration of representation as a strategy for remote control, displacement and abbreviation. For a number of scientific and organizational projects from Western history, Cooper shows how representation, as a means to act at a distance, is the basis of the successes of those projects. Such is the case with the use by the Portuguese East India Company of administrative accounts of acts that took place far away at/or overseas. Such accounts are to be regarded as representations: they make the facts present which, dispersed over different times and places, have occurred. "[S]uch apparently mere descriptions possess significant powers in that they are made to 'stand for' that which is not present" (1996: 129) and thus produce substantial benefits. Namely because it is possible in this way "to control events remotely by making present that which is absent through this process of substitution: 'Events that are remote (i.e., distant and heterogeneous) in space and time can be instantly collated in paper form on the desk of a central controller. (Cooper 1992: 257)'" (Chia 1996: 131). So, our desire to make representations arises from this incentive to find alternative ways to overcome our human limitations. "Understood in this way, the practice of representing is not an attempt to 'copy' an external reality, but to enable us to hold in our hands and to control and manipulate what is intractable or absent from us, i.e., to represent is to 'make present again'. For Cooper, the function of this process of representation is to 'translate difficult or intransigent material into a form that facilitates control'" (1992: 225). The conclusion is that representation has an economic nature: "Representation is simply a device for realizing gains and for ensuring that they come *again*" (Cooper 1993: 255, Cooper's emphasis). In view of the human impulse to overcome human limitations in this way, Cooper and Chia speak of the existence of a "will to represent" (Chia 1996: 130) and place that on a par with the "will to organize". "Representation and organization are therefore two sides of the same coin which issues forth from our primordial 'will to organize'" (1996: 219).

This means that an organization studies that wants to finish with representationalism, simultaneously has to stick to the concept of representation. The big question then is: how do you achieve this in such a way that you not fall victim again to the assumptions about representation that representationalism anchored deep inside us? How do you develop a view on representation that is free of that half-, or unconscious matter-of-coursenesses and that can thereby effectively enlarge our knowledge of organizing and organization?

That is not easy, says Chia, because one has to analyse representationalism in a very thorough and methodical way. To do that you have to think *upstream* as far as possible: upstream against the current of modernist thinking that tends to forget the context of its own truth claims (Chia 1996: 7). And that works best, he says, under the guidance of a selection of postmodern thinkers, in particular Foucault and Derrida. To clarify how persistent representationalism is, what are the problems and pitfalls, and why you ultimately arrive at Foucault and Derrida, he gives an account of the battle which different organizational scientific currents fought with representationalism and the degree of success that they achieved.

The First- and Second-Order Reflexive Organizational Scientists

Criticism of functionalism is primarily attributed to the more reflexive-minded organizational scientists, which, following Chia, I will label the "reflexives". This category includes, among others, Calás and Smircich (1992), Alvesson and Willmott (1992) and Weick (1989). These organizational studies scholars are inspired by the so-called linguistic turn in philosophy and by developments in the philosophy of science. Other names associated with the linguistic turn include among others Nietzsche, Saussure, Heidegger, Wittgenstein and Derrida. To a large extent their work is an elaboration of the awareness, in the words of Wittgenstein, that "the limits of my language are the limits of my world" (1961: 5, 6). By taking seriously this realization, many hitherto obvious things suddenly become less obvious. Representationalism, especially in the guise of the everyday view that language is a means to depict a reality lying ready out there, is suddenly a problem. It could be simply that the opposite is true: that language determines what my reality looks like and can create or cut off realities. This reasoning has far-reaching consequences: it undermines the conception of words and theories as tools to connect to an independent external reality. Related to the linguistic turn in philosophy of science is the development of "the increasing realization that the researcher/theorist plays an active role in constructing the very reality he/she is attempting to investigate" (Chia 1996: 79). Together with the consequences of the linguistic turn, this leads to the idea that the self-image – that of independent, objective observers – to which scientists are traditionally so attached, has become problematic. The scientist himself is in the spotlight now: he is a party in his own research, and is increasingly forced to take that into account.

These philosophical insights invaded organization studies from the sixties and seventies of the last century and influenced the more reflexive organizational scientists. The extent to which this happened, however, could be quite varied and for Chia that is reason to distinguish between first- and second-order reflexive management thinkers (1996: 85). The first-order reflexives acknowledge the problematic nature of scientific objectivity. They let themselves be guided by Whitehead's saying that "it is of utmost importance that we remain vigilant in critically revising our modes of abstraction" (Chia 1996: 34). They conceive of representation no longer as an innocent, "objective" reflection of reality, but as the giving of a presentation "on your own showing" with all the consequences for reality this implies.

However, all this applies, according to this group of reflexives, to the theories of others. In some ways these first-order reflexives claim for themselves a unique position. They accord themselves a meta-position and by doing so their own theories are supposed to be unaffected by the problems that hit the theories of others. In Chia's words: "Each meta-theoretical account is an attempt to outdo the others by claiming a less 'naïve' depiction of how things really are" (Chia 1996: 87). The author's own part is disregarded. This means, according to Chia, that the first-order reflexives, despite their awareness of the constructed nature of organization studies theorising, do not manage to leave representationalist ideology behind them. This is clear from the way in which they write their accounts: often in terms of comprehensive overviews or of superior knowledge, entirely within the tradition of classical representationalism. "Thus, what often starts off as a promising attempt to deal reflexively with the status of organizational knowledge rapidly gives way to an obsessive preoccupation with the slotting of the various theoretical approaches into 2 * 2 schemas (. . .)" (1996: 69). Because for themselves they still see opportunities to work from a privileged and independent position, at the end of the day their subjects reify under their hands. Thus they can observe the extent to which theories of others are social constructions, while their own compilations remain unaffected.

Like the first-order reflexives, according to Chia, second-order reflexives claim alertness, but with more incisiveness than the first-order reflexives. They are aware that the abandoning of representationalist ideology affects also their own theories.

These can not claim a superior reliability, they are – like the theories of others – nothing more than interesting stories and idiosyncratic thought exercises that should not be taken too seriously (Chia 1996: 89). However, this position creates its own shortcomings. The strong awareness of the author's influence on his own accounts, prompts this group of authors to continuously make themselves visible in their texts. With a competition in self-reflective texts as a result. Because of this characteristic, Chia describes those texts as tiresome and prone to the risk of sterility. To show that this organization studies movement ends in a blind alley he cites approvingly Latour who believes that this what he calls "meta-reflexivity" "is in my view, a suicidal attitude, similar (in spite of the contrary impression one might have) to the older idea that a sociological account full of statistics and methodological commitments can defend itself better than a 'plain' journalistic account" (Latour 1988: 169 in Chia 1996: 90). Chia calls the second-order reflexives clearly much more consistent than the first-order reflexives, but "[c]onsistency is, however, part of the language of representationalist epistemology (. . .)" (90), through the pursuit of accuracy of the image.

Gradually it becomes clear how cunning the attractiveness of the concept of representation is as a picture of reality. The venom of this view is in its suggestion that a higher point of view and, through that, superior knowledge are possible. The illusory nature of this view is acknowledged by first- and second-order reflexives, but at the same time they remain under the spell of the representationalist epistemology to such an extent that they cannot really find a way out. If they take seriously their doubts about representationalism they seem to have only the choice between two options that are equally unattractive: either to compete with other authors about who counters the treacherous representationalism most smartly; or to abandon all truth claims. The first option, chosen by the first-order reflexives, almost invariably gets stuck in the trap that it so hard tries to avoid: that of the higher position, so of a better picture, so of a factual reality, in short: reification. The second way-out suffers from such a surplus of self-relativizing, that the work of these authors perishes in sterility.

It may be clear that Chia values the second-order reflexivity higher than the first-order reflexivity. But eventually for him also the second-order reflexives fail to meet the standard required to actually do justice to the revolutionary twentieth-century philosophical insights, because those reflexives restrict their reflection to problematizing epistemology, i.e. the issue of the accessibility of reality. Notwithstanding: "(s)uch recent epistemologically inspired critiques, however, whilst a crucial first step, do not quite reach the heart of the paradoxes raised by the problem of reflexivity." True reflexivity can never be satisfied with that, because in the above approach *reality* (ontology) is still seen as an unproblematic category, and only the *access* to it (epistemology) would be a problem. This is, says Chia, ontological muddling. True reflexivity searches further, namely for the nature of reality (1996: 90, 97). Only by seriously questioning the ontology which is linked to representationalism: the being-realist ontology – i.e. the idea of a reality out there, independent of us and ready to be mapped – you create the conditions necessary to get rid of the epistemological illusion of representation, thought of as superior knowledge from a privileged position. According to Chia (1996: 97, 105) this is the main issue of postmodernism. Thus, the launching of this topic marks the transition in Chia's spectrum to a third organizational scientific current, namely the one which is inspired by postmodernism.

Post-modernist Organization Studies

The linguistic turn in philosophy did not stop at the problematizing of the *images* of reality. If it is true that the limits of language mark the limits of my world, then also the view of the world as an independent reality out there can no longer be maintained. Then you have to face the claim that language shapes our reality, or at least has its contribution in shaping it. Language constitutes reality. This awareness, which breaks with being-realism, is regarded by Chia as characteristic of postmodernism (1996: 97). Within organization studies among others Law, J. (1992, *Notes on the theory of the actor-network: Ordering, strategy and heterogeneity*, unpublished manuscript from the Department of Social Anthropology of Keele University, cited in Chia (1996)), Gergen (1992 and 2003), Hassard and Parker (1993) and Cooper (1992 and 1993) allow themselves to be guided by these post-modernist views. Chia gives a picture of what these developments entail by joining post-modernist philosophers like Rorty and Latour.

Latour points out the inadequacy of the reflection provided by first- and second-order reflexives on the textual rendering of a supposedly-independent reality. This meta-reflexivity, as he calls it, does not work and he dislikes it because "it (meta-reflexivity) makes texts less interesting, less rich and, as we saw, less believable" (Latour 1988: 169 paraphrased by Chia 1996: 90). Indeed, there is a reality, says Latour, but it is not independent and ready to be mapped. For it to acquire shape, direct contact and interaction with the world are needed. Writing is one of the possible forms of interaction with the world, but actually we should not use the verb "depict" for that activity for that is no longer the appropriate name for the game of writing: "[T]he name of our game: displaying the knower and the known and the work needed to interrupt or create connections" (Latour, quoted in Chia 1996: 91). This leads to what Latour calls "infra-reflexivity": an attitude that does not consider texts and scientific discourses any longer as pictures of reality but as part of it and thus makes them more exciting.

Rorty states that acquiring knowledge is aimed at obtaining as much inter-subjective agreement as possible (1996: 22). With this assertion, Rorty joins with Davidson's "coherence theory". The latter says that views can be true or false, depending on the degree of inter-subjective agreement about it, but they represent nothing. Indeed, Rorty will have no trouble to acknowledge that there is a reality, but the latter is, according to him, not depictable. By labelling truth and knowledge as products of social consensus in Rorty's view they become products of social communities. Instead of science which, by the unambiguous definition of its object ("reality") and of its method ("hypothetical deductive") is entitled to universal pretensions, acquiring knowledge now becomes a local affair which for each community can bring different results. As Chia says: "On this view, assertions come to be accepted as true, not because they are accurate representations of an external reality, but because they function as economizing aids that enable the individual and collectivity to cope with their specific set of local circumstances" (Chia 1996: 111). In this way every "interpretive community" creates its own truth and thus partly its reality. By his conception of cognition as a tool for dealing with local circumstances, Rorty's postmodernism can be characterized as postmodern pragmatism.

For Chia the postmodernist progress in terms of reflexivity with regard to the first- and second-order reflexives is to be found in a different conception of reality. "What is real for postmodern thinkers are not so much social states or entities but emergent relational interactions and patterns that are recursively intimated in the fluxing and transforming of our life-worlds" (Chia 1996: 117). Rorty and Latour express this position and within organization studies their insights have fruitfully been used, for example by March (1971/1988), Barnett (2000) and Van Maanen (1995). However, Chia thinks their usefulness for organization studies is limited, because they do not take into account fundamentally enough the phenomenon of representation. Indeed it is, says Chia, too simple to think that representation no longer plays a role of importance in human cognition, which he takes from Latour, or that this role is not interesting, as seems to apply for Rorty.

Regarding Latour, Chia's criticism (1996: 129) is that, after his rejection of representation in the modernist sense, he can no longer attribute any signification to representation. Whereas, according to Chia, representation – be it emphatically not in the sense of depicting – plays a large role in the construction of our reality. A reflexive analysis of the construction processes will have to be able to value the contribution of representation to them. Notwithstanding his appreciation for Latour's reflexive science-historical analyses, Chia therefore considers him not reflexive enough for a real understanding of the genesis of social reality with regard to representation.

Although he says this nowhere explicitly, Chia appears to suggest that Rorty does not match the standard of what postmodern thinking ought to do. Upstream thinking should not be foreclosed at the point where Rorty's constructivism/pragmatism stops: i.e. at a conceptualisation of truth as the unproblematic outcome of social consensus (Chia 1996: 18). The kind of postmodernism at which Chia aims has a clear moral commitment. That postmodernism cannot be satisfied with the social production of truth: the question must extend to how exactly do they function, the mechanisms of exclusion that are at work wherever consensus is being built? Chia finds that Rorty lacks adequate attention for precisely that question. For Rorty, the process of local consensus-building is not relevant as long as the end products of that process are not rejectable. For Rorty representation may play a role in shaping these end products, but that is of no interest: what counts is the outcome. By taking this position, Rorty with all his great contributions to postmodern thought, fails to meet the requirements of the kind of postmodernism that Chia has in mind.

Latour and Rorty seem satisfied with the once-and-for-all excision of representationalism and its pretensions and not to worry any further about representation. Chia cannot agree with this on the basis of his view on representation that we previously discussed, namely that, especially in organization studies, representation continues to play an important role. Chia persists with the connection of truth to representation, even though he, along with Rorty and Latour, abandoned completely thinking about the truth in terms of pictures. He now defines truth in a pragmatic sense: "We say a statement is true in so far as it allows us to economically grasp the complexities of a situation expediently and to thereby enable us to act coherently. *It is this economy of expression which defines the status of truth*" (Chia 1996: 121).

This conceptualisation of truth seizes upon the nature of representation as an activity that enables us "to hold in our hands and to control and manipulate what is intractable or absent from us, i.e., to represent is to 'make present again'" (Chia 1996: 121). So, representation according to Chia has to do with making the world manageable, with getting under control of what initially is beyond our grasp. But if representation remains so important, continuing to reflect on it remains a necessity because the representationalist pitfall continues to undermine it. This continuing reflection is necessary first of all for the understanding of organizing and organizations. Additionally, there is a moral motive: a moral imperative to investigate the precise operation of those representation-supported mechanisms of exclusion that appear everywhere where consensus is being built (Chia 1996: 18).

Deconstruction

For a variant of postmodernism to be fruitful for organization studies, according to Chia, it must meet the following two requirements. On one hand, it should leave behind representationalism as is the case with Rorty and Latour. But on the other hand, and unlike Rorty and Latour, it should persistently take into account the processes of reality-building and, thereby, the process of representation itself. The postmodern philosophers who succeed in establishing this combination are Foucault and Derrida (Chia 1996: 14). Compared to Rorty they are process oriented rather than outcome oriented. Unlike Latour, they acknowledge the role that representation plays in the processes of reality construction. They are interested in the *genesis* of the dominant consensus about reality. Above all, they practice deconstruction: that is to say by analyzing that consensus and meticulously pulling it apart, they reassess carefully what has been discarded in the process of building-up such consensual reality.

Applied within organization studies, the deconstruction[2] oriented postmodernism of Foucault and Derrida entails that "organization is now viewed as the

---

[2]The term deconstruction is usually associated with the philosophy of Derrida. In fact, the term is derived from him. But conceived of as the activity that aims "to 'undo' or to 'dismantle' the conceptual oppositions in linguistic convention which have provided the bases for framing our modern experiences of social reality" (Chia 1996: 145) it is quite possible to bring parts of the work of Foucault under that umbrella. In his archaeological and genealogical studies he tries to trace back the genesis of all kinds of social phenomena, with an eye for the fundamental role language plays therein (Chia 1996: 137 et seq.).

product of our human 'will to order' generating dense relational networks of representation" (Chia: 1996: 144). The new starting point for research now becomes the idea that "organization, as the act of representation when understood in terms of Derrida's 'différance' involves the deliberate process of stabilizing the 'manifold' so that it becomes possible to perceive of the latter as a discrete entity in itself" (1996: 144).

The associated practice of organizational analysis thus becomes an analysis of the way in which the processes of representation that underlie the organized world were enacted: this is deconstruction applied to representation. Organization studies scholars follow back the road to the sifting and the choices made in the course of these processes, and pay special attention to the material that dropped out, or was eliminated (1996: 144). The scientific purpose thereby served, through deconstruction, is situated in the possibility of acquiring knowledge about the mechanism by which some types of interactions are successful and lead to stable forms of organization, and by which other types of interactions completely founder (1996: 161). This also provides insight into how all sorts of false realities can be misleading (1996: 164). Chia points out that deconstruction can yield surprising insights by the radical questioning of matters that in the course of time became gradually taken for granted (1996: 18), and thereby can facilitate change. The moral motive for this deconstructivist approach consists in the wish to do justice to all material and opportunities that in the processes of representation – which, by definition, are processes of saving, economizing and thickening – have been excluded and got lost (1996: 18).

Summarizing Chia we can say that in his approach towards Foucault and Derrida, he finds an answer to the problem of representationalism within organization studies. On the one hand this may be because they, like other post-modernists, succeed in unmasking representationalism as an ideology. On the other hand, it may be because they distinguish themselves in a positive way from other post-modernists like Rorty and Latour, and pay attention to the continued importance of representation. Since for Chia, organizing is equivalent to representing, organization studies will only have a future if it will be dedicated to the study of how social formations are constituted by representation.

Evaluation

The problems that can be caused by representationalism have been indicated previously, where we placed them under the headings of deception and exclusion. Deception, because reification and picture-thinking entail an inability to understand certain social phenomena. Exclusion, because blindness occurs whereby some social phenomena are no longer seen at all. The question is now, if these are the problems of representationalism to what extent can the use of deconstructive philosophy provide an adequate response?

In the case of deception, I tend to think, along with Chia, that postmodernism as a whole succeeds in uncovering the presuppositions of representationalism.

Postmodern thinkers thereby provide us with the resources needed to avoid the pitfalls of representationalism. The first- and second-order reflexives are not sufficiently successful in that respect. They get stuck in a concentration on the epistemological aspects of cognition. They do not arrive at unmasking the being-realist ontology and therefore they keep running into the representationalist trap again and again. Accepting that the post-modernists manage to unmask representationalism, they also seem to realize that this unmasking is not equivalent to its final neutralization. They know that, given the structure of our thinking, reification and picture-thinking, deceptions and illusions remain a permanent threat. This results in a strong and healthy vigilance against unjustified knowledge-claims and premature generalizations among the post-modernists.

In the case of exclusion, Chia states that only some of the postmodernists make a useful contribution and I am also inclined to follow him in this. On his way to this conclusion he deals with the first- and second-order reflexives. It is apparent that the first-order reflexives were not able to do away with exclusion, given the high degree of mutual denunciation which seems to be almost inherent to their work. Neither is the response of the second-order reflexives satisfactory. They direct their criticism rather inwards than outwards and end up in the sterility of permanent self-exposure.

Postmodernism in this case cannot be regarded as a unitary block of thinking. Within postmodernism Chia distinguishes different positions. Rorty is content with the neutralization of the representationalist claims to absolute truth. Thereby, Rorty accepts as unproblematic the various particularistic conceptualisations of truth that take its place, as long as their content is not morally rejectable and they are rooted in a practice. This is in contrast to Foucault and Derrida who consider it to be an intellectual obligation to determine for *any* truth-formation how it was developed and at the expense of what other possibilities. Latour is also interested in that, but he pays too little attention to the role of representation in the establishment of organizational reality. That is why, Chia plausibly claims, only the variants of postmodernism from Foucault and Derrida enable us to counter exclusion within organization studies. In the words of Weiskopf and Willmott (1999: 567): "Deconstructive analysis usefully reminds us of the violence that is incorporated in the very concept of 'organization' which passes unnoticed in mainstream literature and accounts of organization."

This assessment implies to a large extent that I share Chia's view on the merits of postmodernism according to Foucault and Derrida. I am disinclined to reject the existence of an independent reality as a possibility, as postmodernism does according to Chia. But that does not prevent me from wholeheartedly agreeing with the postmodernist's dismissal of picture-thinking and their emphasis on the influence of social and linguistic structures on the construction of our reality.

Furthermore, with Chia, I believe that deconstruction within organization studies can contribute to a richer understanding of organizations "as essentially precariously balanced human accomplishments" (Chia 1996: 209). I appreciate, maybe even more explicitly than Chia, the moral commitment of deconstruction as an activity which seeks to recover what has been obscured and which points to the self-privileging mechanism in the formulation of knowledge claims. Chia speaks rightly of a high degree of intellectual alertness on the part of the post-modernists (1996: 17, 20) against the anti-intellectualism of downstream thinking.

At the same time, I have some reservations. I wonder whether this approach is not too optimistic. A first objection touches on the possibilities for systematically countering illusions. Are those possibilities themselves not too easily taken for granted? It is true, as Chia describes it, that postmodernism is very much alert and aware of the pitfalls of thinking. But is that sufficient to avoid those pitfalls? Can someone be his own critical authority? Can research schools be their own critical authority? Is there not something so cunning in our thinking, whether modern or postmodern, that intellectual operations – and that is what Chia talks about – are in themselves insufficient to prevent deception and almost always lead to some form of ideology and dogmatism?

A second objection relates to the negative nature of deconstruction as presented by Chia. Deconstruction may yield substantial benefits, but at the same time it is a tiresome business. The associations with negativity, of which Chia speaks ("Deconstruction is thus equated with the enterprise of destruction" (1996: 11)), may – as he says – not be entirely justified, but neither are they totally unfounded. Chia himself refers to the postmodern negativity: "It is the cultivation of the intellectual equivalent of what the poet John Keats calls 'negative capability' when dealing with ideas, that marks a postmodern style of thought" (1996: 97) and calls it "not a frivolous activity" (1996: 214). Before you reach any surprising new insights, continuous regression requires quite some effort from both performers and audience. Maybe it enhances the moral level of the efforts, but I see this mainly as a practical issue. The big, actually practical, question is: where to get the energy to perform deconstruction in a serious way? What gives you sufficient inspiration to do that? It seems that post-modernism does not touch that question. In any case, I do not know of authors who are practically alert in this sense and take into account the tiresome nature of a sustained intellectual reflexive attitude, or it should be Foucault's lament in *The Minimalist Self*: "[Y]ou see that's why I really work like a dog and have worked like a dog all my life. I am not interested in the academic status of what I am doing because my problem is my own transformation (. . .) Why should a painter work if he is not transformed by his own painting?" (Foucault 1983: 14).

With respect to these two objections Levinas can offer an elucidating contribution, in my view. I will return to this in Chapter 6, after my discussion of Levinas' philosophy.

The above-discussed concerns regarding Chia's preferred variant of postmodernism suggest that his efforts are laudable but very demanding and, perhaps, not entirely feasible. A further criticism is possible, namely the criticism that focuses on the intellectualistic approach of Chia's post-modernist variant. By its intellectualist nature, that approach would run the risk of losing touch with the lived day-to-day reality of organizations. This criticism has been formulated as follows by Gustavsen et al.:

> But no matter how well the post-modern and post-structuralist schools of thought have been able to identify the cracks in the walls of the fortresses, they have generally failed to consider another problem: the core weakness of the scientific fortresses is not the cracks in

the walls but the ground on which they stand. This ground is slippery and continuously on the move, because it is made up of human practices. The disappearance of the fortresses leave the practices untouched. What remains to do is to relate to practice: to find ways of working with practical problems in practical contexts that can positively utilize the kind of resource represented by research. (. . .) We do not do this by rewriting theory so that it looks more like being 'about' traditional practice than theory – like Bourdieu (1977) or Foucault (1972) – but by being practical, by taking part. (Gustavsen et al. 2001b: 271)

This means that the reflection which began with the linguistic turn passed through two very different elaborations. On the one hand, it has led to the extra alert reflexivity, which – being an eminently intellectual affair – is recommended by Chia for organization studies scholars. On the other hand, that reflection triggered a strong emphasis on practical situations and direct involvement therein of organizational researchers, as expressed by Gustavsen. In the next section this second response is addressed through a description of a current within organization studies in which praxis and practice have become important keywords as an alternative answer to the challenge of representationalism.

Orientation Towards Heidegger and Wittgenstein

Thrownness

This second group of organizational scientists who in their struggle with representationalism turn to philosophy, can be distinguished by their orientation towards the thinking of Heidegger and Wittgenstein. Although these two thinkers are usually thought to belong to different philosophical traditions, they appear to have developed a number of kindred thoughts in their approaches to representationalism. With this observation I can bring under one heading organization studies scholars who let themselves be guided by them as far as representationalism is concerned. This group includes Winograd, Flores, Weick, Shotter, Calori, Reason, Gustavsen and Pålshaugen. In my discussion of their views I will primarily discuss Heidegger's influence on organization studies, and to a lesser extent that of Wittgenstein. The reason being, as we shall see in Chapters 4 and 5, that to a large extent Levinas responds to Heidegger while not at all to Wittgenstein. I will interpret Heidegger's response to representationalism with the help of the expositions on that subject by Winograd and Flores (1986) and Weick (2003).

Winograd and Flores depart from the observation that developments in computer science and organization studies are seriously hampered by inadequate conceptions about human cognition which are deeply rooted in Western thought. The whole set of these beliefs which they label the "rationalist model" and their description of it is very similar to what I have called representationalism in the above. As typical of the rationalist cognitive model the authors (1986: 17 ff) mention the principles of (i) correspondence existing between words and things; (ii) that such correspondence is mediated in a rule-based way by representations; and (iii) that our thinking and knowing proceeds through the manipulation of such representations.

Reification and picture-thinking can be easily recognized when the authors argue that "[t]he rationalistic tradition regards language as a system of symbols that are composed into patterns that stand for things in the world" (1986: 17). This model, which bases the process of cognition on the assumption of mental models or representations of the world, is inadequate, say Winograd and Flores. Their rejection is established by reference to Whitehead's warning on the fallacy of misplaced concreteness (1986: 73). That warning can be considered as applicable to both the assumption that representations are mental phenomena which can be identified in the brain; and to the reified objects in the world to which they are supposed to correspond. Then they argue that Heidegger undermines the rationalist model in a radical way by questioning the distinction between a conscious, reflective, knowing "subject" and a separated "object".

Instead, Heidegger states that "[k]nowledge lies in the being that situates us in the world, not in reflective representation" (1986: 74). That is to say: we do not acquire knowledge by taking a distance, and by observing phenomena as an outsider, but by being actively involved in the world through household, work and relationships. The adequacy of language therefore, is primarily located in the connection of words with the context in which they are spoken.

> Words correspond to our intuition about 'reality' because our purposes in using them are closely aligned with our physical existence in a world and our actions within it. But the coincidence is the result of our use of language within a tradition (p. 61).

Heidegger strongly emphasises that we are embedded in a factual physical existence and a certain linguistic and social tradition to which we belong by birth. He designates that embeddedness with the term "thrownness". This term expresses for him that man is situated and never sets out on his life blankly, but is being dropped in a world which already has its own history. Man has to deal with that in an acting way.

Thus, through the situated nature of our existence, concepts and words have a history. They are formed as a result of events that make it desirable, or necessary, to create those concepts. This means that the level of concept formation and reflexivity depends on our relation to the world. Heidegger distinguishes three positions to describe the way in which the world appears to us, denoted as "ready-to-hand", "unready-to-hand" and "present-at-hand".[3] For a good understanding of the cognitive model that Heidegger offers as an alternative to representationalism, it is necessary to briefly outline those three positions. In doing so, I will rely on the description that Weick (2003) gives of them in an article in which he is looking for the right relationship between organizational theory and practice.

The way in which the world appears to me in the ready-to-hand mode is the most original. It is the way of being-in-the-world that precedes conscious reflection. Indeed, there may be a form of understanding the world and of language, but it is pre-reflexive.

---

[3]I use the English terms because the organizational scientific literature that I consulted is mainly in English. The original German terms that correspond to ready-to-hand and present-at-hand are: *Zuhandenes* and *Vorhandenenes*.

When people act in this engaged mode, they are aware of the world holistically as a network of inter-related projects, possible tasks, and 'thwarted potentialities' (Packer 1985:
1083) rather than as an arrangement of discrete physical objects such as tools. Equipment is
known by its uses and the way it fits into the world (e.g. there is hammering, not hammer).
Measurable qualities of equipment recede unnoticed into the background. Thus, a glass may
measure 15 inches high, but its usability can not be established simply by detached looking.
What is decisive about the glass is that it is a 'piece of equipment for maintaining a body or
otherwise liquidate disobedient in order that we might drink' (Stenner 1998: 70), although
it might also be worshipped as a relic, displayed in a gallery, or used as a receptacle to hold
flowers. Its meaning lies in a wider network of use. (Weick 2003: 467)

So, in the stage of ready-to-hand there is no question of well-distinguished things
having well-distinguished properties. This latter kind of knowledge according to
Heidegger only comes up by the appearance of a crisis in dealing with the world.
This situation, in which the taken-for-granted relationship of ready-to-hand ham-
pers, he denotes as unready-to-hand. A breakdown occurs which compels man, in
order to handle the crisis, to make further distinctions in his life-world:

If an ongoing project is interrupted, then experience changes into an unready-to-hand mode.
Problematic aspects of the situation that produced the interruption stand out in the manner of
a figure-ground organization, but people still do not become aware of context-free objects.
For example, if one is delayed leaving the house to catch a scheduled train, then time and
the train station become salient as do shorter routes, one-way streets, anticipated parking
problems, timetables, back up departure times, etc. Particular aspects of the whole situation
stand out but only against a background provided by the project we are engaged in and
the interests and involvements guiding it' (Packer 1985: 1084). In the case of Heidegger's
favorite example of hammering, as the project proceeds the hammer may prove to be too
heavy for the task. When this happens, its weightiness 'becomes salient whereas before
it was transparent; but I am not aware of the objective "weight" of the hammer (so many
pounds), only that it is "too heavy" to do its appointed job successfully (Packer 1985: 1084).
(Weick 2003: 468)

The recurrent experience of such breakdowns leads to the third position, that of
present-at-hand.

The third mode of engagement, which again involves a shift of experience, is present-at-
hand. This mode occurs when people step back from their involvement in a project and
reflect on it using analyses that are general and abstract and context-free. It is not until this
stage that tools, artifacts, and objects emerge as independent entities, removed from tasks,
endowed with distinct measurable properties of mass and weight, that are manipulated by
distinct subjects. (Weick 2003: 468)

What we call scientific language and objective knowledge will only get shape in
this third position, labelled present-at-hand. For Weick that is the stage in which
theory emerges. Scientific language comes about, according to this Heideggerian
view, because there are repetitive activities with possibilities of potential breakdown for which the making of distinctions becomes relevant (Winograd and Flores
1986: 69). At this stage representation plays an important role. So, Heidegger does
not reject the concept of representation. But he sees it as a derived phenomenon,
which only appears where there is a disruption of our world oriented activities. And
that implies, indeed, a radical rejection of representationalism. The primacy that
Heidegger assigns to being-in-the-world, and to praxis, does not allow for reification

and picture-thinking any longer. There are no pre-given and universal distinctions between things in the world and there are no pre-given, universal pictures in our heads which correspond with them. Representation occurs only when man is already acting in the world for a long time. And the content of representations can always be traced back to the very concrete situations of breakdown to which man had to respond to.

This Heideggerian view on cognition and action has consequences for how management and organization can be conceived of. To specify what those consequences are, Winograd and Flores sketch a situation that can serve as their model of a management situation. It is about a driver who sees happening a lot of things right in front of him on the road.

> Suppose on a clear day, driving a car down a suburban street at 20mph, we see a small child running across the road in front of the car. The problem is clear – some action must be taken or the child will be hit. There are perhaps four alternatives: (1) cut off the engine, (2) put the car in reverse, (3) swerve, or (4) hit the brakes. The choice among these alternatives has been 'programmed' into us and under normal conditions we would automatically use the brakes. Change the conditions to driving on the turnpike in pouring rain at 55 mph with traffic on all sides, and a large dog suddenly dashing across the road in front of us – to hit the dog might result in the car turning over, to swerve might result in hitting the cars on either side of us, to hit the brakes too hard might result in skidding, and so on. The careful evaluation of these alternatives by, for example, looking around to see how close the nearest car is, is a theoretical possibility only if there is sufficient time, but the high speed of the car precludes all these information-gathering activities. Thus we have a situation in which all of the variables are known but where there is not enough time to do the evaluation. In such case we argue that the context makes this an unstructured problem. Managers are often irritated by the tendency of management scientists to focus on the inherent structure of a decision, as in our example of driving, ignoring the context that makes that irrelevant. (from: Decision Support Systems by Keen and Scott Morton 1978: 94). (Winograd and Flores 1986: 145)

The comment by the authors then states: "This driver is an example *par excellence* of the thrownness that Heidegger points out in our everyday life. We do not act as a result of consideration, but as a way of being. The driver's reaction in this situation cannot be adequately described in terms of rationality, even bounded rationality" (1986: 146). This means, according to the authors, that the rationalist conception of management, as being a reflexive, distant, detached way of giving direction from a superior overview, is completely wrong. Organizations do not operate through a cycle of planning-doing-controlling, such as the rationalist model thinks it works. Indeed, in this rationalist view precisely the deception of representationalism is visible, that views things as knowable and depictable in advance. What this view notably lacks is what the authors call the "background", i.e. the whole fabric of more or less random givens, the acknowledging of thrownness.

> The view of management as rational problem solving and decision making fails to deal with the question of background. Saying that a manager is optimizing some value by choosing among alternatives for action is like regarding language understanding as a process of choosing among formal definitions. The hard part is understanding how the alternatives relevant to a given context come into being. The critical part of problem solving lies in formulating the problem (1986: 146).

But in order to do that you must pay attention to that unarticulated background which, according to Heidegger, is being obscured by our Western thinking.

Those who embrace this vision of management will soon conclude that organization studies scholars will have to give up their traditional, observing position. If knowledge is not something absolute and stable, but issues from involvement in an action situation, organizational scientists will have to participate in the activities they investigate. Two quotes from Björn Gustavsen et al. (2001a and b), in which they report on organizational scientific participatory research, illustrate what it means when we consciously want to work from the idea that knowledge and action fade into one another. "The challenge facing the researchers has not been 'how to define an innovation system', but to innovate." Reflection took place from within the innovation process (2001a: 6). And: "Knowledge transmission to a workplace is seldom a mechanical process. Rather, for workplace actors to take knowledge to heart they need to be involved in a process of action where the knowledge becomes relevant. They do not need to be informed, they need to learn. Consequently, the issue of local learning arenas emerges as a key one" (2001b: 234).

Based on the work of Wittgenstein, other authors arrive at comparable positions. John Shotter for example emphasizes Wittgenstein's relevance for organization studies because of his focus on the context of action. He quotes Wittgenstein saying "Words have meaning only in the stream of life" (2000: 351) and explains how Wittgenstein emphasizes the existence of specific "practice certainties", which precede any thesis or theory that we would like to invent (Shotter and Lannamann 2002: 585).

At another point Shotter suggests that the social sciences might benefit from Wittgenstein's thought that "we are already, spontaneously, making sense of our lives in many other ways, very different from the mechanical ways we currently feel are the only rational ways open to us" (1998: 143). The element of breakdown as a transition to a more deliberate form of sense-making and knowing does, under the guidance of Wittgenstein, not get the distinctive place it has with the orientation towards Heidegger. However, Shotter states that in Wittgenstein's work the importance of shocking moments, which enable us to refine or give more depth to our ways of life, is central. (2000: 358).

Language and Organization

Besides the awareness of the embeddedness of knowledge in acting there is another important consequence for organization studies of the views of Heidegger and Wittgenstein. That is the emphasis which is placed on the relationship between language and organization. For Winograd and Flores this is an important theme, for which they entirely focus on Heidegger. From the approach that Heidegger takes, language – at least primary language – is "no longer merely a reflective but rather a constitutive medium. We create and give meaning to the world we live in and share with others. To put the point in a more radical form, we design ourselves (and the social and technological networks in which our lives have meaning) in language" (1986: 78). Language in this view that we already came across in discussing post-modernist organization studies, is a medium through which people shape their reality. And organizations are part of that reality that is permanently being created. They are, in the view of Winograd and Flores, networks created by language and communication.

The impact of language with respect to networks has much to do with the fact that through language we can commit ourselves. Regarding this point Winograd and Flores, inspired by the linguistic theories of Searle and Austin, attribute considerable weight to the phenomenon of language as an important pragmatic function. By saying things we perform speech acts, we position ourselves relative to others and we commit ourselves to others. This happens for example in a promise, a claim, an offer, an acceptance, each of which has its own different practical consequences. "Language is a form of human social action, directed towards the creation of what Maturana calls 'mutual orientation'. This orientation is not grounded in a correspondence between language and the world, but exists as a consensual domain – as interlinked patterns of activity. The shift from language as description to language as action is the basis of speech act theory, which emphasizes the *act* of language rather than its representational role" (1986: 76).

But if acting in organizations consists of communication and speech acts, this has an impact on our conceptualisation of management. We have already noted that authors who are guided by Heidegger and Wittgenstein, appear to consider management as a form of action which, by definition, is bound to a context, to a background. If we find now that those authors assign importance to communication, it becomes possible to describe more precisely that background. Indeed, the unarticulated background that according to Heidegger is obscured by our Western thinking, lies, the authors say, first and foremost in the social and communicative network in which we find ourselves.

Winograd and Flores believe therefore that "[i]n understanding management as taking care of the articulation and activation of a network of commitments, produced primarily through promises and requests, we cover many managerial activities" (1986: 151). Shotter develops similar thoughts based on the work of Wittgenstein. Following Wittgenstein's remarks about the limited effect of explicit (language) rules, Shotter suggests that "[m]ost of what we do is not done by us deliberately and intellectually, by reference to an already existing, framework of rules, external to our current circumstances, but in spontaneous response to 'calls' upon us from within our immediate circumstances", sometimes called an invisible field of forces (2000: 356, 357), namely of practical rules. Shotter characterizes that situation after Wittgenstein as "to know how to go on", and in his turn falls back on the example of driving to show how that works.

> Just as in driving down a multi-lane interstate highway, we sense those cars here as near, and those there as far away, this one as requiring us to move away as it is moving too close, and we possess a synoptic grasp of how 'to go on' in a skillful way in many other spheres of our lives (2000: 357).

Significant are the terms used by the authors to characterize this mode of being that corresponds with Heidegger's ready-to-hand situation. I refer to the description "to know how to go on" by Shotter but also to the position of Winograd and Flores who speak of "our habitual, standard, comfortable being-in-the-world" (1986: 77). This emphasis on a kind of security in thrownness means something to the way in which the authors – within the context of organization and management – see the relationships between the primary mode of being and the modes of being that, in Heidegger's terms, occur after the breakdown. The situation of ready-to-hand, with the corresponding forms of communication and language, for Winograd and Flores is crucial and literally fundamental. That situation serves as a substrate, a reliable ground on which you can build. There is a kind of taken-for-granted inter-human communication and coordination, where things just go as they should go and people, intuitively or otherwise, know what to do. Characteristic of that mode of being is the presence of spontaneous interaction and conversation between people. There is going on what Heidegger calls *Mitsein*.[4] Shotter talks about this mode of being as "a realm in which my activity only has the character it has in relation to yours, in relation to your response to it" (2000: 351) and as a "flow of relationally responsive activity ceaselessly unfolding between us and the others and othernesses around us" (Shotter and Lannamann 2002: 579). Thinking that is oriented towards that flow he calls "withness thinking" (2004: 210 ff.).

That the nature of this situation, which I will refer to with Heidegger's term ready-to-hand, is regarded to be fundamental appears from its characterization as the truly human situation. Winograd and Flores argue that "[t]o be human is to be the kind of being that generates commitments, through speaking and listening. Without our ability to create and accept (or decline) commitments we are acting in a less than fully human way, and we are not fully using language" (1986: 76). And Shotter and Lannamann believe that "[t]he truth of our everyday talk resides in our activities, in how we 'go on' with each other in our practices, and cannot be negotiated in isolation from them" (2002: 584). Shotter assigns it a primordial character (2004: 218).

Summarizing, we can say that the mentioned authors stress heavily the ready-to-hand situation. Undeniably, the other modes of being have their merits – they enable science and objective knowledge – but are, compared to the primary level, mainly supportive. The situation of unready-to-hand for example only emerges after, for whatever reason, a breach occurs within the pre-reflexive, ready-to-hand existence. A digestion of these breakdowns leads to forms of consciousness, which make the denoted things appear as present-at-hand. Within that situation, the role played by representation is important, but in relation to the primary level its performance has a somewhat secondary and serving character. The function of representation is to provide supplements which anticipate future breakdowns in the situation of ready-to-hand. Winograd and Flores again: "But we can partially anticipate situations

---

[4]Peperzak (1997: 66) defines *Mitsein* in Heidegger as the expression of our participation in a common culture (66) and in a common understanding which precedes everything (64). Both at the level of *Das Man*, at which there is no question of consciously dealing with existence and at the level of the articulated *Mitteilung* in which that participation is made explicit.

where breakdowns are likely to occur (by noting their recurrence) and we can provide people with the tools and procedures they need to cope with them" (1986: 158).

Representations are also appropriate for making interactions transparent (1986: 159), as happens in computer software. On this basis, actions of employees in an organization can be coordinated. When the stage of reflection is over, this kind of representation(s) can be considered as a tool that can be used in a taken-for-granted, non-conscious way. Thus, the product of reflection turns into "a ready-to-hand tool that operates in the domain of conversations for action" (1986: 159). It is, in the views of Shotter, Winograd and Flores, the manager's responsibility to supervise this cycle and to be on the alert to increase the possibilities for the range of communicative action.

Implications for Organization Studies

In this orientation towards Heidegger and Wittgenstein two things catch our attention. In the first place the mode of being of ready-to-hand is primary in all respects. This is evident from the view of Winograd and Flores and Shotter that in that primeval relationship to the world all major organizational elements are already given: involvement in the world, speech acts, conversation, being tuned in to one another. Shotter and Lannamann have that in mind when they state that conversation rules in general are not explicit but "are manifested in the spontaneous or 'natural' reactions we provide to the activities of the others around us, in virtue of our *participation* with them in the language-game-interwoven forms of life into which both they and we have been trained" (2002: 585). Those spontaneous forms of communication can nevertheless prove to be inadequate. Then a supplement or awareness is needed, but always with the purpose to arrive at a new, enriched state of ready-to-hand. This is evident from the requirements to which that becoming-conscious is bound. The reflection that occurs after a breakdown (Heidegger) or a shock (Wittgenstein) and which makes use of representation, is not allowed, as was the old representationalism, to take too big a distance from the primarily given practical situation. The reflection should always be aware of that primarily given situation or background.

In the second place, it is remarkable that representation continues to play a role, even though it is no longer the dominant role representationalism assigned to it. As Winograd and Flores express this: "Heidegger does not disregard this kind of thinking, but puts it into a context of cognition as *praxis* – as concernful acting in the world" (1986: 33). What this adjusted role of representation looks like, is an issue on which the various authors have different opinions. Weick characterizes the products of present-at-hand in terms that are still very similar to the pretensions of representationalism and positivism, such as "context-free", "universality" and "abstraction". This may appear from his description of that mode of being that I present here again: "a third mode of engagement, which again involves a shift of experience, is present-at-hand. This mode occurs when people step back from their involvement in a project and reflect on it using analyses that are general, abstract and context-free. It is not until this stage that tools, artifacts, and objects emerge as independent entities, removed from tasks, endowed with distinct measurable properties of mass and weight, that are manipulated by distinct subjects." (Weick 2003: 468).

Therefore, theorizing itself is not problematic for Weick, as long as the connection with practice remains visible. This insight is, he thinks, the main achievement of Heidegger's thinking.

> Theorists may produce better theories if they focus on events such as interruptions (Mandler 1984), breaches (Garfinkel 1963), shocks (Schroeder, Van de Ven, Scudder, and Polley 1989), disconfirmed expectations (Staw 1980), break downs and situations of irresolution (Winograd and Flores 1986, 147). (Weick 2003: 469).

For others, as a result of the thinking of Heidegger and Wittgenstein, theorizing itself has become problematic. For them too representation still plays a role, but the kind of theorizing which representation previously gave rise to, has become completely obsolete. The title of Pålshaugens book *The End of Organization Theory* is clear enough in that respect. Theory as a product on its own is impossible for him, because already its communication requires the interaction with a context. "As a rule, therefore, knowledge acquired through research cannot take on the attributes of a product that can be purchased or acquired in an already finished form. The *communication* of knowledge will usually involve a form of the *development of new knowledge*" (1998: 26). Therefore for him the distinction between theory and practice is not sustainable (1998: 7).

Action researcher Gustavsen would not go that far. He still struggles with the question what the thinking of Heidegger and Wittgenstein really means for the place of representation and reflection with respect to praxis. On the one hand, he is convinced that knowledge creation is local and embedded in local practices and may not be viewed independent of them. The belief in "one best ways", that was common up to the seventies of the last century, we have lost, and rightly so. "Today, this 'one best way' does not attract much interest from people involved in practical efforts" (2001: 103). But on the other hand, does this mean that we give up theorizing? Are there no possibilities yet to produce knowledge with a wider scope, so that you can speak of commonly shared views and broad consensus? Is that aspiration not also a legitimate, natural inclination of a researcher? Should we not say that "[t]he point of being local is to begin 'where we are', not to stay there" (Gustavsen et al 2001a: 15). So the question then is going to be:

> How can the unique property of action research – the fact that it engages in action – be turned into a positive asset in the discourses of society? Are there ways in which action research can transcend the single case without losing the action element along the road? (Gustavsen 2003: 95)

Evaluation

As in the evaluation of post-modernism within organization studies, I want to assess here the value of the alternative to representationalism offered by the above discussed authors who are guided by Heidegger and Wittgenstein. Also I want to present this assessment in terms of deception and exclusion – the negative symptoms of representationalism – by discussing the question to what extent their contributions helped combat these symptoms.

Heidegger and Wittgenstein have both denounced the deception based on the representationalist belief in stable knowledge of stable objects. They have made it clear that it is meaningless to talk about the existence of objects and their properties outside the context of involved action, with its opportunities for breakdown. They indicate the need, for a process of cognition, of an action situation in which learning and knowing can take shape. Within organization studies that idea, I believe, has yielded many benefits. The authors discussed, guided by Heidegger and Wittgenstein, seem to feel encouraged by that orientation to participatory research and to permanent vigilance to avoid reification and picture-thinking.

But for these authors the same holds true as applied to the postmodernist oriented authors: here too the role of representation is not eradicated, even though it has no longer the dominant role it had before. After the (occurrence of the) breakdown and in the situation of present-at-hand, we work, they say, with representations. This means that it would be a mistake to think that for once and always we have finished with the properties of representation that are so treacherous with regard to cognition. Reification and picture-thinking, which were so enlargedly present in representationalism, may keep cropping up and lead to new forms of deception. This is reflected in Weick, who for the description of the present-at-hand uses terms from the representationalist canon, while at the same time he tries to ward off the associated dangers by retaining a connection with the breakdown situations. This is also evident in Gustavsen, who wonders whether there is still room for legitimate generalization, but thereby indicates that the temptation of undue generalizations and abstractions keeps threatening us. And that applies even to someone like Pålshaugen, who wants to break with theory, but at the same time notes that the fascination by representation remains unabated strong.

> Here we find the secret communion between the practitioner and the theoretician. Both of them know that it is an illusion to say that the model models reality. But in the same way that we can not avoid being fascinated by a good film, even though we view it as nothing but a play, an illusion, neither can we avoid being fascinated by a good theory. (Pålshaugen 1998: 12)

Apparently, even after Heidegger and Wittgenstein, representations have an inherently misleading effect because of the way in which our thinking is structured. The dismantlers of representationalism can promote a vigilance against that problem, but they cannot do away with it entirely. Therefore at this point, the comment that must be made is to question whether the awareness of the conditioning is sufficient to counter the illusion-production of representation. How much permanent vigilance and goodwill is needed to cope with the ever-threatening deception?

Here too the same question imposes itself as the one with which I concluded my evaluation of postmodernism: where to find the energy needed for such permanent vigilance? This comment, for the rest, leaves standing the merit of Heidegger and Wittgenstein for combating deception. That merit, I believe, consists in the contribution they made to unmasking the ideological, almost triumphalist nature of the belief in stable knowledge as senseless. Partly due to the impact they had on the discussed organizational scientific authors, reification and picture-thinking are no longer widely-viewed as reliable components of cognition, but as things to be watchful against.

Regarding the symptom of exclusion, I believe the contributions of Heidegger and Wittgenstein are less univocally positive. Organization studies authors who are oriented towards them have no satisfactory answer to this problem. It is certainly true that, thanks to the analyses of Heidegger and Wittgenstein, the exclusion-mechanisms of representationalism have been weakened. This has been achieved because representation is still assigned only a supporting role, in which it can less make its hierarchizing influence felt. In the words of Winograd and Flores:

> What really is is not defined by an objective omniscient observer, nor is it defined by an individual (. . .) but rather by a space or potential for human and group action. (1986: 37).

But the question should be raised when it comes to exclusion, as to whether the alternative orientations of the authors we have reviewed offer any improvement indeed. Is there a reason for the substrate of the ready-to-hand, which Winograd and Flores and, in his own way, Shotter speak about as being the crucial basis of organizations and organizational knowledge, to be trusted in these respects? Indeed, they claim that on that primarily given level, matters in principle operate smoothly. People understand one another because they understand each other's speech acts, people are willing to communicate and through their conversations they keep the organization running. Of course, there may be misunderstandings between people – which belong to the category of breakdowns – but these can be remedied or prevented through reflection which provides better coordination. If reality were really like this, then together with the leaving behind us of representationalism the issue of exclusion would have disappeared. But is this our reality?

The above description relies particularly heavily on the premise that at the ready-to-hand level people are permanently willing to communicate. That premise is a little naïve-romantic and, I am afraid, much too optimistic.[5] The practice in organizations shows too many examples of the opposite. And not all of these are due, in my opinion, to the disruptive role that representationalism still plays in organizations. The examples I have in mind occur at the most original level, which precedes all opportunities to organize and change. I refer to the reluctance of people to talk with other people; to the extensive use of language which indeed does not function but obscures; and to the energy it takes, not so much to overcome misunderstandings, but just to get people to talk to each other at all.

---

[5] Although linguistic usage in this view allows for the possibility to reject commitment. Even then it is presupposed for people to talk about that with one another.

But if that were to be the case, the problem of exclusion would not disappear from within the model of organization studies derived from Heidegger and Wittgenstein. It will continue occurring. It then is no longer merely linked to representationalism, but operating within that model at the primary level, which Heidegger calls ready-to-hand. It manifests itself as a refusal of communication, or as arbitrariness in the distribution of the attention we give to people. This problem is not addressed by authors like Winograd and Flores, Weick, Shotter and others. Willingness to communicate is presupposed with them. Therefore, as a response to the problem of exclusion the orientation towards Heidegger and Wittgenstein is inadequate. In Chapter 6 I will further address this shortcoming, from the perspective of the philosophy of Levinas.

Chapter 4
Levinas on Rationality and Representation

Introduction

In one of the conclusions to Chapter 2 I suggested that the problems for organization studies with rationality, labelled as deception and exclusion, have a clear affinity with the problems that philosophy identifies with respect to rationality. From this affinity I derive a rationale for consulting philosophers in the course of a discussion of problematic rationality in organization studies. In that context, in the previous chapter I investigated some philosophically inspired answers to representationalism. First of all the answers from organizational scientists that are guided by Foucault's and Derrida's postmodernism, and then the answers from those who are inspired by Heidegger and Wittgenstein.

In this chapter and that which follows, I shall deal with the question of the extent to which the philosophy of Levinas can help to clarify the problems identified. For this I will proceed in a different way to the previous chapter. In my presentation of possible clarification from an approach informed by Derrida, Foucault, Heidegger and Wittgenstein, I was able to rely on organization studies authors who had absorbed already into an organization studies framework the views of those philosophers. With respect to Levinas this is impossible, at least as far as the problem of representation is concerned.

As indicated in Chapter 1 there are management authors indeed who are explicitly orientated towards Levinas, as Jones (2003a) and Roberts (2003), but they all seize upon the ethical aspect of organization and organizing. This means that my presentation of Levinas' views on rationality and representation will have to take place in phases.

First, on the basis of the philosophy of Levinas, the questions will have to be addressed as to what is Levinas' personal view on the deficiency of rationality, and any specific answers he has to that problem. The treatment of these questions is the subject of this Chapter 4. Subsequently, and in the absence of authors who, with respect to the deficiency of rationality, already established connections between Levinas' philosophy and the world of organization and management, I will have to make plausible and relevant for organization studies the categories and answers from Levinas. That will be the main focus of Chapter 5.

N. Van der Ven, *The Shame of Reason in Organizational Change*, Issues in Business Ethics 32, DOI 10.1007/978-90-481-9373-8_4, © Springer Science+Business Media B.V. 2011

Connecting Points

Before introducing Levinas, it is important to reiterate that his work offers connecting points regarding the issue that we are dealing with. Levinas is explicit in
his articulation of the problematic nature of the Western philosophical tradition,
which he calls rationalistic because the *mastering* of reality through the *understanding* of reality has dominated that tradition from the outset. In many places
in his work Levinas refers through a single word – undifferentiated, unhindered by
an urge to be nuanced – to that tradition as a monolithic whole. Sometimes in an
appreciative sense, more often in a critical sense. The problems to which he points
can be named in the characteristic terms we have formulated above: exclusion and
deception.

The characteristic of exclusion is the one most emphasised by Levinas. This is
what he does for instance in the Preface of *Totality and Infinity* where he denotes
Western thinking as an "ontology of war" (TI: 22), characterized by the concept of
"totality". Subsequently, a large part of this book is devoted to analyzing the links
between the way in which reason is being conceptualised in the Western tradition
and the tendency, not least through understanding and knowledge, to appropriate or
capture the world.

The term "egology", originating from Husserl, is apposite, according to Levinas.
And that is a term that produces its own, dangerous morality. Thus Levinas presents
his investigation into the inherited tradition of rationality in the first sentence
of *Totality and Infinity* as motivated by the conviction "that it is of the highest
importance to know whether we are not duped by morality."

Deception, i.e. the phenomenon that knowledge appears to be inadequate, is thematized by Levinas in many places under the heading of loss of meaning. Loss of
meaning occurs because reason continually demands underlying meanings but does
not permit signification from outside its own domain (of reason). This leads to the
dilution of meaning and knowledge. For Levinas, this problem is directly linked to
the Western rational tradition dating from Parmenides. Indeed, that rational tradition
has assumed that all scientific and objectifying human activity has its origin in its
obvious, rational necessity for life. It is presumed that reason finds its own ground.
Levinas can not agree with this and, at several places in his principal works (TI: 72,
92; OB: 160), he questions that position. His argument is always that reason cannot
be its own foundation: reason that triggers the objectifying and the bestowing of
meaning, must be preceded by some other original meaning. In much of his work
Levinas' ambition is then to identify that meaning in what he calls the Face of the
other.

In his critique of the Western rationalist philosophy of consciousness Levinas is
forced to further analyze how exactly, according to this tradition, reason proceeds
and leads to consciousness. In the course of this analysis it appears that the concept
of representation plays a major role: the problems that Levinas identifies in many
places within the rational tradition lead him back to the way in which the concept
of representation is conceptualised. In this respect Peperzak (1978) says:

> The central role of representation (*Vorstellung, représentation*) and the primacy of theory and 'egology', which are connected to it, are according to Levinas, characteristic of Western philosophy. The criticism of representation already in his thesis takes an important place. (1978: 30/212)

Levinas' thematizing of exclusion and deception as problems of representation corresponds to another conclusion we could draw at the end of Chapter 2 above: problems associated with rationality may be regarded as problems that are inherent to representationalism. For that reason, following on from this introduction, this chapter will have the following structure: first I discuss the questions in what form representational thinking has been handed down to Levinas and what was his response to it. For this purpose we must go into the work of Husserl and Heidegger. Subsequently, I will investigate the way in which Levinas deals with representation in his own philosophy, and the extent to which that can be regarded as an adequate answer to the problems of exclusion and deception. Finally it will appear that this response from Levinas also implies an answer to our initial question, namely how is change possible.

Prior to that here below, I will give a brief overview of the life of Levinas (1998a), a short characterisation of his work, and a justification of my approach to Levinas.

Life and Work of Levinas

His Life

Emmanuel Levinas was born in Lithuania in 1906 as the son of a bookseller. It was an environment in which he became acquainted naturally with the great Russian writers. Among these, and above all, the works of Pushkin, Tolstoy and Dostoyevsky made a great impression on him. Additionally he received a "modern" Jewish education, in which the Hebrew Bible took a more important position than the Talmud. He experienced the Revolution of 1917 while in the Ukraine. In 1923 he went to study at the University of Strasbourg and he settled permanently in France. His teachers, themselves contemporaries of the Dreyfus affair, led him to develop a love for France as a nation "to which one can get attached as much by mind and heart as by descent" (Levinas 1978: 29; translation NvdV).

During the academic year 1928–1929 he stayed at Freiburg to devote himself to phenomenology and attended the lectures of Husserl and Heidegger. In 1929 he published a long article on Husserl's *Ideen*. A year later he settled in Paris, continued his studies at the Sorbonne and graduated with Jean Wahl on the basis of his thesis on *The Theory of Intuition in Husserl's Phenomenology*. In the same year he translated, along with Gabrielle Pfeiffer, Husserl's *Cartesianische Meditationen* into French.

After his graduation, Levinas opted against an academic career and began working as a teacher at the Alliance Israélite Universelle. He remained philosophically active, however, and moved in the circles of the philosophical avant-garde of that time. Gabriel Marcel, Jean Wahl and Maurice Blanchot were his special friends. In 1935/1936 he published *On Escape*, the first work in which his personal

philosophical insights are discussed. After he obtained in 1939 the French national-
ity, he fulfilled his military service in wartime. His wife and daughter were able to
hide in a monastery near Orleans. It was not until after the War, that Levinas learned
that his Lithuanian family had been killed by Nazis.

In 1947 Levinas published *Existence and Existents* written during his military
captivity from 1941 to 1945. In the post-war years he gave lectures for Jean Wahl's
"Collège Philosophique", on the subject of *Time and the Other* which subsequently
(1947) appeared as a book. Two years later he gathered together a number of articles on the phenomenology of Husserl and Heidegger in *Discovering Existence
with Husserl*. Meanwhile, he had started as the principal of the École Normale
Israélite Orientale, which trains French teachers for Jewish schools and colleges
in the Mediterranean. At the same time he more intensively re-engaged with the
Jewish tradition. He began studying the Talmud under the guidance of the brilliant
Chouchani[1] and this resulted in a stream of writing on Judaism, including *Difficult
Freedom* (1963) and *Four Talmudic Lectures* (1968). Levinas kept separate these
Jewish publications from his philosophical publications, and this is one reason why
he always had two publishers.

Levinas acquired his great reputation through his first major work *Totality and
Infinity*. In 1961 he submitted this at the Sorbonne, Paris and acquired the State
doctoral degree, whereupon he became a professor at the University of Poitiers.
Then from 1967 he was on the faculty at the University of Paris-Nanterre and from
1972 to 1976 at the Sorbonne. In 1971 Levinas received the Albert Schweitzer Prize
for his contributions in the field of cultural philosophy. In 1972 *Humanism of the
Other person*, a collection of articles from the years 1964 to 1970 appeared. In 1974
he published his second major work *Otherwise than Being or Beyond Essence*. In
1975 he published *On Maurice Blanchot*, a collection of studies about his friend,
the writer and critic. A year later, Levinas published *Proper Names*, a compilation
of short essays on his favourite philosophers, writers and poets. After his retirement
from the Sorbonne Levinas continued to publish, for example *Of God Who Comes
to Mind* in 1982.

---

[1]Chouchani was a mysterious combination of clochard, wandering Jew and great sage, who in
the thirties and forties often stayed in Paris. Nobody knew his real name. Chouchani spoke some
thirty languages and quoted as easily from the Talmud, the Kabbalah and the Veda's. Besides
Levinas Henri Nerson and Elie Wiesel came to him to study Talmud. After Levinas once invited
Chouchani in his house, the latter pitched his tent in the attic above the school behind the principal's apartment. There for 3 years he gave, at irregular times, Talmudlessons which often went
on till very late in the night and which were – because of his rude behaviour – not always a plea-
sure. In 1949 he disappeared, without saying good-bye, from sight. Chouchani's genius lied, apart
from his phenomenal memory, in his virtuosity in interpreting texts. Levinas says in that respect:
"Mr. Chouchani was gifted with exceptional dialectical powers; the quantity of concepts that he at
one time and in combination with one another thought through, created as it were the impression
that he was undomesticated in his unpredictable discoveries! The way in which Talmudists deal
with the texts and with Scripture is very complicated and erudite already, but Chouchani managed to extend that ability to other textual fields, and thus to give new turns to an always restless
dialectics." (Poirié 1987: 127; translation NvdV). Through him, Levinas after the war regained
confidence in the books (Poirié 1987: 130).

Levinas' Work: A Principal Theme

A key theme of the entire work of Levinas is the presence of two spheres or dimensions, which seem to be unrelated to one another. These spheres are juxtaposed in the titles of his major works, *Totality and Infinity* and *Otherwise than Being or Beyond Essence*. On the one hand: totality, or the dimension of being, which at other places is called ontology, interiority, the Same; and on the other hand: Infinity, or the Other-than-being, which also may be called metaphysics, exteriority, the Other, the Face.[2] For a brief sketch of the two dimensions the terms "the Same" and "the Other" might be the best place to start. About the Same, De Boer says:

> Ontology is called [by Levinas] a doctrine of the Self or the Same (*le Même*). Wherever the soul travels the world to explore it, it keeps discovering the Same, either in the shape of other selves, or as the comprehensive Self of the world-soul, or as a culture in which it expressed itself. 'Know yourself' means: re-cognize yourself, discover the true self in the shape of the other. In modern philosophy, this principle found its expression in the famous statement of Descartes: I think, therefore I am. Here starts the modern egological philosophy of consciousness, which Levinas' teacher Husserl radically wanted to complete by consistently explaining and understanding everything consciousness experiences in terms of sense-making achievements. (1976: 12; translation NvdV)

The I (self) that wants to swallow up everything along that road and convert it into the Same is understood by Levinas as of a totalizing nature.

Confronting or opposite the Same is the dimension of the Other. In the words of Duyndam and Poorthuis:

> By 'the other' is meant, in an abstract way, what by definition falls outside any totality. That which, in philosophical terms, is transcendent with regard to any whole. In traditional metaphysics and theology, this 'other' is often identified with God, the infinite that we can not grasp, nor with our hands, neither with our senses or our thinking. The other cannot by me be reduced to my world. If indeed it could be absorbed into my world, precisely for that reason it would no longer be different. With this view Levinas joins the metaphysical tradition, which he encounters not only in religion but also in philosophy, for instance in Plato's idea of the good and Descartes' idea of the infinite. (2003: 18; translation NvdV)

In the scope of this short introduction it is impossible to disclose comprehensively the many implications of the terms Levinas uses to indicate these two dimensions, and the mutual relationships between them. But for my objective that is not necessary. Indeed, as long as we know that the problem that concerns us – that of rationality and representation – is located in the dimension of ontology: that is to say in the dimension that Levinas names as the Same.

The perspective of these two dimensions is the framework within which Levinas elaborates a problem that preoccupies him from early in his career. That problem is the existence of what Levinas calls the *il-y-a*. Of that phenomenon Theodore De Boer gives the following description:

---

[2]For a number of key concepts Levinas often uses capitals, but not always. In this book I will, most of the time, write Face and Other with capitals.

(...) an anonymous existence from which things and persons raise themselves by a hypostasis. You can neither affirm nor deny something of this being. It reveals itself in the sleepless
nights in which the eternal silence of infinite space frightens us (Pascal). Levinas calls this
existence *il-y-a*. (1997: 7)

The most oppressive aspect of the *il-y-a* according to Levinas is the endlessness
of the continuous, senseless babbling of being. It frightens him, and already in *On
Escape* (1935/1936) he describes the distaste that the experience of this endless
being[3] provokes in him, and for which he searches an escape. Levinas notes that in
the course of human history all the projects of civilization are aimed at exactly that:
reducing the savage and depressing *il-y-a*. This takes shape through cultivation of
the environment and, at least in the West, through the development of a rationalist
way of thinking in which representationalism is a part. All this indeed belongs to
the sphere of ontology.

However, as Levinas observes, the response of ontology – the development of
being and rationalization in the world – is not adequate to the senselessness of the
il-y-a. The *il-y-a* keeps returning. Here the deficiency of rationality – which may be
called as well the "deficiency of ontology," – comes to the fore. The rationality that
helps us escape the distaste of the meaningless *il-y-a*, leads to forms of closedness,
self-complacency and uneasiness that cause the dispelled distaste to return. Levinas
does not enter into an explanation for this, but stresses this deficiency of rationality
in relation to the *il-y-a*, and he feels strongly about it. Is there no escape indeed, he
wonders. Is this deadlock the last thing there is to be said about it?

Levinas thinks not. He notes that people intensely experience this impasse, but
also that they can find a way out often enough. He focuses his attention on that
escape. What exactly happens that we are able to find a way out? Levinas believes
that to simply describe what happens – to follow the phenomenological method
of which he is so fond – is inadequate. Indeed, that method belongs itself to the
sphere of world-clarification, i.e. to ontology. To break through the senselessness
really, that is to say to find true meaningfulness, we must be outside the scope of
ontology.

True transcendence can only be expected from the realm of metaphysics. It is a
characteristic of true transcendence that it will not fit into the area of ontology: they
are incompatible. In order to be able to say something about that escape therefore,
Levinas resorts to themes of a mystical, metaphysical character. In the confrontation
with death, time, eroticism and the other – such is Levinas' intuition in his early
writings – an opening is offered which really puts the *il-y-a* at a distance, be it always
provisionally. As Levinas' work further develops, his attention focuses increasingly
on the other as the one who pre-eminently offers that opening.

From the moment that the other becomes his central theme, there is one question
which keeps returning increasingly and with growing emphasis. That is the question
that intrigues Levinas in his capacity as a philosopher: a representative of Western

---

[3] Although at that time Levinas had not yet coined the term *il-y-a*.

rational thinking par excellence, who wants to discuss metaphysics in a sensible way. This question is, how do you bring up for discussion something like the Infinite in the Other in philosophical language, which is the language of reason, and of the ontological sphere?

The differences that can be noted between his major works give a good indication as to Levinas' development with regard to that methodical question.

De Boer (1997: 64 ff) offers a comparative description of the two approaches in his article *The Rationality of Levinas' philosophy*. In *Totality and Infinity*, he says, Levinas proceeds transcendentally; that is, he goes back to the constitutive conditions of the experience of a particular domain of reality. In this case, that experience is the Other in his elusive infinity. And that experience occurs as a "crack" in ontology (TI: 171). It appears that "the metaphysical dimension is glimpsed in the 'breaks' of the ontological totality. Metaphysics looks for a toehold in ontology in the places where ontology falls short. The embarrassments of ontology are opportunities for metaphysics. One could call this a 'philosophie de l'insuffiance de l'ontologie'. Ontology indicates its own non-self-sufficiency, at least for those who have ears to hear and eyes to see" (De Boer 1997: 64). Indeed, this produces a very special kind of transcendental thinking in which the constitutive condition is not to be found in ontology but precisely where ontology fails. Thus, this thinking states that, from an ontological point of view you do *not* know what you should expect. The appearance of the other "is something that surprises us 'from I know not where', 'je ne sais d'où'. We can only try to pick up a hint of it" (1997: 65).

In *Otherwise than Being*, De Boer says Levinas applies this method again. Here he speaks of the trace, the echo or reflection (reflet) that the experience of the Other leaves behind in ontology. Something happened, the Unvisible has passed and left its imprints. But in addition to that approach he uses another way to express the metaphysical in a language that is necessarily ontological. This way is by stretching the language he uses, which might even be called a torturing of the language. This is done through the use of iterations, exaltations and superlatives which put the language, and the reader, under pressure. Thus, Levinas speaks about "saying a saying", "meaning a meaning", "independence without parallel" and passivity "more passive than any passivity". De Boer (1997: 67) notes:

> Taking things to excess becomes a philosophical method. L'exaspération comme methode de philosophie. . . ./. . . It is as if ontological language rolls itself up and retreats to a zero point, poised to pass over into the metaphysical dimension. (1997: 69)

De Boer then wonders whether Levinas indeed achieves his goal with these various approaches. Philosophically speaking this question remains open since in all the methods Levinas uses all "attempts to transcend ontology were themselves couched in ontological language" (1997: 73), which is also the basis of reproaches from Derrida.

Nevertheless, De Boer finally judges Levinas' undertaking to be justifiable. For if we consider language, and ontology, as a prison, "we have taken no account of what I said earlier about the 'unselfsufficiency' of ontology, which ontology itself betrays. I have taken the language of ontology as a closed circuit, a totality. But the 'breaks' in this totality point beyond, to the presence of the Other – 'at least for those who have ears to hear and eyes to see'. With this last crucial addition I appealed, outflanking language as it were, to the *experience* of the reader."

The above makes clear the extent to which the relationship between ontology and metaphysics, and even prior to that, the question of the possibility of such a relationship, is at the heart of Levinas' philosophical project.

My Approach of Levinas

The objective of this chapter is to clarify what was Levinas' answer to the problems of rationality and representation which he identifies in Western thinking. In its turn, the exploration of that response has the function, within the whole of this book, to shed light on the problems which organization studies faces as a result of the representationalism which is dominant in the field. This set-up implies a certain selectivity with respect to the works of Levinas that I choose to draw from in this chapter. In this section, I will provide a brief justification for the choices I have made, and doing so I will rely on my presentation in the previous section of Levinas' development and the differences between his major books.

The selectivity in my treatment of Levinas consists in my relying strongly upon works from his early period, namely *Existence and Existents* (abbreviated as EE) and *Time and the Other* (TO) and *Totality and Infinity* (TI). I will refer to a much lesser extent to *Otherwise than Being* (OB).

The importance of EE and TO for my argument lies in the extensive attention Levinas devotes in them to the *il-y-a* and to the first steps taken by the subject to escape from it. These steps are referred to by terms such as "getting into action", "effort", "fatigue", "reluctance" and they are important to me because they enable a connection with elements from organization studies.

The decision to make extensive use of TI is motivated by two reasons. The first reason is that I want to connect with the way ontology functions in that book. As mentioned above, it is precisely Levinas' aspiration to be able to indicate where metaphysics breaks through into ontology. But this objective does not prevent him from using familiar ontological terminology on a large scale, because by doing so he can show where it fails. He can proceed descriptively and phenomenologically, for example when it comes to labour, enjoyment, and scientific cognition. And this ontological sphere may be related – albeit not in a very direct way, but still – to descriptions as we know them from organization studies.

Such links imply that, in our attempts to catch those moments in which "ontology breaks" – and that is what it is all about – we get a fair chance to be able to identify those moments in the context of management and organization. In the following characterization by De Boer (1997: 76) of what happens in TI, several elements can be identified that have their resonance in organization studies: "To 'do' metaphysics is to seek out a Presence *within* ontology, because of an unrest and a *longing* which manifest themselves in the very heart of *theoria* and *praxis*: in the fact that we cannot be at peace with the discovery of truths without commitment and, in practice, with neat borders of well-defined duties and competencies." The unrest and the longing are reminiscent of the utopian thinking that can overtake organizations, the neat borders of the rational schemes people like to work with and which are inherent to "organizational laziness" (Ten Bos: 2004b: 6, translation NvdV).

The chance to find those connecting points arises more rarely in the case of *Otherwise than Being*. The exalted character of the language used in that book (see above) places it at a great distance from the modes of thinking and reasoning practised in organization studies. In Chapter 1 it was already noted that to relate Levinas' philosophy to organization studies is in itself not a matter of course. For this relation to achieve at least some chance of success, it will be unwise to start working from the area of Levinas' work that is most far removed from organization studies.

The second reason is related to the first. The emphasis on the "crack" in ontology makes palpable the relationship between the inroads into rationality and the possibility to speak of "something entirely new": and ultimately – we almost forgot – that is what we wanted to get at. Indeed, in Chapters 1 and 2 we have ended up on the trail of the investigation into rationality and representation, starting from the organization studies question how change is possible. Because of this emphasis on rationality, the danger lurks that the relationship with the question of change has got lost out of sight; and it may have struck already. In TI this relationship is, as will appear, continuously present, because in that book breaching rationality and ultimate surprise are almost synonymous. OB speaks about that breach to a much lesser extent than TI does. That is, according to Theo De Boer, because OB looks more forward at what happens after the rupture, while TI looks backward. He expresses this as follows:

> The quest for a metaphysical foundation of the social contract reaches back to an origin behind or below the pact among free wills which serves as ultimate ontological basis. One could call this a transcendental reduction or a 'way down', a descent to the source. In Levinas's later work we find, as in Heraclites (and Eliot), a 'way up'. Here the train of thought is productive rather than deductive. The metaphysical relation to the Other, which is the terminus of the first way, is now the point of departure, and the region of ontology is developed productively – theory (science and philosophy), praxis (law, institutions, the state), and finally labour (and technology). (1997: 22)

Because OB departs from a metaphysical basis that, so to speak, has been established already, the element of surprise is much less present in that book. One might say that the book has been written for people who are "already inaugurated", and that it tells more about the consequences of the surprise than about the surprise itself. It therefore gives me less connecting points when it comes to change. On the basis of these two motives *Otherwise than Being* will not widely figure in this book.

Section 1: Levinas on Representational Thought Handed Down to Him

Levinas Stands in the Tradition of Husserl

Above we have observed that for Levinas the Western philosophical tradition is characterized by the important position it assigns to representation. To understand what exactly Levinas means by that term and how he formulates his own response to it, it is necessary to further describe the form in which Levinas himself became acquainted with that representation-oriented tradition. His biography shows that in his philosophical training, Levinas was to a large extent shaped by the thinking of Husserl and his phenomenology. Therefore, the way in which that thinking speaks about representation determines, for an important part, the way Levinas himself discusses representation.

This applies both to the content that Levinas gives to the concept of representation, and to his use of a number of terms which he derived from Husserlian philosophy, such as "intentionality" and "intuition". And not only so in the writings in which he explicitly intends to expose Husserl's thinking, but also in the works in which he develops his own philosophy at some distance from Husserl. The conception of representation with which Levinas works in those last books remains formulated in Husserlian terms. For this reason it is important first to determine how Husserl understood representation according to Levinas. Thus, the following discussion of Husserl's thinking on representation is based fully on Levinas.

Representation in Husserl According to Levinas

Fortunately there is no lack of expositions by Levinas on the work of Husserl and the place of representation in it. His first thesis *The Theory of Intuition in Husserl's Phenomenology* (abbreviated: I) reveals that,[4] as do the articles from various stages of his life, bundled together in *Discovering Existence with Husserl* (abbreviated as DE).

From these, representation in Husserl comes across as an act of consciousness that leads to knowledge. Namely, that act of consciousness by which man makes something into an object for himself (I: 59) and which, for that reason, is sometimes named as an "objectifying act" (I: 62) or as the "constitution of the object" (I: 62). In this respect much emphasis is laid on the active role of consciousness, which primarily, already from itself, and in a vague way, reaches towards something; which thing, secondary to the reaching, in the act of perception – called "intuition" by Husserl – is then given as an exactly knowable object. The active role of consciousness in representation, consisting in this primary "reaching towards", is labelled by Husserl as "intentionality". Intentionality refers to consciousness as an independent

---

[4]The Dutch Husserl-specialist Theodore de Boer (1997: 3) notes in this respect: "Levinas's dissertation is still one of the best works on Husserl."

source of meanings which want to connect with things outside consciousness, in such a way that knowable objects result from it. Thus, representing things is also always an act of signification, *Sinngebung*, by consciousness.

According to Levinas, Husserl was led to this conception of representation and cognition from a deep dissatisfaction with the views on cognition which were dominant in the nineteenth century, and which Husserl summarizes under the heading of "naturalism". Naturalism for him stands as an approach to the world in which the interest in things has been narrowed just to the question of their *existence*, while neglecting their *meaning*, which should be sought in consciousness. He considers this to be an obvious, natural, but at the same time naive way of conceiving the world. Naturalism is a view "which affirms existence while ignoring its meaning and mental horizons" (DE: 64).

The effect of this approach to the world without consciousness, is that the facts and objects which are so confirmed in their existence, in fact lack meaning. Facts and objects are "opaque" (DE: 74), i.e. unsayable. They suffer from ambiguity, bloodlessness and what Husserl calls "abstractness". This may sound strange when we reflect that naturalism considers itself in its approach to the world as concrete and hard because it focuses on the tangible and measurable aspects of things. But the term abstract is understandable when we look at Husserl's view, which situates meaning, and thereby concreteness, in consciousness and in the frameworks ("horizons") that consciousness entails. To seize upon things merely from the aspect of their physical existence, and as such wrested from their sense-horizons, that is what Husserl calls really abstract indeed. In the words of Levinas: "Without bringing to light what reveals – the phenomenon as access – what is revealed – being – remains an abstraction" (DE: 118).

Husserl observes that naturalism is dominant in the field of science and that has its own consequences. First, in the form of an inadequate science: "All these sciences are dogmatic: they posit their objects without worrying about the self-evidences that allowed that position, and of which they lose sight. And thus they are insufficient as science. The natural attitude is at the origin of the equivocations and crises in which the very meaning of the operations escape the scientist who, as a technician of theory, carries them out with certainty" (quote from Husserl in DE: 72). But subsequently also because the abstraction and ambiguities that attach to the results of current science cause a widespread scepticism about the human cognitive capacities. In order to remedy this state of affairs in science Husserl considers it necessary to subject to criticism the "natural attitude", which looks only at the *existence* of the world. "This attitude must be radically changed. First, the meaning of this *existential thesis* which the natural attitude naively presupposes – the meaning of existence – must be clarified. Second, we must overcome the scepticism which is possible precisely because the meaning of this thesis is obscure" (DE: 12).

This programme may be implemented by focusing on the phenomena of consciousness and Husserl's phenomenology may be understood as a many-phased project in which he precisely tries to do that. An essential part of that phenomenology is the attention it pays to the getting away from the natural attitude, which is a prerequisite for the study of the phenomena of consciousness. Precisely because of the naturalness of the natural attitude, the detachment from it is an act which must be performed in full awareness. Husserl brings about this detachment through what he calls "putting reality between brackets", or the "phenomenological reduction". Thereby the "natural" question on the existence of reality is being postponed, allowing for questions on the meanings of that reality. Thus, acts of consciousness and phenomena of consciousness come into sight, which Husserl sees as the origin of these meanings and, therefore, of the objects as they appear to us.[5]

Amongst those acts of consciousness representation takes a privileged position: "We must, therefore, observe first that, for Husserl, being is correlative to theoretical intuitive life, to the evidence of an *objectifying act*. This is why the Husserlian concept of intuition is tainted with intellectualism and is possibly too narrow. (. . .) The characters of usage, value, etc., can exist only as grafted on a being that is the correlate of a representation" (I: 94). The way in which representation operates therefore belongs to the main topics of research that Husserl studied by way of phenomenological reduction.

The view of representation as described above, that is as an objectifying act, is that which Levinas learned from Husserl. And while Levinas, as we shall see, in his own philosophy moves far away from Husserl's thinking precisely with regard to the position of representation in it, he remains committed to the Husserlian conception of representation as the act of objectifying cognition. This is demonstrated by the fact that up to his last books and in many places Levinas uses "representation" and "objectifying cognition" as synonyms. Furthermore, Levinas reverts to expositions of Husserl for an explanation of the functioning of representation and, when it comes to objectifying cognition, the continued use of typical Husserlian terms such as intentionality and intuition.

Representationalism

The determination of the content of Levinas' conceptualisation of representation serves a purpose. It takes place within the context of the finding in the earlier chapters that representationalism leads to problems and of our turning to Levinas for possible clarification of those problems. From such a perspective it is important not only to note that Levinas assigns an important role to the concept of representation in the Western philosophical tradition and that he calls that role problematic. We must also be convinced that the concept of representation as it functions within representationalism shows sufficient similarity to the view of representation that Husserl and, in his footsteps, Levinas hold, before we can explore subsequently Levinas' response to these problems. Otherwise it is not sensible to consult Levinas

---

[5]Levinas (1998b: 72, 73) about the phenomenological reduction: "The phenomenological reduction is a violence which man – a being among other beings – does to himself in order to find himself again as pure thought . . . To transform man's 'technical' thought into spiritual activity, it will therefore be necessary to refrain from presupposing the world as a condition of the mind. Every truth that implicitly contains the "thesis of the existence of objects" must thus be suspended."

in these issues. Therefore, the objective of this section is to compare the characteristics of representation in representationalism with those of representation in the sense of Husserl and Levinas. In doing so, we must realize that Levinas uses his own concepts and philosophical categories.

While the term "representationalism" does not occur in his vocabulary, according to De Boer (1997: 80, 38 note 21, 54 note 74), Levinas does indeed present a view of the world that can be labelled as thing-ontology,[6] presented in contradistinction to "existential ontology" by which he means the ontology which was developed after Husserl. And that thing-ontology is related by Levinas regularly to the operation of representation (e.g.: DE: 115, 120), which connection actually creates the combination which has been called characteristic of representationalism. However, as it will appear when we below carry out the comparison, the precise content of the representation component in that combination, is different in Levinas than in representationalism.

In Chapter 2 the following was said about representation within the context of representationalism:

> A representation can be described as something mental (an act, but also the product of that act) which within the human mind gives a reliable reflection of an entity from outside the human mind. (The) representation may be expressed in signs or words. The concept of representation presupposes a certain arrangement of the world. Namely, in the words of Chia (1996: 70), "that a fundamental split exists between the world and the word and that the world is made up of discrete and identifiable material and social entities which can be faithfully documented using precise literal concepts and categories." From this perspective in this world view four presuppositions can be distinguished which are essential to arrive at the concept of representation:
>
> a. A representation is separated from that which it reflects ('the thing itself').
> b. Notwithstanding any separation the reflection is reliable and usable for cognition, thinking and speaking: there is correspondence between the representation and that which it reflects.
> c. The things themselves have a clearly identifiable, stable identity; they are separated from one another by clear boundaries.
> d. Combining (b) and (c): also the representations, being reflections of those things, are thus separated from one another by clear boundaries.

The first thing which may strike us in this description is the use of the term representation – mainly – as a substantive, while Husserl and Levinas predominantly perceive of representation as a verb: for them it is an activity of consciousness. In my view this does not mean that a comparison is inadequate a priori. Because, if we go through the above assumptions (a) to (d) and examine the extent to which they can be related to representation in the sense of Husserl and Levinas, there appear to be all kinds of relevant links between those characteristics and their perception of representation.

However, to carry out this comparison, it is necessary to bridge the difference between verbal and substantive use of the word representation. My proposal would

---

[6]See p. 31 for a definition.

be to look for that bridge through the "object" as it is understood by Husserl. The object, namely, is essentially linked to representation, because it arises as the result of the act of representation. Husserl locates the object in consciousness and as such it has a substantive character, comparable to the "reflection in the mind" of representationalism. If we view the object the same way as Husserl views it, a comparison between that object and representation in the sense of representationalism becomes possible. Such a view allows us to examine the extent to which the assumptions that we have been able to identify for the latter, also apply to the object. Similarities in those assumptions can in this way be related to Husserl's and Levinas' act of representation.

The Relation to Representationalism

Premise (a) reads as follows: a representation is separated from that which it reflects (the thing itself). To examine whether this premise is true for representation in the sense of Husserl and Levinas, it must, according to the above indication, be reformulated as follows: the object of representation is separated from the thing itself. The question then becomes: does Husserl (according to Levinas) agree with this principle?

In approaching this question we immediately run up against a difference with representationalism that leads back to Husserl's rejection of naturalism. As indicated, naturalism departs from the independent existence of the world and things and situates objectivity precisely there: in the independence of the outside world with respect to the subject. Separation then becomes an issue. Objectivity for Husserl, on the contrary, is connected to the attribution of meaning. Because for him the process of sense-making, which originates in subjective consciousness, proceeds by an association with perception and thereby constitutes the object. The "thing itself" is no more than a feeder and just completes content which already exists. By preference it is put in brackets in his study of the object by Husserl. Therefore, whether or not it exists independently is not really an issue for him.

So, assumption (a) belongs to the naturalism which Husserl detests so much. His usual reaction to naturalism therefore can be regarded as applicable to this premise: an independent existence is perhaps not untrue, but stressing that in no way contributes to our understanding of the world. So, in this respect Husserl's thinking on representation differs from representationalism, which does emphasize the separate, independent existence of the outside world.

Because of Husserl's approach to the natural attitude, the bottom also falls out of premise (b) for him. Adjusted for the verbal use of the word "representation", it should be read as follows: notwithstanding the separation, the reflection is reliable and usable for cognition, thinking and speaking; there is correspondence between the object of representation and that which it reflects. Because of the way it is worded, this premise is already closely associated with (a). And if for Husserl the independent existence of the thing itself is not an issue, then for him the problem of the reliability of the reflection does not appear as pregnant as it does for representationalism. Indeed, that Cartesian problem arises precisely because of the independence which representationalism postulates under (a). Because Husserl puts the question of an independent existence between brackets, object and subject come to stand less opposite to one another as separate poles. "The subjective phenomena are not given as distinct from the object they intimate. Their relation is not comparable to that of a sign or an image to the thing they signify or represent" (I: 6).

Since Husserl then designates subjective consciousness as the place of the constitution of the object, subject and object move into one another to a certain extent,[7] and reliably bridging the distance between those separate poles is no longer an urgent issue. That is why Levinas can say that "[i]t is not by the fact of being reflected that the relation between thought and object is defined, but by the meaning of the object and its existence. Hence what we have to know is not whether the object is faithfully reflected in consciousness, but the meaning in which it appears" (DE: 64). So, also regarding assumption (b) we find a difference between Husserl's thinking and representationalism.

This does not apply to the presuppositions (c) and (d) where in the last one, adjusted for Husserl's language, again should be read "the objects of representation" instead of "the representations". For the comparison we are performing I combine the two assumptions (c) and (d) because the central point of both statements is the same: namely, that the world consists of clearly identifiable, separate entities, the idea which we called reification in Chapter 2.

When it comes to the content, this idea connects – apart from a different interpretation of the term "reification" – to Husserl's view, when he continues to conceive of the world as made up of delineated entities. For this conception he does not use the term "reification", which he reserves for the view that the world is to be considered in terms of the physical nature of things, as in naturalism. He actually, sharply denounces that view (De Boer 1997: 4). But for Husserl objects in a non-material sense, equally understood as identifiable, defined entities, remain to be the primary knowable data of the world. This is evident from his descriptions of how the access to the world can be found. This access, according to Husserl, cannot be achieved other than through the human apparatus that is equipped to deal with those entities. That apparatus is human reason which, in representation, constitutes objects that are characteristically obvious – that is that they may be identified as entities. Indeed for Husserl "to know" is primarily "to know in an objectifying way", which is performed in representation and is conceived of as a matter of the intellect. These elements of his view are important characteristics of representationalism as well.

If we sum up the comparison we carried out between the assumptions of representationalism and those of Husserl's thought on representation, we find that the assumptions (a) and (b) are not shared by Husserl. The central point of (c) and (d), namely: the object-oriented thinking, we do find indeed in Husserl.

---

[7] De Boer (1997: 3): "Instead of setting the world as object antithetically against subjective consciousness, which would leave us with the insoluble problem of the relation between them, Husserl is interested primarily in the mode of being of the world and of consciousness."

In the previous chapters we noted that the problematic aspects of representationalism: deception and exclusion, are to a significant extent related to the object-oriented, reifying (in the sense of entity-delineating) operation of reason. It is precisely with respect to that element that the assumptions of representationalism and Husserl's thought appear to have much in common. On the basis of that relationship, the question that concerns us in this chapter may be regarded as legitimate. Namely, the question whether Levinas' efforts to deal with the problematic aspects of Husserl's thought on representation also contain an answer to the representationalism of which organizational scientists and philosophers have found that it leads to deception and exclusion.

Levinas' Assessment of Husserl's Thought on Representation

From the above the conception of representation Levinas inherited from Husserl has become clear. Before we examine below the place which Levinas accords to representation in his own philosophy, it is important to know how Levinas assessed representation in the sense of Husserl. That is the subject of this section.

When it comes to representation, Levinas' assessment of Husserl is ambiguous. On one hand, Levinas stresses that by the attention he pays to the "horizons" of knowing, Husserl offered opportunities to break through the object-oriented thinking. The narrow focus of naturalism on bare objects "does not grasp their meaning, but only an abstraction in an inevitable misunderstanding; it is because the intention in its 'bursting forth toward the object' is also an ignorance and a failure to recognize the meaning of that object, since it is a forgetting of everything that intention only contains implicitly and that consciousness sees without seeing" (DE: 115). To clarify exactly the contribution of Husserl to philosophy, Levinas points to statements by Husserl in which he does *not* insist that the status of gateway to the world is limited to objectifying cognition (ED: 117, 119, I: 223). Through the importance he attaches to the *meaning* of things in those statements, Husserl attributes also to that status non-objectifying acts, such as practical acts, value-judgements or acts of the will.

These other acts feature that they do not take the way objects appear to us – physical or not – for their starting-point, but their mode-of-being. The mode-of-being or modality of an object refers to the context of meaning of an object viewed from the subject. The object may for example be a tool or an aesthetic object. This focus on the context suggests the presence in Husserl of a certain space to consider the world in a different way than as a collection of objects which the intellect can identify.

Levinas recognizes this focus in among other places Husserl's statement in the *Cartesianische Meditationen* that "[t]he fact that the structure of all intentionality implies a 'horizon' prescribes an absolutely new method to phenomenological analysis and description" (DE: 115). Levinas loves to refer to that space that Husserl seems to offer, and indeed he is prepared to play down those elements of Husserl's thinking that point to the latter's attachment to object-thinking. Thus Levinas says in *The Ruin of Representation* (DE: 120) that the fact that Husserl himself treated the above-mentioned horizons as objects, does not detract from the influence of the innovating aspects of his work. And on the basis of the openings that Husserl offers, Levinas feels justified in saying that "[t]he practical and aesthetic categories are, as we have asserted, part of the very constitution of being, in the same way as the purely theoretical categories" (I: 53).

But to say something like this, Levinas is obliged sometimes to stretch his interpretation of Husserl rather far, as he himself admits in the sequel to the last quote: "However, it would be twisting Husserl's thought somewhat to speak here of equivalence. In Husserl's philosophy (and this may be where we will have to depart from it), knowledge and representation are not on the same level as other modes of life, and they are not secondary modes. Theory and representation play a dominant role in life, serving as a basis for the whole of conscious life; they are the forms of intentionality that give a foundation to all others (...) This is what causes the intellectualistic character proper to Husserlian intuitionism." (Idem)

This last quotation shows a more negative assessment by Levinas of Husserl's conception of representation, and that is the other pole of the ambivalence. The negative element is located in the fact that the objectifying cognition, and hence the focus on objects in Husserl, keeps primacy over other relationships to the world, such as practical action or aesthetic action. "Hence, the mode of existence of the existing world that is revealed to us is the same as that of objects given to our theoretical attention. *The real world is the world of knowledge.* The characters of 'value', 'usage', etc., attached to things are attributed to them by us but do not constitute their existence" (I: 62). This characterization of Husserl is repeatedly represented by Levinas, at several places in his thesis (e.g. I: 62, 63, 65 and 94).

The ambivalence about the value of Husserl's thinking pervades the whole work of Levinas. Probably the assessment that he gives on p. 62 of the *Theory of Intuition* is representative of his attitude towards Husserl. There Levinas points to the primacy of the objectifying cognition by which Husserl's thought is ultimately characterized. Indeed, he immediately adds that Husserl later relativized that primacy to the benefit of non-objectifying acts but "the assertion of the dominant role of theory, perception, and judgment in our life, in which the world is constituted, is a thesis that Husserl has never abandoned. For him, representation always will be the foundation of all acts."

This assessment, I believe, reflects Levinas' final judgement, and determines how Husserl's thinking functions within the work of Levinas. Because of his adhering ultimately to the objectifying way of knowing about representation, Husserl on his own account is a representative of Western thought since the work of Plato. He is an outstanding representative indeed, who does not know how to deal with the deception and the exclusion of that ancient rationality-tradition.[8] By the attention he paid

---

[8] Van Riessen (1991: 162, 163) says in this respect: "Husserl's central thought is that in the objectifying act the same determines the Other completely. With him the creative capacity and the total

to the horizons of cognition, it is true that he provided impulses for breaching the primacy of representation. But Husserl himself did not go beyond these impulses. Only his student, Heidegger, could break the power of objectifying thinking on the basis of those impulses.

The Influence of Heidegger

Levinas made acquaintance with Heidegger's work through his friend Jean Wahl in 1927. He was immediately fascinated by the work, and that is understandable because of Levinas' early recognition of the limitations of the rationality-tradition together with his enthusiasm for the openings suggested in Husserl's work. It was no doubt stimulating for the young Levinas to discover the thinker from the Black Forest who went on from where Husserl stopped.

In 1929, when Heidegger took over the Chair of Husserl in Freiburg, Levinas enrolled for his lectures. He had perhaps some special feeling that he would be the witness of a revolution in philosophy. In his thesis, Levinas says that he was inspired by Heidegger's "powerful and original" philosophy (I: LVI). With his publication of *Martin Heidegger and Ontology* (1932), Levinas was the first to introduce Heidegger's thinking to the French public.

The step by which Heidegger definitely leaves Husserl behind, in the eyes of Levinas, is where he dares to say that an access to reality is possible that does *not* seize upon the object-character of things in the world (I: 154). That is an approach to reality that seizes upon being and the modes-of-being of things, and which thereby cancels the primacy of the objectifying knowing. "With respect to being (in the verbal sense) it is evident indeed that it can never be conceived of as an available object, as a being (in the substantive sense)" says De Boer (1989: 175; translation NvdV). Levinas himself formulates the meaning of Heidegger as follows.

> The presence near to things referring to, initially and most frequently, unsuspected hori-
> zons – horizons that nonetheless guide that very presence – indeed also announces the
> philosophy of being in Heidegger's sense. All thought that directs itself to *a being* stands
> within the being of that being (which Heidegger shows to be irreducible to a being), as
> within the horizon and site that commands all position-taking, the light of a landscape,
> already guiding the initiative of the subject who wills, works, or judges. All Heidegger's
> work consists in opening and exploring this dimension, unknown in the history of ideas,
> to which he nonetheless gives the most well-known name of *Sein* [Being]. In relation to
> the most traditional model of objectivity, it is a subjective field – but subjectivism "more
> objective than all objectivity. (DE: 118)

----

freedom of the representation get priority. In the representation the opposition between subject and object is cancelled because the object is incorporated into the world of the subject (the same). But also individual thinking can no longer stand out, it becomes one with the universal ... Thus the individual can in representational thinking become creator of the world. In this respect for Levinas there is no difference between Husserl's philosophy and idealistic creation philosophy. In both cases the I becomes causa sui with at the same time too little and too much responsibility" (translation NvdV).

The idea that appeals most to Levinas in this philosophy of Heidegger, is that consciousness is relativized. Under the regime of classical, thing-oriented ontology consciousness, being the seat of objectifying power, i.e. of representation, took the place of origin of the world. There consciousness counted as the place where, through representation, things become knowable and get constituted into objects and such without consiousness itself being dependent on something else for its own existence. So, there consciousness was also its own origin and as such took an unassailable position in classical ontology, Husserl's phenomenology included.

The philosophical significance of Heidegger's position is that by highlighting the fact that consciousness is conditioned, he undermines the totalizing, imperialist character of representation. Consciousness exists within a context of prior experiences of a practical, social and historical nature that have their determining influence on the operation of consciousness, but have been forgotten. Or suppressed, because "precisely these are obscured within classical ontology, by a system of eternal values and an interpretation of human existence from categories of an eternal nature" (Van Riessen 1991: 89; translation NvdV).

We already came across the anti-thing-oriented central idea of Heidegger in the description of how organization studies uses Heidegger's work. Much of his work consists of systematically exploring that context of forgotten experiences and horizons and thereby the "thrownness" of consciousness. Given Levinas' objections to the limitations of the rationalist philosophy of consciousness – for him synonymous with the Western philosophical tradition – the new thinking of Heidegger marked no less than a very necessary and thus exciting revolution.

What exactly were the consequences of this revolution for the idea of representation Levinas has described in his article *The Ruin of Representation* from 1959. In my discussion of this article I do not bother too much about the fact that Levinas extends some merits, which at other places he specifically attributes to phenomenology as developed by Heidegger (in opposition to Husserl), also to Husserl. That will have to do with the nature of the article that appeared as Levinas' contribution to the compilation *Edmund Husserl 1859–1959*, released to commemorate the hundredth birthday of Husserl (of course in combination with the ambivalence of Levinas regarding Husserl that we already noted).

The thrust of the article is that thanks to phenomenology, it is not so much the concept of representation itself which has been blown up, but what Levinas calls "the sovereignty of representation". By this he refers to the long tradition in philosophy that conceives of knowing as a full presence of the knowing subject to a fully present object, a subject-object relationship from which nothing escapes, and which can be characterized in terms of omniscience (DE: 115). Phenomenology undermines that view by showing that in cognition it is never solely the object which is at stake. There are, around the object and the subject, always horizons, which also play a role in the illumination and discovering of the object. But most of the time we are unaware of these horizons, they are implicit.

Therefore, the intentionality of knowledge goes hand in hand with the forgetting of everything that intentionality only contains implicitly, and which consciousness sees without seeing. By concentrating on that forgotten experience, clarification of that which takes on meaning through the operation of consciousness: i.e. clarification of its objective sense takes place (DE: 115). For Levinas, this represents a welcome break with the cognitive tradition in which a sovereign consciousness comes to perfect knowledge through representation. But, this being so, also for him the role of representation has not finished. Representation in the sense of intending objectifyingly remains in place. This is evident when Levinas re-defines the new phenomenology, which finishes off representation in the old sense, in terms of representation: "(...) a phenomenology (...) where representation finds itself placed within horizons that it somehow had not willed, but with which it cannot dispense (...)" (DE: 121).

The difference with the pre-Heideggerian view of representation thus consists of an awareness which henceforth ought to accompany representation permanently. Namely, that representation is not omniscient: continuously many things escape consciousness, which nevertheless contribute to its contents. However, Levinas says there is something in the nature of representation that does not want to realize that. Inherently representation seems to forget its own conditionality, seeing itself as the origin and the objects which it constitutes as absolute in the sense of being unrelated to sources outside consciousness. Thus:

> (r)epresentation deals with beings as if they were entirely self-supporting, as if they were substances. It has the power to disinterest itself – be it only for an instant, the instant of representation – from the condition of these beings. It triumphs over the vertigo of the infinite conditioning that true thought, and thought that is true, opens up in these beings. Without traversing the infinite series of the past to which my today nonetheless refers, I embrace this day, in all of its reality, and derive my very being from these fleeting moments. (DE: 112)

In other words, our representational faculty fools itself (and ourselves) and permanently creates illusions. Even after the Heideggerian-turn. The difference being that, after Heidegger, we are more alert (as we have concluded already in Chapter 3), and thanks to his analyses we are better equipped to emasculate imperialistic pretensions and to pierce the illusions. But the question is whether that is enough against the power of representation. Ultimately, Levinas does not think so.

Levinas' Critique of Heidegger

The elements of Heidegger's work about which Levinas is most enthusiastic are his criticism of Husserl's intellectualism and his appreciation of the actual human existence. "For Levinas, the basic advance and advantage of Heideggerian ontology over Husserlian phenomenology is that it begins from an analysis of the factual situation of the human being in everyday life, what Heidegger after Wilhelm Dilthey calls 'facticity'" (Critchley 2002: 9).

As we have seen, he did not hold back in the praise he offers to Heidegger for these merits. But, already soon after his acquaintance with Heidegger's work, he started to take more distance from him. And that distance only increased in the course of his philosophical life, to the extent that at one time he had the nickname of being the "anti-Heidegger" in France. It should be mentioned that up to his last writings he nonetheless continued to recognize Heidegger's merits for philosophy.

The drifting away of Levinas from Heidegger originated from a new kind of oppression that Levinas began to feel with respect to his work. Heidegger had finished off the dullness of thing-ontology, but the result, i.e. existential ontology, at closer inspection turned out to be no less depressing. What had disappeared, compared to Husserl, was reification: the focus on the fixed object. "Objects are uprooted from their dull fixity to sparkle in the play of rays that come and go between the giver and the given" (DE: 118).

But what remained was a focus on knowledge and understanding. Because the reason why Heidegger looked for the "openness of being" as the environment in which things can appear, was his deep desire to find out the truth and to understand the world. For Heidegger, in a sense, "to live" becomes the "understanding of being". In this focus on the *Seinsverständnis* Levinas recognizes a new form of thirst for power and even totalitarianism. "Levinas' objection is that philosophical understanding in Heidegger pervades the whole of life" says Van Riessen (1991: 94; translation NvdV). Precisely that which Levinas admired in Heidegger – the connection between philosophy and life – turns out to be the point at which he ultimately can not follow him (1991: 93).

Levinas realized already in the 1930s that, despite Heidegger's garish break with the philosophical tradition, there was a continuity with that tradition at a deeper level. In the last resort thing-ontology had emerged from the drive to understand the world, and that was precisely the motive by which Heidegger was driven. Clarity, light and brightness, that is what thinking was about since the Greeks. In that area, according to Levinas, Heidegger had achieved much, because thanks to his analyses, even though continuous vigilance is required, the deception caused by thing-ontology gets less opportunities.

That does not apply however – and that is Levinas' major objection – to the exclusion which was inherent in thing-ontology. Indeed, exclusion is intrinsic to all understanding. For Levinas, when it gets a dominant position, understanding is by definition totalitarian. The reason is that there are things that refuse existential clarification, such as the relationship to the Other, "an enigma, something ultimately refractory to intentionality and opaque to the understanding" (Critchley 2002: 8). According to Levinas, within the Heideggerian universe, there is no room for those transcendent matters precisely because understanding of being is the ultimate horizon there.

> [T]he Heideggerian ontology that exceeds intellectualism is unable to describe this non-comprehensive relation because particular beings are always already understood upon the horizon of Being, even if this is, as Heidegger says at the beginning of Being and Time, a vague and average understanding. (Critchley 2002: 11)

The other appears there only in the context of what Heidegger calls *Mitsein*. "The other might at best become my colleague, comrade or co-worker, but not the source of my compassion or the object of my admiration, fear or desire" (Critchley 2002: 13). Levinas therefore can not reconcile himself to Heidegger's existential ontology.

The problem thereof is not only that – as before – good old representation is being maintained in it. In fact, also for Levinas, the objectifying act remains a necessity. And if permanent vigilance is required against the dangers of illusion which cling to representation, it is still Heidegger's merit that he combated them by means of his analyses, because in his cognitive order representation gets a more modest and conditioned position than it had in representationalism. No, Levinas' main problem is that understanding of being and beings in Heidegger has the final word. For Heidegger, there is nothing outside existential ontology.

This state of affairs motivates Levinas to step outside the framework of phenomenology and to enter the area of metaphysics. At this moment, it is most important for us to emphasize that Levinas' intention is – as he says in the preface of *Existence and Existents* – to leave the climate of Heidegger's philosophy, which is characterized by attention to the development of being (EE: 4). The true transcendence in that atmosphere gets caught in a fix. I will try to clarify in the following section what exactly is the significance of this move by Levinas, by giving a description of Levinas' anthropology. It will show that within the Levinassian universe, a special role is assigned to representation which, as mentioned, also for Levinas has not finished. In constructing his own views, Levinas partly builds upon useful insights of Heidegger, especially the conditioning of representation. Also partly, and in a completely original way he interweaves representation with the transcendence that the dimension of metaphysics entails.

Section 2: The Position of Representation in Levinas' Own Philosophy

In the overview of the major lines of Levinas' philosophy, we found that the issue of rationality takes an important place in his work. Throughout his philosophical life he struggles with the question of how the relationship between rational thinking and what seems to escape rational thinking should be understood. Since representation is regarded by Levinas as a direct manifestation of rationality -and he sometimes uses it as a synonym for rationality – that struggle may also be seen as a determination of the position of representation within Levinas' philosophy. It is my intention in this section to indicate the role Levinas assigns to representation within the field of forces of *il-y-a*, ontology and metaphysics, and which characterize his philosophical universe. On the basis of the reasons I gave in the introduction to this chapter, I will focus mainly on Levinas' work prior to *Otherwise than Being*.

The starting point for my descriptions is what already early, in *Existence and Existents* and *Time and the Other* was the starting point for Levinas' own philosophy: the experience of the *il-y-a* and the response thereto in the hypostasis. The hypostasis, the process of coming-to-stand-on-its-own of the subject with regard to the *il-y-a*, is understood by Levinas as a layered process. The first steps within what I call the first phase of the hypostasis are most extensively covered in EE and TO.

I therefore derive my descriptions of that first phase primarily from those books. I situate a second phase in what Levinas calls "the separation". He works out that phase particularly in *Totality and Infinity* and, for that part, I therefore follow the descriptions of TI. In my presentation of the hypostasis it will appear that representation, and therewith rationality, gets assigned an intriguing place within the whole of the hypostasis.

Il-y-a and Hypostasis

Il-y-a and hypostasis within the work of Levinas form a central pair of concepts. The combination is of great significance for Levinas' description of the human condition. As we already saw in the introduction to this chapter *Il-y-a* with Levinas denotes being, but being in its specific appearance of formless, undetermined being. He at times calls it a noise, a roar. It is frightening, on the one hand because of its unstoppable character: it is unlimited, and continues endlessly. But on the other hand, and more so, because of the horribly indifferent character of the *il-y-a*, its colossal neutrality. The aspect of unlimitedness generates weariness regarding the endlessness and the meaninglessness, the neutral aspect evokes anguish. Levinas encounters it in insomnia.

Hypostasis is the breaking apart of a being from the *il-y-a*. It is the process of substantiation, taking a distance from the surrounding being, at first by assuming a position in space and time and next by creating a world, that is by naming things and by developing consciousness. It is: becoming a subject. Levinas describes the hypostasis as a process that contains several phases. The process starts with choosing a position with regard to the *il-y-a*, passes through the phase of reinforcing that position without any role for consciousness, and results in a stage in which consciousness plays an important role.

The First Phase of the Hypostasis

The conceived point of departure for the hypostasis is a situation of aversion against the *il-y-a*, in combination with the necessity for the emerging subject, if it is to become really a subject, to choose a position with respect to the anonymous *il-y-a*. In the above, we used the formulation "taking a distance" to indicate this process, but that tells only the half story. The – emerging – subject will not be able to repress the *il-y-a* completely. In the taking up of its own being the subject will also have to entertain a relationship with the *il-y-a*, that is: with that being which at the same time arouses fright and disgust. As Levinas writes in EE: "The questioning of Being is an experience of Being in its strangeness. It is then a way of taking up Being (. . .)The question is itself a manifestation of the relationship with Being. Being is essentially alien and strikes against us" (EE, 9).

Disgust and Laziness

So the issue is one of entering into a relationship with something repulsive. Weariness and sloth characterize this situation and form the expression of the reluctance which holds the emerging subject in its grip.

The weariness has to do with the impossibility of escaping the boundless being, perhaps even more so in hypostased form than without hypostasis, because hypostasis presupposes a kind of coming to terms with being and therewith acceptance of being. In all cases one rule applies: you have to be. There is "a commitment to exist, with all the seriousness and harshness of an unrevokable contract" (EE: 12) and the weariness is about exactly that: "[T]he weariness concerns existence itself . . ./. . . (O)ne has to do something, one has to aspire after and undertake" (EE: 11,12).

The sceptic believes falsely that it is possible to avoid the situation, but the *il faut* is inevitable. The nausea is not so much a content of consciousness (it finds itself at a too early stage in the hypostasis for that), but something which happens, primarily a *refusal* indeed, a refusal to exist: "Weariness by all its being effects this refusal to exist" (EE, 12). This weariness thus does not have any link with action. Weariness cannot quite realise action.

With sloth, or indolence, this is different. Levinas links sloth to human action, namely the beginning of action: "Indolence is essentially tied up with the beginning of an action: the stirring, the getting up (. . .) It may inhere in the act that is being realized, in which case the performance rolls on as on an ill-paved road, jolted about by instants each of which is a beginning all over again. The job does not flow, does not catch on, is discontinuous – a discontinuousness which is perhaps the very nature of 'a job'" (EE, 13). The emerging subject has erected itself, but incessantly falls back. It keeps starting up. The same repugnance that precedes the beginning of action returns here. The refusal of existence pervades the indolence as well and manifests itself precisely in that repeated backslide from action. "And indolence, as a recoil before action, is a hesitation before existence, an indolence about existing" (EE, 15).

Levinas stresses that all this is not at all agreeable. The pleasures of the hypostasis are reached by the emerging subject only in a later stage, the phase of enjoyment. There he speaks about play, here about the necessity of "one must try to live." Sloth at this stage is linked with repugnance against the constraint to exist. The opportunities which are offered to the subject at this stage, above all, present trouble and sorrow: the subject's concern is to be "concerned with itself (. . .) It possesses riches which are a source of cares before being a source of enjoyment" (EE,15).

Fatigue

Whereas sloth is somewhere stuck in the middle between a beginning of action, the loss of the beginning and the next restart, Levinas places fatigue as an essential part of activity. The subject has already taken up its own existence, or, more precisely, is incessantly engaged in taking up its existence. But existence takes a lead over the subject, the subject cannot keep up well with existence; the subject is a moment behind its existence. This relaxation of the grip on its own existence, that is fatigue. "It struggles behind the instant it is going to take on" (EE, 22). "Effort is the very effecting of an instant" (EE: 23). Fatigue is about the exertion that is needed for that. That effort gives the activity a double character: "Action is then by essence subjection and servitude, but also the first manifestation, of the very constitution, of an existent, a *someone* that is" (EE, 23). Effort and fatigue thus are part of the genesis of the subject, which, according to Levinas, may be succinctly characterized as the taking upon itself of existence by the *existent.*

The Second Phase of the Hypostasis: The Separation

Compared to the tragedy and gravity of the first phase of the hypostasis the second phase strikes us because of its much more pleasant features. Once the substantiation of the subject has started off, this movement develops further in a way Levinas describes mainly in positive terms. Levinas often calls the hypostasis after the phase of the fatigue a "separation". Namely between the indeterminate being and the emergent subject, because the detachment gets a more clear shape at this stage. The most elaborate descriptions of this process are to be found in TI. The separation in those descriptions is characterized first by enjoyment, then by dwelling, labour, possession and finally representation.

Enjoyment

Enjoyment is a name for the stage in the substantiation of the subject in which the subject no longer just melts with the surrounding being. It has acquired a relationship with that being. There is, at a certain point, more than deprivation, fatigue, hunger and thirst. There is now also the relationship with those contents: the love for life, which is a new content in itself, namely the enjoyment. Levinas speaks of a position of man "at the second power" (TI: 113) and he expresses that as follows: "(...) where the attachment to the contents that fill it provides it with a supreme content. The consumption of foods is the food of life." (TI: 114)

The nourishment which is enjoyed by the enjoying being is taken from what Levinas calls "the elements". By that he means wind, earth, sea, heaven, air and all the rest which supports man and which constitutes, after the separation, the environment of the enjoying being. Elements are not to be considered as things, but as qualities which offer themselves to the senses. They can be felt, smelled, tasted but they cannot be fixed or known as objects. This corresponds with the affective, sensory character of the enjoyment which at several places is stressed by Levinas.

The role the enjoyment plays in the process of hypostasis lies in the particular form of independence which it introduces. Preceding the enjoyment there is a situation of indeterminacy: the being coincides with the whole from which it derives its nourishment, which can be interpreted as pure dependency. The enjoyment according to Levinas' description causes a change in that situation. A distance is being created, the dependency can be suspended and in this way arises the paradoxical figure of a being which has detached itself from the world from which neverthe-less it still feeds itself (TI, 116). The enjoyment is a decisive step in the process of breaking away from the *il-y-a*.

The enjoyment, however, has a problem: the elemental, which it lives from, has a somewhat ambiguous nature: it provides nurture, but does not give any guarantee for the future. Enjoyment lacks security. "In sensibility itself and independently of all thought there is announced an insecurity which throws back in question this quasi-eternal immemoriality of the element, which will disturb it" (TI: 137). Therefore something else will be needed to compensate for the deficiency which sticks to enjoyment: labour, which operates from the *house,* or centre, of each per-son. The separation between the separated being and the surrounding world will deepen because of that.

Dwelling, Labour and Possession

The human answer to the uncertainty of the enjoyment is: to increase the distance to the elemental. Levinas calls this a turning into oneself and this occurs as a dwelling in the intimacy of such a *house*. To dwell is like "a recollection, a coming to oneself, a retreat home with oneself as in a land of refuge" (TI: 156).

The *house* provides, by the shelter which it offers man, the opportunity to find new relations with the elemental. The element is now available in a new way: it can be seized upon from a sheltered spot. Man "gets a foothold in the elemental by a side already appropriated: a field cultivated by me, the sea in which I fish and moor my boats, the forest in which I cut wood" (TI: 131). Thus the dwelling, by suspending the enjoyment and by its distance to the elements, enables labour, and labour provides us with greater security against the elements.

This results in some more opportunities, because apart from being grasped by labour, the seized element now also can be tied up: "The element is fixed between the four walls of the home, is calmed in possession" (TI: 158). One implication of this seizing by labour and possessing by fixation is that the element's charac-ter changes: it becomes substance, it falls apart into things and thereby loses the elusiveness of the mere qualitative being which characterizes the elements.

Levinas stresses that at this stage of the separation we cannot speak yet of know-ing or thinking. Labour and taking-into-possession are the work of the hand, "the organ of grasping and taking, the first and blind grasping in the teeming mass" (TI: 159), and not of the mind that sees and represents. But through dwelling, labour and possession a number of conditions will be fulfilled that are going to make possible representation and knowing, which form the culmination of the separation. Levinas says that dwelling has this effect because "the subject contemplating a world pre-supposes the event of dwelling, the withdrawal from the elements (. . .), recollection in the intimacy of the home" (TI: 153). Labour and possession do so by snatch-ing substances – things with fixed contours – from the elements. They provide the "mobilization of the thing, grasped by the hand" (TI: 163). It is therefore, based on the possession of things, now possible to bring up representation as a topic.

Consciousness, Representation

The final step of the hypostasis, which is step towards knowing and thinking, is being taken with the development within the subject of consciousness, rational thought or what Levinas calls the light. That step is characterized by the appearance of representations (conceived of in Husserl's sense, i.e. as objectifying acts) and is made possible by the preparing work of labour and possession. This appearance of representations is considered by Levinas as the apex of the hypostasis: the separation between the subject and the surrounding being are being radicalized in it. "[L]ife in the world is consciousness inasmuch as it provides the possibility of existing in a withdrawal from existence" (EE: 37). "Existence in the world qua light, which makes desire possible, is, then, in the midst of being, the possibility of detaching oneself from being." (EE: 43). The subject now has its own world.

Arriving at this stage, Levinas pays great attention to the character of representation. What interests him is its illusory nature, which we came across already in our discussion of Levinas' reaction to Heidegger. The illusion of representation consists in the ability of the representing consciousness to see itself as origin of the world. This is shown best in philosophical idealism which departs from the idea that a priori the world of objects is being constituted by thinking. But it applies basically to any intellectualistic, cognitive view in which representation plays a role. "Representation consists in the possibility of accounting for the object as though it were constituted by a thought, as though it were a noëma" (TI:128). It is evident for Levinas that this is illusory. He takes much trouble to show that thinking is conditional: only if preliminary conditions are satisfied – i.e. through dwelling and labour – man can arrive at thinking and knowing. With this peculiarity, that thinking subsequently tends to forget its own conditions: it sees *itself* alone as the condition for the world instead of the other way round. That is the illusion – but sometimes for Levinas also the genius – of representation.

For Levinas this illusory nature of representation is not necessarily to be valued negatively. His appreciation for the achievements of the hypostasis and the escape from the *il-y-a* is too big for that. But he points to the substantial problems connected with this treacherous nature of representation: loss of meaning and a particular, with respect to the totalitarianism of the original *il-y-a*, new form of totalitarianism. "reason is singular. And in this sense knowledge in the world never meets something really different. That is the deep truth of idealism" (TO: 53; translation NvdV).

Impasse: The Deficiency of Representation

This means that ultimately the hypostasis results in an unsatisfactory ambivalence. On the one hand there is the achievement of the escape from the *il-y-a* which cannot easily be valued too highly. But on the other hand, there is the continuous return of the *il-y-a*, and this in two guises, moreover. The *primeval il-y-a* succeeds at times in breaking through our rational insights and control, because of which the threat of being flooded by broken out elements remains constantly lurking. On the other hand the loneliness that belongs to reason, and which therefore is given with the high level of rationality of developed subjects, entails its own version of the *il-y-a*. That *il-y-a* manifests itself in the closed, totalitarian nature of our rational and ideological thinking that is linked to the misplaced sense of sovereignty and the forgetting of its own origin, which are characteristics of representation.

The totality that belongs to this second manifestation – which I will call the *veiled il-y-a* – is no longer that of the primeval *il-y-a*, but it still is a totality. It has its own specific forms of aversion and disgust, which however are reminiscent of the supposedly exiled primeval *il-y-a*, especially in the experience of meaninglessness and discomfort that it entails. So, the *il-y-a* sticks; man never really escapes from its atmosphere where it may be present in its original and in its veiled form.

> In the hypostasis of an instant – in which a subject's mastery, power or virility are manifested as being in a world, in which intention is the forgetting of oneself in light and a desire for things, in the abnegation of charity and sacrifice – we can discern the return of the *there is*. The hypostasis, in participating in the *there is*, finds itself again to be a solitude, in the definitiveness of the bond with which the ego is chained to its self. (EE: 84)

Here Levinas outlines a fundamentally depressing paradox: of man who is nowhere as free as in his spontaneous thinking in which he is the origin of his own world; but, at the same time, in no way more locked up and lonely than as though chained like this to his own thinking. Van Riessen formulates this as follows:

> One final aspect of the loneliness must be mentioned: precisely because the subject, by the struggle for self-maintenance, is involved in the world in an enforced way; through that way no breaking of the loneliness can come about. Neither the sensory experience, with the 'enjoyment' which is a part of it, nor knowledge, can break up the circle in which the subject continues to refer to itself. All experiences and all knowledge, finally return to the subject and leave it eventually alone with itself. (Van Riessen 1991: 112; translation NvdV)

Against this background we understand the exclamation of Levinas (TI: 90) who wonders: "Who can punish the exercise of the freedom of knowing? Or, more exactly, how can the spontaneity of the freedom that is manifested in certitude be called in question?"

A Second Narrative: The Other

So far Levinas' narrative has been set up rather schematically. The hypostasis is presented as an essentially linear process that starts with a laboriously emergent subject and that results in the separation. During that process the conditions are being created gradually to achieve the form of human rationality that manifests itself in representation. "[The objectifying] intentionality is a necessary moment of the event of separation in itself, to whose description this section is devoted, and which is articulated starting with enjoyment in dwelling and possession" (TI: 122).

But from the outset Levinas has a second plot in mind. He introduces that plot, however, in a systematic way only from the end of Part II of TI, after his explanation of the importance of dwelling. This second narrative says, in a nutshell, that the conditions considered so far are not sufficient for representation to occur. A new condition is what Levinas calls the "gift", which in turn depends on the appearance of the Other. Below I will go into that in more detail.

The effect of the second plot is highly significant because through it the whole of Levinas' book changes completely. The first narrative continues to follow his argument, but at the same time he steps outside its framework, with the effect that a whole new story is created. The second narrative provides a different way of looking at the same issues and thereby enables us to break through the oppression with which we are saddled by the first way of looking, i.e. up to the previous section.

Prior to my treatment of this second narrative, it therefore is important to indicate how it must be understood. Not as an argument that can not be reconciled logically with the first narrative and thus shows an inconsistency in Levinas' thinking. By adding a second narrative, the story as a whole turns over, and that is a wanted effect. Indeed, it is the very occurrence of the surprise that Levinas wants to describe.

The Gift

The first narrative, which we have hitherto followed, presents enjoyment, dwelling, labour and possession as prerequisites for representation: these create the distance which is necessary for knowing, first with respect to the elements, then with respect to the things. But arriving at this point, Levinas states that these are not sufficient conditions – more is required. The reason is that enjoyment and dwelling are still, despite their distance, in a way involved in the non-I. The separation of the enjoyment and the possession is not radical enough yet. That means that I must free myself from property. "But in order that I be able to free myself from the very possession that the welcome of the Home establishes, in order that I be able to see things in themselves, that is, represent them to myself, refuse both enjoyment and possession, I must know how *to give* what I possess." (TI: 170).

Thus, Levinas arrives at relating objectifying cognition, thematizing and defining things to my possession being contested by the Other (TI: 209), to abolition of the inalienable property (TI: 75), to the provision of things to one another through the word (TI: 139, 174). The meaning of these statements is that, at the basis of the generalization which is a characteristic of objectifying knowing, there is an ethical event (TI: 173). With regard to this Wyschogrod (2002) says:

> Levinas sees signification, the capacity to generalize, as an ethical event. (...) To be sure, the thing is first mine but language which designates it thereby giving it to the other is a dispossession, 'a first donation'. Generalization as an invoking of the world in acts of nomination is an offering of the world to another. (p. 195)

In this respect Levinas assigns an important role to language because that is the medium through which we make knowledge available. Speech is a teaching and "does not simply transmit an abstract and general content already common to me and the Other. (...) [It] founds community by giving, by presenting the phenomenon as given; and it gives by thematizing" (TI: 98).

How, according to Levinas, does this work? For an answer to that question we have to read the sequel to the aforementioned quote on the necessity of donation:

> Only thus (i.e. in the gift, NvdV) could I situate myself absolutely above my engagement in the non-I. But for this I must encounter the indiscrete face of the Other that calls me into question. The Other – the absolutely other – paralyzes possession, which he contests by his epiphany in the face. (TI: 170, 171)

Whereby for the Other and the face can be filled in: the distressed, needy, maladjusted fellow human, who in particular is indiscrete because he calls upon me to share my possessions with him. Van Riessen says in this regard:

> The last and most definitive distance between the subject and reality is caused by the critical presence of the other. Levinas refers by that to the criticism which is based in the face of the other – the outsider. (. . .) In the encounter with this strange other, an indiscrete question is asked, which contests the legitimacy of the newly acquired autonomy of the subject and the possessions it has collected. (1991: 165; translation NvdV).

Levinas describes the positive impact thereof in his characteristic language as follows: "[The face] is the commencement of discourse rationalism prays for, a 'force' that convinces even 'the people who do not wish to listen' and thus founds the true universality of reason (. . .) as basis of knowledge" (TI: 201). Whereby rationalism, true universality of reason and knowledge, stand for the objectifying thinking that takes place in representation and that indeed starts right there.

Again: The Deficiency of Representation

In fact, after bringing in the second narrative we find ourselves back again at the point where we already were: with representation considered as a possibility of the subject and as the culmination of the hypostasis. The story became fuller and richer indeed, because not only enjoyment and dwelling, but also the Other is mentioned now as a condition for the possibility of representation. But that does not change the ambivalence of the final result: the intriguing ability of man to constitute his own world in the objectifying knowing. Splendid on the one hand, characterized by Levinas in terms of freedom and genius. But at the same time depressingly lonely, blind and imprisoned in itself: an egology, *une force qui va*. The introduction of the second narrative, which adds an ethical origin to the springs of representation, does not change anything to that situation so far. The above-quoted exclamation retains its full strength: "Who can punish the exercise of the freedom of knowing? Or, more exactly, how can the spontaneity of the freedom that is manifested in certitude be called in question?"

Actually, as this impasse shows, according to Levinas, the *il-y-a* is not really overcome. The hypostasis, with rationality as its apex, represents a gaining of independence with regard to the *il-y-a*. But this emancipation appears to be fragile. The hypostasis is never sufficiently strong to eliminate the *il-y-a* completely. The sea of the *il-y-a* continues to lash the island which is formed in its midst, and also retakes possession, sometimes in original shape, sometimes in veiled shape, of the achievements of the hypostasis. The *il-y-a* cleaves. It returns into the heart of the rationally ordered world of man. The achievement of human time changes into a new endless continuum, namely that of a planned and closed future. The achievement of an orderly and defined world into a collection of dogmas and reifications, or, from the aversion against them, into new undecidedness and indifference. The highest form of victory over the *il-y-a* – i.e. rationality – appears to be the carrier of the same nasty qualities as those which characterized the *il-y-a*: meaninglessness and indifference.

Representation Under Criticism

From this point, where the deficiency of rationality takes oppressive forms, the second narrative appears to imply more than just the donation given under the influence of the Other. Equally important, in any event within the framework of this research, is that the Other appears to be able to break the impasse of representation and thus to renew representation continuously and keep it going. Indeed, the Other calls me to order, also at this level of intellectual imperialism. "[I]f freedom situates me effrontedly before the non-me in myself and outside of myself, (. . .) before the Other it retreats" (TI: 87). The other is the only one who can burst the illusion of my self-created universe. The way in which this happens is presented by Levinas in other terms than he uses with regard to the gift, they are more adapted now to the self-sufficiency of representation. If the other breaks through this self-sufficiency, this feels like the breaking of the autonomy of the I, like being brought up for discussion, like being whistled back by a referee. "It involves a calling into question of oneself, a critical attitude which is itself produced in face of the other and under his authority" (TI: 81).

How does Levinas see this exactly? How can the face do this? Because the face, with its summons, breaks the laws by which usually, knowing is bound. These laws prescribe that knowing is always a matter of referring: to horizons, backgrounds, or other knowledge in terms of which new knowledge can be formulated. Resulting in an endless game of mutual referrals. The face, on the contrary, as far as it calls upon us, expresses *itself* (TI: 51). It derives its meaning for us from nothing else than from its presence. In this sense it is absolute, detached, an independent source of meaning. Thus the face can be the basis of renewal in the game of references which is language, and it can give the objectifying knowing a new impetus. "The commencement of knowing is itself only possible if the bewitchment and the permanent equivocation of a world in which every apparition is possible dissimulation, where commencement is wanting, is dispelled" (TI: 98). "The face is the evidence that makes evidence possible" (TI: 204). "The way in which the other presents himself, exceeding *the idea of the other in me*, we here name face. This *mode* does not consist in figuring as a theme under my gaze, in spreading itself forth as a set of qualities forming an image. The face of the Other at each moment destroys and overflows the plastic image it leaves me, the idea existing to my own measure and to the measure of its *ideatum* – the adequate idea. It does not manifest itself by these qualities, but *kath'auto*. It *expresses itself.*" (TI: 50, 51)

Viewed this way, within the second narrative, the apparition of the other plays a double role. What Levinas presented as an additional prerequisite for representation in the gift, he resumes in the impasse with which representation ends. For exactly that, which contributed already to the creation of representation, will ultimately contribute to the questioning of representation, and thereby to its constantly increasing quality.

Levinas sometimes joins these two moments together, as on p. 84 (TI), where he expresses this coincidence as follows: "Morality begins when freedom, instead of being justified by itself, feels itself to be arbitrary and violent. The search for the intelligible and the manifestation of the critical essence of knowing, the movement of a being back to what precedes its condition, begin together." Wherein "the search for the intelligible" stands for the activities of representation which makes the world understandable; and the "critical essence of knowing" for the critical surveying of the illusion of representation. Both are based on the apparition of the Other.

What applied to the outcome of the hypostasis, which tried to detach itself from the *il-y-a* in the first narrative, applies equally to the breaking of ontology in the second narrative: it is only temporary. The stroke of the infinite is but a moment. The essential difference between this last release and the hypostasis' release is that now there is a genuine transcendence, which exceeds the atmosphere of ontology. Representation, as the culmination of the hypostasis, offers no more than an "everyday transcendence" (Van Riessen 1991: 112) that remains trapped in the atmosphere of ontology and the cleaving *il-y-a*. Nevertheless there is a connection. Because where the everyday transcendence of hypostasis fails (or in the words of De Boer, where the ontology becomes embarrassed (1997: 64)), there the "true transcendence" gets chances: "Philosophy can get on the track of 'genuine transcendence' by searching for something that hinders or withholds 'everyday transcendence'" (Van Riessen 1991: 113; translation NvdV).

The Impact: Shame and Change

Shame

So, the collapse of the illusion of representation, as well as its renewal, are led back to the appearance of the Other by Levinas. What is special about this, is that the impasse to which representation brings us, is – for a moment – truly and tangibly broken. Indeed, the relationship between me and the other escapes from the grasping, totalizing movement of representation and therewith of the atmosphere of ontology with the adhering *il-y-a*. Ontology "breaks", and for a moment the atmosphere of the infinite – i.e. metaphysics – manifests itself. "[T]he relationship between me and the Other does not have the same status as the relations given to objectifying thought, where the distinction of terms also reflects their union. The relationship between me and the Other does not have the structure formal logic finds in all relations" (TI: 180). It puts matters upside down.

If, according to Levinas, representation is characterized by imperialism, freedom and spontaneity, but because of that also by loneliness, autism and illusion; then the infringement of that by the Other is in being called back, being questioned, and also in truth and the relationship and the possibility of a new beginning. Levinas speaks of the "indiscrete face of the Other that calls me into question" (TI: 171) and he stresses the impact it has: "[I]f freedom situates me effrontedly before the non-me in myself and outside of myself, (. . .) before the Other it retreats" (TI: 87).

Based on the meaning of such passages, which occur scattered throughout the work of Levinas (TI: 88, 1982: 247, 248, 1996: 85) I believe that the term "shame" covers a lot of the experience of the subject in these key moments.[9] Provided that it is understood in the sense of shame for one's own rationality that manifests itself in representation, because in representation the subject functions as origin and the rest of the world as deduced from that origin. The breaking of that illusion, by the Other who does not fit in, pushes the subject from its center and generates shame. This is expressed in the following quote from TI: "Shame does not have the structure of consciousness and clarity. It is oriented in the inverse direction. Its subject is exterior to me" (TI: 84). I call this shame "rationality shame".

An illustration of the occurrence of this kind of shame I found in the form of a story. It is called *The man who lives with dogs in a camper* and it is presented by Van Dinten in his book *Met gevoel voor realiteit* (which can be translated as *With a sense of reality*). Van Dinten describes a trip with a colleague through the United States. On their way they decide to stay for the night in the village of Bishop.

> After we had checked in in a hotel, we walked to a restaurant. In a petrol station we passed a camper. A man got off: I estimated him to be in his late thirties, he was a bit dirty and unshaven. He caught my attention because he looked somewhat helplessly around. Behind the windscreen three dogs watched us.
>
> As we walked along, he spoke to us. He said he had no money and asked whether we could give him some so that he could refuel. He was very gentle, showed no aggression at all. I gave him five dollars.
>
> I asked him whether he always travelled around with those three dogs. "It are no dogs sir, it are people." I thought he had not understood me, pointed at the dogs in the cabin and repeated my question. Again he replied: "It are no dogs sir, it are people."
>
> My colleague asked him whether for him there was no difference between dogs and people. He said that there was a lot of difference, that dogs gave much more love and were much better life partners. We looked at him, paused for a while. My colleague said that, even then, there are still so many differences that dogs cannot be called people. He looked at us a little longer, still without any aggression. He gave the five dollars back to me and walked away. I knew nothing to say, felt myself crude, rude and aggressive. (Van Dinten 2002: 253)

In this short fragment the most important elements of Levinas' second narrative seem to figure. To begin with, there is the perfectly natural tendency of the knowing subject, here embodied in the storyteller and his colleague, to define the world. Their personal way of sense making is supposed to be obvious to everyone. Then, in response to that, there is the enigmatic silent gaze of the addressed dog-man, which

---

[9]See the Preface for some characteristics of shame.

suggests sorrow and resistance, but is totally defenseless. This causes a deep sense of shame and even guilt with the storyteller.

I find the choice to speak about this confrontation-effect in terms of shame confirmed by Van Riessen (1991), where indeed she does not describe this key moment, but rather the long-term impact that experience of these key moments brings about within the subject and that she describes as "hesitation":

> In Levinas hesitation plays a role, both in his ethics and in his phenomenology of Eros and death, that can be described as an embarrassment with the situation of difference, the awareness that the other can not be grasped and represented and that it is equally impossible to imagine what would be good for her. Hesitation means the willingness to avoid creating any idea of the good from the self, but instead to adapt it to the situation and to the demands of the other. (p. 238; translation NvdV)

An element that is associated in some places with this experience by Levinas, is the phenomenon of powerlessness that occurs. The I loses its autonomy, is no longer completely its own master. The control over the self makes place for heteronomy: control by the Other. This goes so far, that at some places Levinas compares the appearance of the other with the approach of death. Van Riessen (1991: 187; translation NvdV) says in response to Levinas' descriptions in TI of the paralysis which the Other may cause: "This heteronomy of the self is most apparent in the relationship to death and on that basis Levinas draws a comparison between death and the Other."

And this applies equally to *Otherwise than Being*: "Also in OB Levinas compares the vicinity of the other with the approach of death. Both are a thwarting of the activity of the subject and confront him with the situation where he 'no longer is able to do anything', i.e. passivity" (Van Riessen 1991: 234; translation NvdV). That passivity is heavily emphasized, suddenly a force majeure appears which paralyzes the subject in a mysterious way. In the eyes of my defenseless, humiliated interlocutor is a commandment, and in that a moral impossibility is expressed: "[H]is face expresses my moral impossibility of annihilating" (TI: 232). I can no longer exercise my power.

Change

But for Levinas, there is more than just shame and powerlessness. At the same time there is surprise and the possibility of a new beginning. These opportunities for innovation were discussed above a few times as effects which may originate in shame. The reception of the face brings about "the new in a thought (...) The absolutely new is the Other" (TI: 219). De Boer speaks of "the true novelty in the monotony of the history of being" (1997: 60) and emphasizes the surprise that is the effect of the Face: "The absolute alterity, which cannot be interiorized, genuine alterity, irreducible to the Same via calculated prediction or appropriating interpretation, this alterity is revealed when the Other enters. 'The absolutely new is the Other'. His presence as 'visage' and 'visitation' is unexpected, since it implies that judgement is passed on the Self" (1997: 12, 13).

The impetus which issues from the Other is expressed by Levinas also in terms of energy, for instance when he exclaims "Whence does this transcendental energy come to me?" (TI: 170). Elsewhere, he answers this question in saying that the subject "is brought into motion by an unknown other, whose fate does not leave him indifferent. That the unrest in his existence is more important than the rest" (Van Riessen 1991: 247; translation NvdV). "The relationship with the Other puts me into question, empties me of myself and empties me without end, showing me ever more resources" (Levinas 1998c: 94).

Also with regard to this generated change energy the story of *The man who lives with dogs in a camper* offers opportunities for illustration. It seems as if this element of Levinas' second narrative is missing. That is true in that the fragment does not speak about the innovative impulse which can issue forth from the feeling of shame. But the reflection that Van Dinten performs in his book as a result of this and other events, testifies to the effectiveness of that impulse.

Necessarily, after the impact of the Other, rationality regains the lead. For humans there is no other way of thinking and knowing than through the faculty of representation. But the moment of decentring of the subject, the stroke of the Other, only for a split second, however short, turns representation upside down. Thus, that moment could provide genuinely new contents and therewith, change. The representational thinking subsequently repossesses its totalising position, the innovative impulse is betrayed as it were by the rationality that creates itself a new – and perhaps improved – order. Until this one is breached also by an Other, which keeps change going. Meanwhile, thanks to the Other, representation may gain in quality and meaning and therewith the order of objectifying knowing and science.

This means that Levinas' second narrative connects some of the key elements of our investigation: the deficiency of rationality and the desire to break through it. The deficiency of rationality lies in the illusion-producing nature of representation that brings us into an impasse of which deception and exclusion are the symptoms. Breaking through them is achieved in the second narrative by the radical resistance of the Other who opposes himself against the imperialist nature of representation and by the shame this opposition generates in the knowing and thinking subject. This leads to reflection and to new forms of rationality.

Evaluation of Representation in Levinas

The concept of "representation" is a continuously recurring theme in the work of Levinas. It played a major role in the philosophy of Husserl in which, for a large part, Levinas was trained; and in his own work it keeps returning right up to his last books. Levinas uses the concept of representation, understood as an act of the subject by which it constitutes its world in a meaningful way, in the sense of Husserl. What concerns Levinas particularly with regard to representation is that this meaningfulness may fluctuate. The big problem with that, is that a great loss of the meaning of concepts and objects may occur.

This focus on loss of meaning by Levinas can be understood against the background of his thinking on the subject. The subject is a project that, by means of the hypostasis which culminates in the use of reason and representation of the world, struggles out of the grasp of the *il-y-a*, which stands for the meaningless, frightening anonymous being. The problem of the hypostasis is that the emergence from the *il-y-a*, and therewith the acquisition of meaning, is never a guaranteed permanent one. All forms of rationality and bestowing of meaning are susceptible to the return of the *il-y-a*.

With regard to the thing-ontology and representationalism this is easily observable: the fixated objects get dull and lack life in many respects, and Levinas praises Husserl for his efforts to overcome that loss of meaning by postulating sensemaking by the subject. He notes, however, that Husserl cannot break free from thing-thinking completely and that besides he makes the subject absolute. In that respect he has more confidence in the approach of Heidegger. Heidegger shows that representation never exists in isolation, but is embedded in horizons of a linguistic, practical, and social nature. Representation derives its sense giving from those horizons, and therefore becomes within this existential ontology much richer and truer than in combination with the thing-ontology. Levinas considers this contribution of Heidegger to philosophy as a major achievement.

Nevertheless, he already soon finds that loss of meaning – the deficiency of rationality – is not stopped by focusing on the conditions of representation. The deception continues. Indeed, representation plays – also within existential ontology – a role still, and Levinas feels more strongly than Heidegger about the obstinate illusionary character of representation: even if you are conscious of conditioning, it takes a lot to be constantly aware of it, if indeed such a thing is possible at all off one's own bat. The illusion to be of your own unconditioned origin cannot easily be taken away. The self-sufficiency and loneliness that are involved, are guises of loss of meaning in which Levinas sees the return of the *il-y-a*. To counter that loss of meaning, something completely different is needed. Something which "from itself" has meaning. For Levinas, that is the face of the Other, who, by his call upon me, unmasks the lack of foundation of my illusionary sovereignty. The genuine relativization of representation therefore, in his view does not come from horizons of being, but from an atmosphere outside being, from metaphysics.

This reasoning is consistent with another objection of Levinas against thinking which Heidegger put in motion, namely that the problem of exclusion has not been addressed. Indeed, Heidegger offers opportunities to monitor reification and finishes with the blindness in thing-ontology for phenomena that are difficult to categorize. But also outside representation, in the being which is the area where Heidegger situates the sources of meaning, in particular ethical significance is not available just like that. Indeed, this might be Levinas' main objection to Heidegger. With respect to ethics, the "openness for being" offers Levinas little or nothing. It stands in the long Western tradition of fascination for being and understanding thereof, which Levinas qualifies as totalitarian. Being may be beautiful and splendid, but it is indifferent in moral terms. For Levinas this comes too close to the *il-y-a*.

From the above it becomes clear, I think, that Levinas offers a thorough and entirely original contribution to discussions on the problems associated with rationality and representational thought. He always approached these problems from the perspective of "loss of meaning". To overcome the loss of meaning that manifests itself as deception, to some extent he follows Heidegger, who finds meaning in the horizons, the situating of life. At the same time Levinas, through his second narrative, states that this derivation of meaning is insufficient to fully counterbalance the misleading nature of representation. The real energy for that response is derived by the subject from the encounter with the Other, the truly critical instance and guarantee against deception.

Thus Levinas offers additionally a response to the problem of exclusion. Once the critical Other is accepted as the final basis of truth and meaning, a place can be given to what is outside of all order as long as ontology – i.e. representation, constitutive consciousness or the anonymous horizons of being – determines what is and what is not.

These outcomes of Levinas' answers to the problems of representationalist thinking led us back in the last section to our initial question from Chapter 1: how is change possible? In that chapter, a relation was suggested of change problems with problems that seem to be inherent in rationality on the one hand, and the resistance of people against encapsulation on the other. Chapter 2 entered further into the rationality problems and there we noted that representation, with its deception and exclusion, blocks change. Along that road, we arrived in the present chapter to the question which is also Levinas' theme: "Who can punish the exercise of the freedom of knowing? Or, more exactly, how can the spontaneity of the freedom that is manifested in certitude be called in question?" His answer to that question: that happens in the encounter with the recalcitrant Other, brings – in one single gesture – the issue of radical opposition against encapsulation into the argument. A demonstrable relation appears to arise between the imperious nature of rationality, resistance against that, its breaking in shame and the renewal of rationality. These elements come together in Levinas' second narrative that responds to our original question to the possibility of change.

Chapter 5
Levinas Translated to Organizations

Introduction

In the previous chapter with a view to Levinas' response to the deficiency of rationality, we have sketched a picture of his philosophy. Two significant and complementary themes were addressed extensively. First of all the *il-y-a* understood as a frightening, anonymous being and subsequently, hypostasis understood as the genesis of the subject that wants to wrest itself from the grip of the *il-y-a*. The hypostasis leads to the development of the rational faculties of man, often referred to by Levinas as the ability to represent things. At this stage the escape from the *il-y-a* appears to be only partially successful: it keeps returning into the heart of the rationalist universe in veiled ways. This failure of rationality, which manifests itself as prejudice, meaninglessness and monotony, makes itself feel like a deadlock that is only broken by the intervention of the Other – needy, indiscrete, sad –, who does not fit into my rationally organized order. The Other unmasks that order as being egological and imperious and causes me to feel ashamed. But at the same time that break is the possibility of a new beginning, and also of improved rationality. It is Levinas' answer to the question how the deficiency of reason, previously presented under the labels of deception and exclusion, can be countered. In the previous chapter I referred to this response as Levinas' "second narrative", presented in *Totalité et Infini*.

The intention of this chapter is to relate what we have explored to the world of organizing and organizations. A translation of these ideas of Levinas into the context of organized life will be proposed. The following type of questions will accordingly be addressed: what does the *il-y-a* mean in the context of work and organization? What is the relation between organization and representation? How can we, with respect to organizations, talk meaningfully about the Other, the Face and shame?

It is important to note that Levinas himself never made these connections between his philosophy and the world of organizations. Indeed, he pointed out, specifically when it comes to the implications of the encounter with the Other and the responsibility which then arises (TI: 79), a whole research field of human interaction lies unexplored. This is consistent with observations by organizational studies scholars who indicate that in their field any human interaction at all is a

N. Van der Ven, *The Shame of Reason in Organizational Change*, Issues in Business Ethics 32, DOI 10.1007/978-90-481-9373-8_5, © Springer Science+Business Media B.V. 2011

neglected topic. Smith (2001) thinks that because of the permanent exclusion which is at work in organizations, many dialogues lead to nothing more that an accumulation of humiliations for employees. "Before such humiliation can be managed and their worst effects dissipated, their character needs to be understood" (2001: 541). And Jacques (1996) argues that relational practices have remained relatively invisible within organization studies for the following reasons: "(1) Such work practices get labelled as appropriate to the home rather than the workplace; (2) There is no language to describe such practices as competent work behaviours; (3) Such activities are gender coded as pertaining to 'women's work'" (1996: 178). This chapter may be regarded as a contribution to an approach to the problem mentioned under (2): the lack of an adequate language.

The chapter attempts to introduce into organization studies a certain vocabulary that is alien to it. But, because of this, the opportunities to talk about issues for which until now no language was available within organization studies will increase. This in itself is change already, and because of that it will, I hope, enhance the possibilities within organizations to manage and change.

The translation of Levinas' philosophy to organizations in this chapter will be performed in two different ways. The first section departs from the terms of Levinas' philosophy and examines how those terms can be understood in such a way that they become meaningful for organizations. I will do this on the one hand, by exploring whether and how the story of Levinas resonates in organization studies literature. And on the other hand, where such resonance is missing, I will present my own proposals for a translation of Levinassian concepts to the context of organizations. The construction of this section essentially follows the line of thought of the second section of Chapter 4. That means that first of all the *il-y-a* will be discussed, and then that part of the hypostasis which has a clear parallel in organizations: representation, which is synonymous with rationality in Levinas.

This leads to a translation of the deficiency of representation for the world of organizations. I subsequently perform a similar translation with regard to the appearance of the Other and to the shame and the change that accompany that appearance according to Levinas. This section culminates in a series of propositions about the way Levinas' use of the concepts of rationality, the Other, shame and change may acquire meaning within the context of organizations.

The second section provides a translation of Levinas' views, showing on the basis of a number of real-life organizational cases, what his views may look like in practice. The starting point of this section is again the second narrative of *Totalité et Infini*, but on this occasion in combination with the propositions arising from Section 1. The wording of Levinas' thinking, which ensues from that combination and which is tailored to organizations, is what I propose in interviews with practitioners, along with the question of the extent to which they recognize the matters presented. Does that second narrative, translated to organizations, correspond with events in the everyday life of organizations? And if so, what stories can be told about these events? The cases are the records of those interviews. They also deal with, as part of the second story, the question of the extent to which the described experiences offer connecting points to arrive at change.

Section 1: The Organisation Studies Literature

Il-y-a, Hypostasis and Representation Translated to Organizations

Levinas describes from a human perspective the field of forces of the *il-y-a* and the hypostasis. Therefore, the hypostasis he elaborates in stages, is the hypostasis of the emerging subject, sometimes referred to as psychism or individual. Levinas never discusses such ideas from a perspective of larger social groups, such as organizations in which several people work together.

What he does, however, is to indicate the elements of social life in terms derived from the hypostasis. Actually, these are connected always with the most developed stage of the hypostasis: that of representational thinking, i.e. rationality, where the two narratives of Chapter 4 come together. Thus, Levinas considers the act of objectifying knowing to be embodied in the collective social activity we call "science" (AE: 160). Justice (AE: 128) is a corollary of truth finding, which the objectifying thinking is aimed at, and the same applies to the assessing of interests of politics and the constitutional state (TI: 46, 47, 241). In his formulations Levinas makes it clear that these collective social activities are to be regarded as instantiations of rationality: of the hypostasis at its most developed stage. In line with this application of hypostasis terms to larger societal formations by Levinas, I consider that organizing and organizations are manifestations of the hypostasis, also at its most advanced stage.

I can substantiate this position in part by pointing to parallels which exist between descriptions of organization and organizing in management literature and Levinas' descriptions of the hypostasis at the level of the subject. This will be done – partly and indicatively – in the sub-section on "Representation". For the elements of Levinas' views on the *il-y-a*, hypostasis and representation, which have little or no resonance in the organization studies literature, I will propose a translation of Levinas' views to the world of organizations. The *il-y-a* is the first Levinassian concept for which that has to be done.

The il-y-a

If organizations are to be regarded as an embodiment of the hypostasis, how exactly could the *il-y-a* be related to them? To answer that question we need to recall the distinction made in Chapter 4, between the primeval *il-y-a* and the veiled *il-y-a* of rationality. The primeval *il-y-a* stood for the frightening atmosphere of vast indifference in the infinite spaces of Pascal. The veiled *il-y-a* refers to the phenomenon that the experience of meaninglessness and monotony, known from the primeval *il-y-a*, can be linked to the achievements of the hypostasis, such as rationality and culture.

Organizations can very well be related to the primeval *il-y-a*, namely by considering them as a response to it. At all places where people, from their individual hypostases, join together to counter the elements through dikes, fire-brigades and irrigation projects, we may speak of a collectively experienced primeval *il-y-a*, and of a collectively-given response to it in the form of organization. And the threat of an erupting, primeval *il-y-a*, (e.g. hurricanes or tsunamis,) constitutes a permanent motivation for maintaining or indeed creating organizations. To the *il-y-a* which returns in veiled guise also a relation can be indicated: organizations themselves appear to be its bearers. This is illustrated by the haunting effect that can emanate from massive office buildings or from the monotony of a restrictive work regime, but also by the people- devouring road from Ben Okri's quote in Chapter 1.

The two guises of the *il-y-a* that are at issue here, and their interdependence, flow together in the following quote from the article *Strength is ignorance; Slavery is freedom* by Willmott (1993):

> [L]acking instinctual closure, the openness or indeterminacy of human existence is accompanied by an imperative to accomplish (normative) closure 'for all practical purposes' (Garfinkel, 1967). The sense of order bestowed by this 'second nature' provides a way of coming to terms with a fundamental 'lack' in human nature (Bauman 1976). (Op. Cit.: 531):

In this passage, the "fundamental lack in human nature" stands for the experience of fright and meaninglessness that existence in its primordial form entails. The "normative closure" and the pursuit of order stand for the response to that fundamental lack, but also for the closedness and tightness of that response. This can be seen as consistent with the thinking of Levinas that the *il-y-a* can return in disguised form as an effect of the hypostasis, namely as an atmosphere of deep monotony and meaninglessness, an echo of the primeval *il-y-a*, which evokes disgust and repugnance. Along that road organizing, being the embodiment of the hypostasis, can also be seen as the embodiment of the veiled *il-y-a*.

Representation

Above I indicated the culmination of the hypostasis as follows: representation, that is objectifying thinking, can be related to organizing and organizations. In this section I will substantiate this claim by reference to the article *Formal Organization as Representation: Remote Control, Displacement and Abbreviation* by R. Cooper (1992). This article has already been mentioned when we discussed the orientation towards Foucault and Derrida in Chapter 3.

However, the parallels that can be identified between representation in Levinas and a particular conception of organizing along this path, touch only a part of Levinas' story about hypostasis and representation. It will appear that these parallels originate in their common focus on the striving for control, to the extent there are similarities between Levinas' description of the hypostasis and such description of organizations as Cooper provides. This focus in Levinas is visible only in his first narrative, as we noted in Chapter 4. That narrative is based on the striving for control in which the subject, through dwelling, labour and possessing, arrives eventually at representation, aroused by the desire to arm himself against the elements and the threatening world outside. That narrative therefore can be related to ideas of organizing and organization of which we will discuss the resonance in management science on the basis of Cooper's article.

The differences between Levinas and Cooper (1992) are related to Levinas' second narrative. That was the one in which the appearance of the Face is presented as a condition for initiating and critically maintaining the representation. That second narrative does not resonate, neither in Cooper, nor anywhere else in the management literature where the issue of "representation" is being treated. In the sub-sections "Who is the Other in the context of organizations?" and "Shame and change translated to organizations" it must become clear whether, based on the themes of "the organization-Other" and shame for organizational rationality, Levinas' second narrative still can be found in the literature.

The applied translation which is the issue of this sub-section – namely the transposition of the hypostasis-component "representation" from subject-oriented terms to organization-oriented terms – will therefore concern only Levinas' first narrative: the one which departs from the control motive. A quote by Critchley (2002) in which he speaks about the theme of "separation" in the work of Levinas, serves as a starting point. That theme has been discussed in Chapter 4 as an element of the hypostasis. Critchley explains, within the separation, how the transition takes place from labour and possession to representation. In doing so he emphasizes, as in Levinas' first narrative, the motive of control which guides the subject. Critchley does that, following Levinas, by highlighting the word grasp (*prendre*) for both the seizing of things in labour and for the understanding of the world in objectifying cognition.

> Taking up the analysis of separated existence in part 2 of Totality and Infinity, ontology is the movement of comprehension, which takes possession of things through the activity of labour, where conceptual labour resembles manual labour. Ontology is like the movement of the hand, the organ for grasping and seizing, which takes hold of (*prend*) and comprehends (*comprend*) things in a manipulation of otherness. (2002: 16)

This quotation indicates for this Levinassian analysis that the subject is driven to representation mainly by a strong striving for control. The desire to protect oneself against the threat of the elements forms the background for this.

According to Cooper (1992) "organizing" is exactly that: the pursuit of mastery through working with representations: in the title of his article he equates organization with representation and thereby he has the following in mind:

> The function of representation is to translate difficult or intransigent material into a form that facilitates control (. . .) This is how the Voyager 2 spacecraft can bring the planet Neptune on to the computer screens of the Houston space center, how geologists can probe the depths of the earth for minerals and oil and how medical doctors can see inside the human body by means of X-ray tomograms. All rely on specific technologies of representation (1992: 255).

Representations make accessible the inaccessible and unknown, and thus enable objectification and control. Cooper stresses that this is a sense-making process performed by the organizing instance. This is in line line with the conception of representation in the subject according to Husserl and Levinas: representation is about "the need to make transparent what is opaque, to make present what is remote, and to manipulate what is resistant" (1992: 255) and it is not just about the collection of information. "It is this principle of economy which makes the logic of representation more fundamental to the understanding and analysis of organizations than the traditionally more limited concept of information" (1992: 257).

To show the element of sense-making Cooper refers to Jeremy Bentham who considered organizing primarily as classification, that is to say: as the imposition of meanings to the outside world. "In Bentham's eyes, all factories, schools and prisons are materialized classifications, lists, hierarchies, and statistics" (1992: 265). That this is not a form of representationalism is demonstrated by the rejection in Cooper of the concept which views organization and its environment as two radically separate poles. In the same way that there is in the representation of Husserl and Levinas interaction between subject and object and that these two to some extent move towards one another, so according to Cooper also in organizing there is some border blurring: "As we have noted, inside and outside are not separate places; they refer to a correlative structure in which 'complicity is mixed with antagonism (. . .)'" and "Organization as an active process of displacement or transformation denies and defies such categories as inside and outside" (1992: 262).

The imperialist character that Levinas had found in representation on the level of the subject is fully recognizable here: "As we have seen, representation is really a reversal process in which a disadvantage is turned into an advantage – for example, chair and glove embody this power. This is essentially how the Portuguese extracted compliance from the heterogeneous elements – social, technological, natural – that constituted the maritime organization of their East Indies Company" (1992: 258). And the establishment of an organization "becomes a center to the extent that it incorporates relevant features of its periphery and makes those features work for it" (1992: 269).

The Deficiency of Representation

Viewed from the perspective of all those successful projects which Cooper presents, organizations look like a Western success story with representation as a pivotal plot. But then, what about the deficiency of rationality, also called the deficiency of representation? That deficiency was discussed in Chapter 4, in the exposition of Levinas' views on representation, immediately after the presentation of the qualities, even the genius, of representation. There, Levinas' thesis is that simultaneously with the appearance of representation, illusions also occur which cause deception and exclusion. A deadlock sets in, which Levinas interprets as a return of the *il-y-a* at the level of representation.

In Cooper's article there is no question of problems with representation indeed. On the contrary, control through representation has the final word, covering all continents. But from the world of organization studies there is a range of widely differing voices to be heard as well.[1] In Chapters 1 and 2 I have suggested some of these, which demonstrate a faltering of the control of representational thinking and the points at which the loss of meaning occurs. As an instance I referred to Reason and Torbert (2001: 3, 4), who note that the prevailing rationality has become completely alienated from practice and therefore misleading. I also referred to Mintzberg (2004), Gustavsen (1998: 108) and Starbuck (cited in Koene 2001: 92), who decry the rigidity of management rationality.

In such instances, I am not just speaking about rationality in the caricature of a narrowly-defined sense of the word in which it is concerned only with planning and efficiency. Among the organization studies approaches which were presented as problematic in Chapter 1, there were quite a few that apply principles which reflect a broad conception of rationality in terms of cognitive views. By this, I refer to the circumstance that these approaches assume that the relationship between people and things and between people and people is always marked by the meaning that people attribute to those relationships, and by preconditions, including the existence of other people as independent centres of sense-making. Examples of this include approaches such as empowerment, flat organizations and HRM, in which the elements of signification and motivation play a prominent role. Management authors who recognize the importance of sense-making for the acting and thinking of people, also in organizations, include Mayo (1933) and Peters and Waterman (1982).

In their approach to organizations these management authors and the associated trends provide evidence – mostly in an implicit way – of their presupposition that acting and knowing, through representation, are never unconditional. They believe no longer that the world is a collection of fixed and humanly independent entities that are simply reproduced in the representation. This is reflected in the importance these approaches assign to values and to the need for meaning in employees. This importance is such that, when it comes to align employees with organizational interests, the management of culture becomes a serious matter. This is what Willmott (1993: 524) implies in saying that corporate culture management has left behind it the notion that an underlying consensus in organizations is already given, and instead that consensus should be constructed by manipulating values. In fact, these organizational approaches thus use the ontology which Levinas calls the existential ontology, even if they themselves do not refer to it in philosophical terms.

Within these broad-rationalistic organization studies movements the treacherous deficiency appears to manifest itself equally as clearly as in the narrow-rationalist movements. In the same way – but in his case at the level of the subject – Levinas could identify that deficiency, not only starting from thing-ontology but also starting

---

[1] As Munro (2000: 405) indicates, Cooper himself also has pointed to the oppressive effects of rationality and representation, and to the need to counterbalance that.

from existential ontology. For, – attesting to a certain broad-mindedness – despite the awareness that other people belong to the conditions of the possibility of organization, and thus are prior to representing, organizing thought, this relationship gets turned upside down. The moment at which control is sought and representational thinking is deployed by an organization, the illusion that adheres to representation comes into effect: the illusion that representation itself, unconditioned, is the center of the world. And with this illusion come loss of meaning, deception and exclusion.

So, the reversal which occurs is linked to the desire for control that representation strives for. Furthermore, desire for control is not lacking in organizations. As we saw in Cooper, control can be viewed as the essence of organizing and organizations. Thus in this article the emphasis lies, as it traditionally has done, on control of the elements and of material requirements. The novelty of the above-mentioned, organization-culture-oriented approaches, compared to the traditional control as Cooper discusses it, is that, precisely because of the newly acquired awareness that people are their own centres of meaning, paradoxically then that striving for control focuses on people. Jacques (1996: 98), in a quote that we already came across, thinks that after the rationalization of physical input, it is now the turn to the rationalization of human input. Collinson (2003: 542) states that "[w]ithin the workplace, employee subjectivity could become an increasingly 'contested terrain'. In recent times employers have extended their control strategies ever deeper into employee subjectivities with their concern 'to win hearts and minds' and to shape employee attitudes, emotions."

Peters is, as we saw earlier, also very clear about this. Of the means he thinks can help to create meaning – such as vision, symbolic action and recognition – he says that they constitute a control system of which the manager has to make use in the most conscious way (Peters, quoted in Willmott 1993: 530). That this may lead to loss of meaning actually, is seen by Willmott (1993: 518) who speaks of the tightening of thought and emotion of employees in the efforts of management "to colonize the 'softer' features of organization." Willmott puts the emphasis here on the loss of meaning that occurs in the shape of totality: exclusion, namely of people's own sense-making.

Giddens does so too, according to the following quote that Willmott (1993: 539) presents from him: "The reflexive project of the self generates programs of actualization and mastery. But as long as these possibilities are understood largely as a matter of extension of the control systems of modernity to the self, they lack moral meaning." This becomes manifest as oppression and heavy-heartedness, in line with the effect of the control systems of modernity about which Weber noted already that they lack moral significance (Willmott 1993: 539). Here we face the veiled *il-y-a*.

Besides this, there is the deception, that is being misguided by one's own efforts to organize, that can occur with organizers. Also among those who have the best of intentions with regard to their employees through managing culture. Grit and Meurs (2004: 221) call these the "visionary hard-luck pilots" and say of them: "The bad thing is not that these managers have a vision, but that they in advance are fully convinced of their vision, or indeed that they assume that they are the only ones who have a clear vision and direction available. With this attitude, the seamy sides or harmful effects of the management's good intentions cannot be identified. The vision has thus become a dogma." Being this misguided is also a manifestation, in the context of organizations, of the veiled *il-y-a*, i.e. of the deficiency of representation that Levinas has indicated at the level of the subject.

In Chapter 4, the impasse in which the subject finds itself in the finished hypostasis was described as the tension between a successful defence and control of the primeval *il-y-a* on the one hand, and a possessive, lonely imperialism suffering from lack of meaning on the other hand. The parallel to these at the organizational level which we came across just now, can be put in similar terms: we find the deadlock whereby the necessary control appears to be associated with the appropriating, manipulative imperialism of representation, resulting in loss of meaning and in a permanent shortage of creative and motivated employees.

Simultaneously, in Chapter 4 we noted that, at the level of the subject, this deadlock can be broken. This is possible because something escapes from the totalizing movement of representation, namely the Other who means *himself* and appeals to me. How does this operate at the level of organizations? With regard to organizations it can be claimed, in accordance with the basic line of Levinas' philosophy, that there also, despite the deadlock, people often enough know to make their getaway. Regularly people escape from the closure of a planned future and the totalitarian compulsion of rational structures. There is sense-making within organizations. It does occur that traditional rigid control systems are replaced by systems that allow more freedom to employees. It actually happens that bosses who could organize matters arbitrarily, afterwards want to account for their actions. And that organization studies scholars, who never seemed to worry about forcing their rationally justified ideas upon organizations, open their minds to completely different voices from the factory floor, in the face of such practice.

If my concern is to translate Levinas' philosophy to organizational language, then it is important to be able to designate – behind these breakthroughs – the appearance of the Other. However, to reach that point we first need to answer another question: what does the Face look like within the context of organizations? Levinas himself (TI: 244) speaks of the Other in terms of the widow, the orphan, the stranger. But these categories are not very relevant for organizations. Therefore the question is: who is the Other in the context of organizations?

Who Is the Other in the Context of Organizations?

To answer this question we have to recall certain parts of the hypostasis as described in Chapter 4. Because the way in which Levinas describes the subject affects the way his thinking can be extended to organizations. According to Levinas' descriptions man does not arrive at activity just like that. There is also something like disgust, repugnance against coming into action. This reluctance is related to an aversion to life in general. The taking upon itself of its existence takes the subject a lot of effort indeed. Through laziness, fatigue, enjoyment, labour and possession this genesis of the subject takes place, which ultimately culminates in representation.

Both organizations and man within the context of organizations can be described in terms borrowed from the hypostasis. For organizations I have already performed that above. There it appears that organizing and organization can be linked to the hypostasis in its most crystallized stage: the stage of representation, that is to say, of rationality. That means that organizations are strongly marked by an important feature of rationality according to Levinas, namely: the tendency, in its representative thinking, to consider itself as the origin of the world. Representational thinking is troubled by the illusion that its existence is self-evident and mirrors a pre-given order. It is not aware of a situation which preceded that order, it forgets its own origins. That is why, for organizations – in this condition of blindness – weariness or sloth are non issues, any more than the refusal of existence which pervades the getting into action. They conceive of labour as something which according to Levinas is only its partial truth: a play, or "(. . .) labour mystique, which appeals to themes of joy or freedom through labour" (EE: 22).

But, as opposed to organizations, people cannot simply be linked to one of the hypostasis stages. Neither can people in the context of organizations simply be linked that way. Levinas' description of the genesis of the subject is linear, but should be understood, I think, in such a way that man permanently carries all hypostasis stages within himself. He can continuously experience them. It will be clear for instance that in our intellectual work we deal with representations. But we also know of the laboriously getting into action, through repugnance and sloth.

The fact that, to people in organizations, many stages of the hypostasis can be linked, and to organizations just one stage causes a tension between organizations and the people who work there. This tension has been described by A. Witteveen (2004) as follows.

> For organizations, the manufacturing of happiness is daily business. Towards an employee, or towards a client – they essentially pretend nothing less than to bring heaven on earth. Organizations know exactly what that heaven looks like. Tailored to the individual: the ideal work environment, challenging tasks, inspiring colleagues, a balance between career and private life, digital fragmentation of everything that could be unpleasant. Happy people making other people happy (our motivated employees, your complete customer satisfaction, social responsibility, loyal vendors, rejoicing shareholders). 'Thou shalt be happy' applies nowhere as strongly as in organizations. Who in a team interview indicates that he is not happy, is suspect and will by colleagues and managers be bombarded with advice and action. In order to get the happiness offender back on the track of his individual happiness. (Witteveen 2004: 2; translation NvdV)

Organizations, being social phenomena in which preparedness for action is already taken for granted, tend to ignore the problems of the early stages of the hypostasis, like weariness and sloth. But individuals, working in organizations, do not forget those origins. The very thing organizations ignore keeps returning for people: the trouble to collect oneself and to organize oneself in the middle of an anonymous, threatening existence.

Besides there is still another factor. As we saw in the previous sub-section the *il-y-a*, in veiled form, returns at the level of representational thinking. Organizations themselves appear to be bringers of it. Here the veiled *il-y-a* stands for the experience of meaninglessness and futility, relating to the lonely and totalizing nature of representation. The veiled *il-y-a* brings back the disgust and repugnance evoked by the original *il-y-a*, from which the subject tried to escape through the hypostasis.

The two factors combined – first the discrepancy between the hypostasis-stage of organizations and the stage in which people find themselves, and secondly the veiled *il-y-a* that sticks to organizations – can, with employees who are sensitive, arouse repugnance and disgust against organizing and organization. This can manifest itself as a refusal to be organized, as job-refusal, melancholy or less articulate resistance. In all these cases there is an amount of suffering by the employee within the organization.

On the basis of the above, can we now say anything more about what the Other looks like in the context of organizations? I propose to consider the individual, who suffers from the rational blindness and the associated deficiency of meaning, to be the Other as meant by Levinas, and now transposed to the context of organizations. This description implies a certain measure of incompatibility for this Other with organizations. Given the taken-for-grantedness of their own existence and given the claims of rationality and justified order that organizations have, the suffering of the Other – his revulsion and his disgust – appear as incomprehensible and unreasonable. Whoever confronts the organization with that repugnance and weariness really is an outsider.

Does this view on the relationship between people and organizations, and the profile of the Other that it entails, resonate somewhere in the management literature? The issue of the effect of early hypostasis-stages in the lives of people is treated by Collinson in his article *Identities and Insecurities: Selves at Work* (2003). There he objects to a common approach to people within organizations, which seizes upon their rationality and autonomy. Opposite that approach he states (2003: 529) that there should be more attention given to the insecurity that people experience in organizations and that can have an existential, psychological, social and economic character. He believes that "[b]y exploring the workplace construction of selves (...) a greater appreciation of subjectivity and its insecurities can enhance our understanding of the ways that organizational power relations are reproduced, rationalized, resisted and, just occasionally, even transformed" (2003: 535).

The theme of the discrepancy between organizations as the embodiment of rationality and employees who may find themselves in completely other stages of the hypostasis, is reflected in the quote from Ten Bos (2004b: 4) that I already cited: "The difference of orientation between people who move towards an idea *and* organizations that move from an idea, explains why people are always the central problem in organizations." Organizations take rational action for granted, but along with that also they find some forms of resistance incomprehensible, as highlighted by Townley, Cooper and Oakes (2003: 1052): "There is an implicit assumption that (...) there can be a degree of rationally motivated agreement among participants." While disgust against organization can, for an organization, never appear as rational and thus is placed outside the rational order: it does not fit in.

Parker (2003: 196) refers to that when he says: "[I]f some general rules or orientations are specified to the satisfaction of rational people, then important questions about how and why people actually act and account for their actions are in danger of becoming a lesser concern." The incomprehensibility of people for organizations matches an emphasis which Davies (2002: 165) finds in Levinas' descriptions: "[T]he other is never first encountered cognitively." He does not let himself be silhouetted against the horizons and references which the objectifying knowing uses to insert something new into the existing knowledge patterns in order to thus appropriate it. Precisely because of that property, the Other as we described him now for organizations, resembles the infinity with which Levinas associates him. It is like Ten Bos (2004b: 5) says: "Only in this way, that is because of his incompatibility with the rational play of references, infinity can enter the picture."

Looking back on this sub-section, we can say that based on the organization studies literature a translation can be made according to Levinas of the Other in the context of organizations, namely in terms of fundamental incompatibility. The question, raised in the section on representation and which remains unanswered, is whether thereby we also found a parallel in that literature for Levinas' second narrative, namely the one in which the Other criticizes representation and thus keeps it constantly renewed. Working on the translation of representation we did not find such a parallel, working on the translation of the organizational Other we just now found a trace of it, namely in the quotation from Ten Bos. However, in that quotation nothing is said about the capacity of infinity to renew the representation. Therefore, the second narrative can neither be found in its entirety in the literature, nor from the perspective of the organization-Other.

Shame and Change Translated into Organizations

Shame

What then does the confrontation with the Other within organizations – that is the "organization-Other" – look like? In my discussion of this topic, in this sub-section, and deviating from what until now I did predominantly, I will not speak of "organizations" and "organizing", but of "organizers". By that I mean people as far as they are engaged in organizing, and with that I have in particular in mind: bosses and managers, but also for instance management consultants and trainers. This is in line with Levinas' own language. As we saw in his writings already, he sometimes attributes properties and practices to societal institutions like "jurisdiction" and "science". But for the rest he is consistent in describing the encounter with the Other as an encounter between individuals and not between larger formations. Analogous to Levinas' different approaches, I have in the above on the one hand assigned properties to "organizations" and "organizing". But, on the other hand, in order to describe the encounter with the Other in an organizational context, I will start from the individual: the organizer (boss, manager, organizational scientist) who faces the Other.

So, here the organizer figures as the embodiment of representational thinking, that is, rationality. The characteristics of rationality are that it manages to order the world by its objectifying thinking, but that at the same time it falls prey to the illusion to be the center of the world and therefore has an imperialist character. Now, what happens when the I of the organizer perceives the pain in the eyes of the organization-Other, which pain is directly due to the loss of meaning that the organizer's rationality entails? "But if freedom situates me effrontedly before the non-me in myself and outside of myself, (. . .) before the Other it retreats" (TI: 87). The Other is the only one that can pierce the illusion of my self-created universe and superior freedom, as we said in Chapter 4.

Looking for descriptions of this enigmatic confrontation, I draw a blank within the organization studies literature. I managed to find, in an article by Deuten and Rip (2000), a description of a kind of embarrassment which can be regarded as a lagging-behind-effect of that confrontation. Deuten and Rip in their article investigate how managers involved in product development discuss their projects. For that purpose they noted down the statements the product developers made in that respect and they reconstruct the image the developers have of their projects. The embarrassment which I have in mind is to be found in the following passage in which Deuten and Rip report on the responses to their reconstruction of one of the projects. It concerns the development of a new industrial enzyme, called gemmase, and the reactions come from the managers, Orlans and Bentrom, who led the project.

> Our rewriting the product development process of gemmase enhances understanding, but also unsettles actors. When Orlans and Bentram read our analysis, they recognized the points we made as real and valuable – but also felt slightly uncomfortable being positioned as characters in a story, and seeing their own modernist terminology between quotes.[2] Managers typically write (i.e. produce texts and stories) in a modernist vein, assuming their own agency, and assuming readers who will follow them in their exposition, and who can be routed and re-routed. (Deuten and Rip 2000: 89)

---

[2]Orlans and Bentrom for instance expressed the following statements:

> Then, you need to be convincing, with the team, together with this guy [coordinator of production], and say, listen, this is extremely disappointing and by now nobody believes that it will come to anything, but believe me, we've had this experience before and things will turn out right in the end. And that's how it went with the [gemmase] project (. . .). So, again, it wasn't the first time. That helps you to go on. (Deuten and Rip 2000: 84)

> What we emphatically tried to do was to create this 'sense of urgency' with the team members, so that they would put in just a bit more effort than they were used to. When stories appeared in the media about environmental problems due to phosphate in manure, I brought these up in the project meetings, as a message that our customers were really desperate for this enzyme. And, of course, we had committed ourselves to bring it on the market before a certain date. So people accept this bit of additional effort, if you have a clear product concept, so that everyone knows what should be done. My experience is that people then have no problem at all to work an hour longer each day, or come back during the weekend more often. The enthusiasm, the idea that we can really achieve it, is so great that everyone puts up with all that. (Deuten and Rip 2000: 84)

The embarrassment in question here possibly is the equivalent for organization studies of the reluctance of which in Chapter 4 it was said that it was not so much the core moment of a confrontation, but rather the long-term effect these multiple core moments bring about in the subject. Van Riessen described that feeling in the presented quote (1991: 238) as "an embarrassment with the situation of difference, the awareness that the other can not be grasped and represented and that it is equally impossible to imagine what would be good for her."

But, as said, the confrontation with the Other himself is not at issue here. A description thereof in the context of an organization I found in a literary tale, namely in the story of Bartleby the Scrivener, written by Herman Melville.[3] In this story Bartleby can be seen as the organization-Other, and his boss, the lawyer, as the organizer.

> *Bartleby* is the story about a clerk of a lawyers firm at Wall street in the middle of the 19th century. Bartleby has been hired by the firm, together with two other clerks, to copy legal documents. This is a very dry and husky sort of business, but Bartleby surprises everybody by his fervour, accurateness and productivity. That is why the lawyer, as the boss of the firm, is very pleased with this new worker, even if to him a more cheerful character than the pallid, withdrawn figure of Bartleby would have been welcome. His enthusiasm however gets tempered when, on the third day, Bartleby refuses to do a job that for this type of business is very common. Copies of documents have to be compared with the originals and everyone of the clerks is regularly being asked to do that. So also Bartleby, but he tells his boss that he doesn't want to, or, in his words: "I would prefer not to". The lawyer is completely taken aback for a moment, but business calls. He concludes to come back to it at a later time.
>
> But this scene repeats itself and every time Bartleby uses the same formula: I would prefer not to. The boss starts brooding. Normally he would not have any problem with firing one who refuses his job, but some way he is being disarmed by Bartleby's attitude. The formula he uses to express his refusal has much to do with that. The boss has been touched and seeks to talk with Bartleby but that appears to be impossible. On the request to be at least a bit reasonable comes the answer that at this moment he prefers not to be a bit reasonable. This situation brings the lawyer into a clew of conflicting feelings and thoughts, ranging from decided rejection of Bartleby to melancholy and solidarity with a lost person.
>
> The affair escalates when, at a certain moment, Bartleby announces that he prefers not to copy anymore. It must come to dismissal now, Bartleby is being told to have left in 6 days. When on the seventh day the boss finds him at the office it takes him great effort not to get into a black temper. At the same time he feels unable to be cruel to Bartleby. He wonders what his conscience would prescribe him at this moment. The lawyer chooses as solution to self abandon the building: he moves his office, leaving Bartleby behind. In a cleared out room the boss once more says goodbye. He has to tear himself away from Bartleby, the man he wanted to get rid of. The landlord finally does what the lawyer could not: call the police to remove Bartleby. When the lawyer hears about this his reaction is ambivalent: "At first I was indignant; but at last almost approved. I do not think I would have decided upon this course myself; and yet, under such peculiar circumstances, it seemed the only plan". Bartleby dies in custody with the police.

---

[3] In their extensive discussion of *Bartleby* Ten Bos and Rhodes (2003: 406) point out that this story stems from the early days of American industrial capitalism, when the robber barons built their empires. The new, more rationalized, labour relationships that go with them and that will dominate the next century and a half, are characterized here by Melville in a concise manner in the stage of their emergence.

What happens here? Rationally speaking, there is not very much the matter. There are agreements between two parties in an employment relationship. One of the two parties is not complying with the agreements, so the other (the boss) is entitled to terminate the employment relationship. But that is not what happens. The boss is paralyzed and unable to react against Bartleby. Of course he has, physically and legally speaking, the means to react, but a mysterious inability has come over him. And that seems to be related to the perception of a reluctance in Bartleby, coming from very deep, which does not lead to aggression or explanation of his behaviour, but to a kind of captivating melancholy. It breaks the boss' natural pattern of action. "[The face] involves a calling into question of oneself, a critical attitude which is itself produced in face of the other and under his authority" (TI: 81). Here happens at the level of the organization what Levinas wanted to describe for philosophy: "It is this resistance, this point of exteriority to the appropriative movement of philosophical conceptuality, that Levinas seeks to describe in his work" (Critchley 2002: 17). Levinas relates this moment to the experience of "no longer being able to be able" (TA: 82; translation NvdV) and associates, as we saw above, the Other also with death.

What does this moment feel like for the organizer? In order to describe that experience, in Chapter 4 we used terms like being whistled back and abruptly recalled. This is succinctly summarized under the heading of "shame", but then specifically in the sense of shame for the exertion of one's own rational faculty, which is being ashamed. It is important in this context to point out that rationality always has something euphoric about it and – unless there is question of malice – is in good faith. We basically assume that the organizer wants the best for the organization and creates order, with a view to improving the situation for all concerned. The fact that rationality creates illusions and may prove to be imperialistic does not detract from those good intentions. So on the side of the organizer generally, there is a sincere belief in organization and rational order. This means that the experience of being whistled back as though by a referee is the more painful. Not only are intended plans blocked by it, but the value for which the organizer stands and which he believes in, is unmasked and put down as the arbitrariness of freedom (TI: 84).

Is there anything we can say about the injury suffered by the organization-Other? With what exactly does he confront the organizer in such a way that the latter gets put off? To answer that question we have to go back to our translation of the Other. Ultimately, the injury that leads to the confrontation is the meaninglessness that the organization-Other experiences, and so on two levels: first, the meaninglessness associated with the primeval il-y-a, and secondly the meaninglessness associated with the veiled il-y-a that sticks to representation. These two varieties of meaninglessness can appear concretely in ways that are contrary to one another.

For the suffering under the threat of the primeval il-y-a, the organization-Other can seek compensation within the organization in the form of an attachment to fixed routines, a clear definition of tasks and a clear professional identity. Any resistance to change that threatens to affect one of those matters, can thus be an expression of the grief of the Other. Willmott (1993: 544) sees this thematized in Giddens:

"Giddens is also almost unique amongst leading social theorists in accepting the importance of repression and the unconscious in his theory of agency. In particular, Giddens makes an important connection between the reproduction of routines and the sense of security derived from 'the regrooving of established attitudes and cognitive outlooks'".[4] The grief associated with this can appear as sorrow indeed, but also as aggression or courteous resistance (Argyris 2003: 1185, 1188).

In the suffering from the meaninglessness of the veiled *il-y-a* that is associated with the intrusive rationalized universe, the exclusive nature of representation according to some authors plays a major role. Pålshaugen (1998: 49) points to the need for people to have a say in defining reality and Smith (2001: 540) believes that the bad point of organizations consists not so much in the repression they cause but in the exclusion they create. "It is striking that Elias's argument stresses the fact that subordinate groups are 'outsiders' rather than that they are dominated. He emphasizes their exclusion rather than their exploitation." The grief that comes from that exclusion, and which is thus specifically organization-related, may to the organizer manifest itself – like with the primeval *il-y-a* – as sorrow, but besides as the cynicism or weariness that were described already in Chapter 1.

Change

When an organizer is confronted by this grief, the encounter with the Other may occur – and therewith shame for his own imperialist action that caused the meaninglessness for the other. But there is more, because in Chapter 4 the encounter with the Other, through the associated surprise, was related to possibilities of new beginnings and to change and correction of the representation. The unrest raised by the Other questions established truths and intrudes into the neat borders of well-defined duties and competencies (De Boer 1997: 76). Transposed to organizations, I believe this means the following: the confrontation forces the organizer to take seriously reluctance of the organization-Other and it prevents him from maintaining dogmatically his familiar rationality. He must listen, hard intervention is not an option, as Bartleby's story illustrates. Based on the reply from the recalcitrant other the organizer tries to arrive at new insights and a new form of rationality.

Voices from the organizational literature that reflect this relationship between encounter, surprise and change are to be found in writings of Sutton, Maas and Gustavsen et al. Jacobs (2003: 56) says with regard to Sutton's *Weird Ideas That Work. 11,5 Ways to Promote, Manage, and Sustain Innovation*: "Sutton's starting point is that, whoever wants to overcome tunnel thinking and self-overestimation, should organize within the organization diversity and contradiction." Maas (2004) writes about interventions in organizations. He suggests that successful interventions stem from the ability to let go of old concepts and to create new ones. For this,

---

[4]These "established attitudes and cognitive outlooks" of the organization-Other might as well be regarded as forms of rationality as is the rationality of the organizer. They embody for the organization-Other the hypostasis-stage of representation. Therefore, the injury here originates partly from a conflict between rationalities, each of which generates its own blindness.

intensive interaction is required among stakeholders, and reflection on the interaction, and more especially so where barriers and blockages arise in the interaction. So here the emphasis is on breakdowns in the interaction that, in all their negativity, produce opportunities for change. One aspect of Maas' research that struck him was "that the talking about fixations or blockages in the interaction with the person who got stuck in such a situation, can be understood as the production of context variation" (2004: 116), i.e. as the creation of opportunities for new visions and insights. Barriers and blockages in the interaction must therefore according to Maas in organizations be at the focus of attention.

Gustavsen, Finne and Oscarsson (2001b) begin their book by noting that for change, almost by definition, something is needed which stands out beyond what exists already. That is, something transcendent. "Since change means to transcend structures and motives that are, it can, by definition, not be understood by looking at "what is", how, then, can we approach change? (2001b: 238). The resonance with Levinas' identical question – "How can something really new come about?" (e.g. EE: 94–96, TI: 55–56, 218) – can not be overlooked. One of the possible answers provided by Gustavsen et al., is the taking seriously of the sense-making of employees. But one cannot do that by imposing or seeking patterns and regularities within a representational frame of mind. So, being organizational studies scholars and looking for innovation, "we must turn from a concern with regularities and representations of past events to unique, 'once-occurrent events of being'" (2001b: 239). For that purpose, one should allow oneself to be surprised in the interaction with employees. "The core point, however, is that it is in conversation that we meet 'the other'. 'The other' may be steered by norms unknown to us or guided by smart and hidden strategies; what we encounter is what the other says (. . .) What happens here must have the force to transcend what the actors bring with them – or are steered by – when they meet" (2001b: 253).

Does this mean that, starting from the thoughts on innovation of Maas and Gustavsen et al., the second narrative of Levinas is to be found in organization studies literature? Or, the same question in another formulation: do the key moments, on which these authors focus in the interaction between organizer and employees and which lead to innovation, have exactly the character which the encounter with the Other has in Levinas? The answer is negative. It is true, there are parallels to point out. Namely, first of all in the emphasis of Maas and Gustavsen et al. on the imperialism of rational thinking that is looking for abstract concepts and universal regularities. And then in their view that the breaking of those despotic tendencies in encounters with people may be associated with organizational change and renewal. But those mentioned authors do not speak about "shame" and "being whistled back". Whereas Levinas characterizes the shock in the interaction between people – which leads to opportunities for change and innovation – in terms of shame for one's own rationality. This means that, also in respect of "shame and change", no complete resonance of Levinas' second narrative is found in the organizational literature.

Propositions as a Result of the Translation So Far

The above is an attempt to make key concepts in the philosophy of Levinas meaningful within the context of organizations. The combination of performed translations results in a number of propositions that together constitute a scheme that provides guidance in finding key moments of insight development within organizations. These propositions are as follows.

1. People, including employees in organizations, are exposed to the threat of meaninglessness that is based in the *il-y-a*. Both that of the primeval *il-y-a* that evokes disgust and from which the subject breaks away only with difficulty; and that of the veiled *il-y-a* of rationality, the monotony of which can evoke repugnance.
2. Organizations are manifestations of the most crystallized stage of the hypostasis: that of rationality and representation. In accordance with the illusion-producing nature of representation, organizations can forget their own origin in the hypostasis. Then they no longer know how the laboriously getting into action and preparedness for action is taken as a matter of course. Organizations tend to ignore the disgust, both with regard to the primeval and with regard to the veiled *il-y-a*.
3. The discrepancy that arises in this respect between organizations and employees may in some cases lead to tensions. On the side of the employee the growing resentment may manifest itself as attachment to routines, refusal to work, melancholy or otherwise-articulated resistance. In each of these manifestations there is a certain degree of suffering of the employee within the organization. He is the Other within organizations.
4. On the side of the organization, represented by the organizer, this resistance and suffering appear – given the pretensions of reasonableness and accounted for order that organizations have – as incomprehensible and unreasonable.
5. This discrepancy may lead to confrontations between the organizer and the employee, in which the organizer is touched by the repugnance of his employee and recognizes that repugnance as an existential problem. He discovers the imperialist nature of his own aspiration to organize.
6. The confrontation with his pretensions arouses feelings of shame with the organizer. This forces him to take seriously the employee's repugnance and prevents him to maintain the established rationality dogmatically. He must listen, hard interventions are not an option.
7. Based on the response of the recalcitrant other, the organizer tries to arrive at new insights and at improved, and more inclusive forms of rationality.

As announced in the introduction to this chapter, the translation that leads to the above propositions has been performed in two ways. First, departing from Levinas' descriptions, we have sought to find parallels of his thoughts in the organizational studies literature. These parallels are then considered and discussed as translations of elements of Levinas' ideas to the context of organizations. Secondly, and where these equivalencies are missing, I made my proposals on how the terms and ideas of Levinas may acquire significance within the context of organizing and organizations. By way of evaluation, it may be appropriate at this stage to identify briefly which elements of Levinas' philosophy have been found to resonate in the organization studies literature and which did not.

The *il-y-a* with some difficulty can be found, especially in the writings of Willmott (1993) and Ten Bos (2004b), from which I have quoted. Partly, I added my own suggestions for ways to make that term meaningful in the context of organizations.

Representation according to Levinas' first narrative, which focuses on the striving for control as the motive to arrive at representation, has a clear parallel in management science, namely in the article by Cooper (1992). I did not come across representation conceived of as a result of the confrontation with the Face (Levinas' second narrative).

The deficiency of representation, which manifests itself according to Levinas as the oppressive feeling and meaninglessness of the veiled *il-y-a*, we found as a theme in some writings, particularly by Ten Bos (2004b), Willmott (1993) and Giddens (1991).

With regard to the Levinassian Other, needy and incompatible with the order that representation creates for itself, a good translation can be made on the basis of the organization studies literature. For a characterization of this organization-Other, I could draw on writings from i.a. Collinson (2003), Parker (2003) and Ten Bos (2004b).

The shame which according to Levinas occurs in the confrontation with the Other, has no parallel within the organization studies literature. For a description of that confrontation within an organization in terms of embarrassment, I had to resort to a literary narrative. As regards the manifestation of the injury that underlies the confrontation, I was able to link up with texts from i.a. Argyris (2003) and Smith (2001).

The finding that some elements do, and others do not, or barely, resonate in the organizational literature has implications for how Levinas' second narrative can be transposed to the context of organizations. That second narrative is the one in which the Other is presented as a condition for the representation, either through the gift or through the constant renewal of representation under the influence of the Other as the ultimate critical authority. This second narrative in its terse form, in which shame for one's own rationality plays an important role, is not reflected in the organization studies literature in a complete and explicit way. Only the autobiographical fragment of Argyris, presented in the Preface, is to be regarded as evidence of the occurrence of this phenomenon. In a less terse form, it can indeed be found in e.g. Gustavsen et al., Maas and Sutton who stress the importance of encounters and debates among employees to arrive at new ideas. But the lack of rationality shame makes the difference with the ideas of Levinas too great. Answering the question of what this second narrative on representation looks like *in its entirety* in the context of organizing and organizations, therefore will have to take place mainly on the basis of the cases that are presented in Section 2 of this chapter.

The above scheme of propositions supports the identification and the presentation of those cases, because it gives meaning to at least some of Levinas' concepts within the context of organizations.

Section 2: Cases

The Second Narrative Translated

The Identity Card Department

For about 4 years I work as the head of the Identity Card Department of a big municipality. It is the Department's responsibility to take in requests from citizens concerning identity papers, to judge them, and to comply with or reject them. This regards for instance passports, driving licenses and certificates of residence.

One of my employees is Ruud. He is with the Department already for a very long time and deals mainly with certificates of residence. With Ruud I have a problem: I do not get hold on him. There is nothing wrong with his production: he's a really hard worker, he is never sick and the clients are very satisfied with him. But internally, as far as the cooperation within the department is concerned, he is very negative. He ducks out of any form of internal consultation – excluding gatherings in the pub – and refuses to think with the others about radical changes in the organization and functioning of the department. In fact, he lets his colleagues be saddled with the supple operation thereof, and with every change up to the last it remains uncertain whether he will be obstructive or not. A negative effect radiates from his attitude, and I often think: this is not acceptable! You can not just unpunished back out of everything like that? Imagine if everyone would behave that way! If we really do want to have the open, communicative approach that we propagate, then Ruud just should be involved and adapt his behaviour.

Recently, we completed a project which aimed at improving the department's telephonic accessibility through the cooperation with a call center. The project was to provide a more efficient handling of incoming calls and brought with it major changes to the internal organization of the work in the department. In order to consider all implications once more, I had planned on the day before the start of the new system a consultation with all department employees and the external consultant who had supported the project. The consultations would take place in the private space of the department.

At the appointed time all people concerned had gathered except Ruud. He was still sitting just behind his desk. I asked him to sit with the group but he did not. It made me angry, but I decided to just start. After half an hour from the corner of my eye I saw in a flash that Ruud drew up his chair and sat about one metre outside the circle. I pushed on a little for him to come and sit with us. But he did not respond. In an effort to at least verbally engage him into the circle, I asked him his opinion about the call center. He replied in a barely audible murmur something like that he didn't mind. At that moment the thought went through me: "There's someone sitting there who can not do otherwise than he does. This reluctance must indeed come from very deep. As if he hates all this." And at the same time I suddenly saw myself sitting there, in yet another consultation with my colleagues and I felt a deep embarrassment. What the hell is this about? And why should I at all costs draw over the line someone who does not want to be there? Why should a person adapt oneself to this circus?

The meeting continued with the things we had to arrange yet. At the end Ruud immediately stood up and went back to work at his desk.

I still do not know how I feel about this. The cooperation with the call center soon after the start turned out to be a happy choice. All employees were satisfied, even Ruud made compliments. But that did not really help me in my puzzle. What was going on here? If Ruud had frankly said: "I don't do that", a good talking-to would have been given to him. You therefore perhaps could call it cowardice that he did not say that, but that's not what it feels like. With him it comes from very deep down. It is: up to here and no further, I just can not. It was a kind of defencelessness that made I could not be angry anymore.

I indeed would like to ask Ruud some questions. Why do you work so hard and at the same time back out from everything? I would like to discuss with him. If there would be only Ruuds, would not that be a big problem?

The story *The Identity Card Department* confirms the second narrative of Levinas *in its entirety*. In it we come across: the deficiency of rationality, the resistance against that, rationality shame and a new beginning in the form of intense reflection. In the remainder of this section, a number of this kind of cases will be presented. Any of those cases has its own remarkable qualities, be it as a part of the storyline, or other aspects that allow us to perceive Levinas' second narrative in organizations. In my presentation of the cases I shall be guided by those salient aspects, but at this point it is important to note that each case in its own way reflects the *whole* of Levinas' narrative within the context of an organization.

The Importance of Completeness

I want to emphasize here that completeness of Levinas' train of hought, because precisely that feature makes the difference with regard to the fragmented reflection of his thinking in the organizational literature. The fact that the cases are complete is the reason that they are presented.

The importance of the completeness of the narrative is related to the objective of my research. That objective is: to establish a connection between the philosophy of Levinas and thinking about change in organizational science. In a case in which one of the elements of the narrative would be missing, that objective would not be met. Then there would no longer be question of Levinas' narrative, or it would be impossible to establish the connection to the organizational theory. To illustrate this point, I will briefly touch upon each of the said elements with the intention to imagine that element is absent and then to consider the implications of its absence for my argument.

Suppose that in one of the cases there would be no question of a deficiency of rationality, which in Levinas has the character of myopic closedness. Then the rest of the storyline would be a lot harder to comprehend. Why then would there be resistance to rationality, and a confrontation and shame?

But if the deficiency of rationality comes to the fore in a case, without giving rise to resistance, then it is not obvious that this would lead to a confrontation and to embarrassment for the rationality deficiency.

If shame were missing, after the manifestation of the rationality deficiency and the resistance thereto, then change – not as a tactical move but as repentance and radical reversal – would be hard to imagine.

And if, finally, in the case no change would occur, not only the Levinas' narrative would appear incomplete, but also no connection could be made with organization studies' thinking about change.

Collecting the Cases

Prior to the presentation of the cases, I briefly want to discuss how they are gathered. The main idea behind this collection is as follows. If it is true as Levinas describes: the becoming ashamed of one's own rational actions by the Other, and the turn around which because of that takes place in the subject, all that just happens.[5] Then, using Levinas' descriptions, all that should be traceable in its entirety in reality. Levinas is not a moralist, in the sense of a specialist who tells us what *should* happen, but he is – at least in *Totalité et Infini* – a phenomenologist who wants to talk about *what manifests itself* in and through the phenomena. For me the issue was to catch those moments in which Levinas' second narrative occurs palpably within an organization. Indeed, that would make clear that, partly because of the language he offers us, certain aspects of reality may light up for us in a new way.

As a means to this end I chose the form of interviews with what I referred to above as "organizers", that is, people who are professionally involved with organizing and organizations, such as managers, consultants, organizational studies scholars and trainers. The first step in the interviews used to be that I told the interviewee about Levinas' second narrative and about my ideas, summarized in the above seven propositions, what the event of the narrative could look like in organizations. Then I put the question to them whether they had ever experienced such an event themselves, with themselves in the role of the thinker. So events they would come up with, should apply to situations where they themselves acted as organizer and in which they had experienced the shame for their own reason in a confrontation with people who were supposed to comply with their ideas and schedules. For further clarification I indicated to them that I wanted to know:

---

[5]It is possible to hear in the phrase "it just happens" the resonance of a theme that since Kierkegaard appears frequently in continental philosophy. Namely what Kierkegaard calls "the decisive moment", Heidegger "Ereignis" and Lyotard "événement", to mention only three names from a range of thinkers that is far longer. Obviously, each of those thinkers has his own interpretation of the notion which sometimes is labelled as "event" (e.g. Van Riessen 1995: 83) but that does not preclude that a common feature can be identified. This shared characteristic according to Safranski (1995: 219) lies in the fact that "the event" in all these thinkers refers to the occurrence of the "completely different", whereby the "horizontal time is cut by a vertical one." These associations to "it just happens" in the context of a study of Levinas are not unjustified, because the impact of the Face can be seen as Levinas' interpretation of "the event". However, in this study when I say that "it just happens", I use the verb "to happen" in less loaded sense. What I mean to say is simply that "it" (that is: the impact of the Face and everything that goes with it) *appears in an observable way* in our reality. My intention is thus to contradict that such phenomena would be unlikely. Or that they would be desirable indeed, but (as for instance Bauman 1993: 125 says) systematically and successfully neutralized.

- whether they recognized the phenomenon of the refusal to organize or to be organized, also to be conceived of as a form of aversion to existence;
- whether they experienced that as the identification of the violent nature of organizational rationality;
- whether that confrontation was an impulse to seek new ways and led to new insights.

By way of example, so that the interviewees could get a more precise idea of what I was looking for, I presented them one of my own experiences through the following case.

The Man Who Wanted to Write a Dissertation

As part of the research done to prepare the present dissertation I was looking for examples of shame in organizations. My interest was in shame which could be related to the use of reason. A well-known organizational consultant agreed to my request to interview him on that subject.

The conversation started with mutual acquaintance, but soon we got on the topic that had to be the theme of our exchange. Namely, experiences of shame, felt as a confrontation with one's own imperialism, which had been experienced by my interlocutor in the exercise of his profession, and which were directly related to the organizational rationality he uses in his work. We needed quite an amount of time to arrive at a clear idea of the experience of which I was seeking illustrations. That went as follows. My discussion partner, time and again, brought up incidents of which he thought they came close to what I was looking for. I listened carefully to each case, and in an immediate response I indicated to what extent the content was in line with what I was looking for. It appeared that any story of my interlocutor that contained elements that supported the case in question, was unusable for my purposes. It was for instance about just a different kind of shame than that I had in mind; or there was no question of shame, but of disgust; or there was a certain anticipation of resistance, and therefore not a surprising confrontation. This went on for about one hour until my interviewee said: "That what you are looking for in my past, is that not exactly what you are currently practicing in discussion with me? You have your schemes in your head, you know exactly what you want. And on top of everything that I bring up, you put your prefabricated grid and then you cut everything off which does not fit in the grid." This was exactly what I meant by imperialist rationality. I told him so. And I told him that after this remark from him my shame was not far away. It was only because he did not give me the impression of being hurt – he looked quite amused – that embarrassment about my own performance did not fall upon me. But if my interlocutor would have been visibly uncomfortable, misunderstood and cornered, I would have taken that to heart. And it would lead to a different approach next time. Yet, we noted, it is also true that writing a dissertation would not succeed without schemes and concepts. Writing is a form of organizing, and if I wanted to make the book I had in mind, I could not escape a process of selection, logical ordering and reasoned presentation of my material. That is: I could not escape rationality, unmistakably imperialist.

If interviewees indicated that they had ever experienced anything like this, I asked them to tell the core moments of such an incident as factually as possible. I wrote down literally their descriptions of those core moments, and thus these have been preserved in the cases.

From the outset in the interviews I stressed that people possibly might not recognize themselves at all in the described phenomena. Such an outcome of a conversation occurred frequently. But that was not problematic for my research, as long as there was also a number of people who actually did recognize themselves. Indeed, the aim of the interviews was not to show that the second narrative has a universal validity. The aim was to show that the second narrative, despite its absence in the literature and the neglect of the associated symptoms in daily practice, simply occurs.[6]

Based on the above, you can also say that the focus during the interviews was in part directed at counteracting the neglect of the second narrative. Something had to be called back into the consciousness of the interviewees, that for some reason had disappeared from it. That there was neglect involved was often confirmed by the way the interviews proceeded. If interviewees were able to dig up events at all, these often appeared into consciousness only after long searching and digging. This despite the intensity of the key moments they could then describe. Exposing the neglect of a perhaps trivial, but also important, phenomenon is another way to express what the interviews were partly about.

I am aware that objections may be brought against the way the cases have been collected as described above. The question may be raised whether violence has been done to the interviewees by presupposing that there could be question of forgotten experiences. To be true, it is hard to imagine a different approach, when it comes to catching Levinas' second narrative, because Levinas himself speaks about a forgotten experience. But the danger of a certain pushiness on my part was surely not hypothetical. I indeed tried to show the interviewees that I was aware of that danger, for instance by telling the above case, but I am not sure whether that in all cases was sufficient to remove the discomfort.

Another possible objection is that I heard too much of what I wanted to hear from the interviewees. I was looking for a phenomenon described in full detail, where the description was presented to the interviewee before the interview. I cannot exclude that people will say they recognize the phenomenon and say they have experienced something like that, and then invent a story. Apart from my intuition that the providers of the cases all spoke about authentic, personal experiences, and reinforced by the fact that they often could produce minute details that never contradicted one another about the core moment, I have no defence against this objection of wishful hearing.

Finally, therefore, these cases should be judged on their plausibility. Are they credible? Can it be like this in reality? Stories from and about organizations, even if they are invented, can be considered as alternative ways to understand organizations. This is shown for example by the way Kaulingfreks (1999: 64) and Ten Bos and Kaulingfreks (2001: 137) use fragments from Kafka's work. Stories can often come closer to reality than methodically accounted for social scientific studies

---

[6]The statement that it "simply occurs" therefore does not mean that the confrontation with the Other occurs in *everyone* and *continuously*. This raises the question whether some a priori sensitivity or certain conditions, apart from the presence of others, are required for the confrontation to take place. I will, within the framework of this book, not deal with this question. For beginnings of discussion of this issue, see Visker 2005: 22, Van Riessen 1995: 83 and Bernasconi 2002: 246.

can, as has been stated among others by Rhodes (2000), Czarniawska (1997) and Case (1995). And the traditional scientific methods have, according to the Parker et al. (1999), contributed to the tendency that "[r]aw human experience, in organizations or anywhere else, is often unrepresented in organization studies." The issues that concern us, such as disgust, existential insecurity and shame, can be counted among the "raw human experience", on which stories can give us more insight.

Translation in Tenfold

Below I present some ten cases, each of which reflects the second narrative of Levinas in its entirety. The presentation of the cases is organized according to the four basic elements of the second narrative: the deficiency of rationality, the resistance against that deficiency, rationality shame and a new beginning. In respect of each basic element I present one or more cases. These I connect, by case, with a number of key ideas from Levinas relating to that element of his thinking. In doing so, I will refer to quotes from or about his work which have been addressed already in the exposition of his thought in Chapter 4. By connecting these citations to the cases they can light up again. Wherever needed, I will add to them extracts from the propositions or other passages from Section 1 of this chapter, for a correct understanding of those citations in the context of organizations.

The Deficiency of Rationality

Standardization at a Brewer's Company

When I was still at the beginning of my career, I was invited as external consultant to work on a project at a major brewer.

The company included a group of 20–30 larger and smaller breweries at home and abroad. These brewers worked until then each according to its own historically developed practices and locally specified guidelines. The Executive Board had conceived the idea that it would be good to more standardize the different practices. That would make the control from the company's management more uniform and simpler and that would bring efficiency gains. Moreover, automation announced itself and that could rely on the standardized practices. The first step in the process of standardization was to establish uniform administrative procedures. A project group was composed with the mandate to draw up those procedures.

The project group included approximately 35 men, divided into two teams of equal size. One team was formed by external consultants. Of this group I was the first man. The second team consisted of people from the company, led by a 55-year-old financial director of one of the branches. Within the project as a whole he was the second man, the ultimate responsibility for the project's leadership was on me.

So I had to deal a lot with this financial director. The cooperation was difficult. Not because the man was unpleasant. On the contrary, it was a nice man, with a strong commitment to his local branch where he had moved up from accounting clerk to his current position. The problem was that he tended to consider the practices and guidelines of his own location as the most appropriate across the board. They should therefore be the standard for all other locations. I objected that the intention of the project was to combine the best practices of all locations and, where necessary, to design new ones.

We debated about this for 3–4 months, but those talks were not successful. I foresaw that, with this man around, the planned streamlining and efficiency gains could not be achieved and that the project would fail. What should I do? I struggled with that question. I finally removed him from the project. That meant for the financial director that he ended up in pre-retirement, for him a very undesirable outcome.

At the farewell-reception that was offered to him by the company, he spoke to me about the issue. He remarked to me that I should think about whether I had done well and whether in a subsequent and similar situation I should not act differently.

I feel uncomfortable about this case.

More often, I have had to dismiss or move people against their will. But always there were reasons for that which meant that I did not feel uncomfortable. In this case it is different. Here the question is left open: was there no other way for me to solve this? My decision came from tunnel vision: a narrow rationality that only focused on the benefits of efficiency gains. Because the man in question did not have the same idea as I had, he was forced to leave, harmless and full of good intentions. It was as if an innocent was convicted.

If I were to be in the same situation now, I would take him more seriously. I would confront him with his own limitations and thus bring him at a different level of consciousness. I would more play along with his survival instinct. He might have coped with that.

About the deficiency of rationality we saw on (p. 103) that this can manifest itself as oppression and as the feeling of being locked inside oneself. "The achievement of an orderly and defined world changes into a collection of dogmas and reifications." Applied to the sphere of organizations it was found (p. 114) that rationality can be seen as "normative closure", which on the one hand is a response to the meaninglessness of existence in its primeval guise, but which on the other hand creates new anxiety. That anxiety was labelled as the return of the *il-y-a* in disguised form and associated with the oppressive feeling that may be aroused by the mirroring of office buildings and strict labour discipline. As appears from the case, other examples could be the described striving for efficiency and the associated tunnel thinking. To that manifestation of rationality, what has been said of rationality applies in general: it helps us to organize the world and to put the primeval *il-y-a* at a distance. But it simultaneously is a source of oppression.

The deficiency of rationality may impose itself through the confrontation with the Other, as we saw with the Brewer. But it also can already be present as a vague feeling of discomfort, associated with an otherwise deliberately chosen rational course of action. That is the way it seems to be in the case of the *Credit Card System*.

Credit Card System

During my stay in South Africa as a consultant I was hired by a major bank to provide support to one of the developmental projects of the bank. The job concerned the part of the bank that deals with the processing of credit card transactions. At that time there was an improvement process that should result in a new organizational structure, clear work processes and good Service Level Agreements with the contributing banks and credit card labels. I was hired as project manager, which meant I had to lead the organizational implementation of the improvements.

My project was part of a program that included several projects and that was led by a strong program manager who knew what he wanted and set out clear lines to achieve his goals. When I started, I had a conversation with him in which he told me to be happy with a European project manager. We discussed the way we wanted to work and we agreed that a strict schedule with associated budgets and deadlines was crucial. We therefore started, in close collaboration with the people who would have to carry it out, to draw up a comprehensive plan.

From the outset it was clear that strict observance of the established planning was the key to the success of the project. For me, as project manager responsible for implementation, this meant that I constantly had to hurry up people to ensure that deadlines were met. Meanwhile I was aware that a Dutch kind of directness could have a counterproductive effect, so I did my best to express my exhortations as diplomatically as possible.

An important role in the improvement process was played by Susan, the product manager of one of the labels of the bank's credit card. I very often needed information from her, to provide it to others who then had to work further on its basis. One of the times she had to provide me information we had already moved the original deadline and made a new engagement for ultimate delivery at a certain date before 17.30. When at that time I had not received anything, I called her, in accordance with the agreement on tight schedule control. I asked her why she still had not delivered and whether she understood the importance of the project. Susan muttered back, said I had no idea of all the things she was busy with and hung up. I regretted this course of events and felt confused. Fifteen minutes later I received a mail from Susan. In it she wrote that she had more things on her mind and that, if once more I would address her like that, she would let go the entire project. She demanded an apology from me. I felt shocked. Professionally, I had approached her legitimately on the deadline, but there was more at stake here. Susan was not functionally angry, she was really angry. I felt personally touched and ashamed that I spoiled someone's professional life. I had transgressed my personal standards.

I've offered my apologies to Susan. I also decided to more follow my own sense of keeping pressure and to less hurry up employees.

The "own sense of keeping pressure" and the "personal standards" which are at issue here suggest the existence of a discomfort that already preceded the confrontation. The reference to own standards indicates that there is a suspicion of a situation of greater meaningfulness, against which the actual situation may stand out as less meaningful, and therefore as unsatisfactory. This is one of the things hinted at in the quotation from De Boer at p. 79 in which he designates ontology as fragile and loaded with a presumption of its own inadequacy, "at least for those who have ears to hear and eyes to see." The appearance of the Other seizes upon the perceived deficiency and may lead to people becoming acutely aware of that deficiency and discomfort. This can give rise to a change of behaviour.

It is important to consider that the deficiency of rationality does not only occur in the forms of rationality that appeared in the two previous cases, namely as a striving for efficiency and as a tight activity planning. On p. 117 I indicated that the veiled *il-y-a* also manifests itself when it comes to so-called broad, comprehensive rationality. That is, with organizers who have an eye for culture and emotions in organizations, who take people seriously as centres of sense-making, and advocate open and transparent communication. Thinking can, in all its professed openness, become blind and dogmatic, however paradoxical that may sound. To show that also inspired organizers can get entangled in their own logic, I referred at p. 103 to Grit and Meurs. They point out that managers with a vision run the risk of believing so much in their vision that it acquires a dogmatic dimension. Something similar is reflected in the case *Personal Coaching*.

Personal Coaching

It is part of my job to act as a personal coach to managers. Several years ago I did that for a young, very talented manager of an insurance company. The discussions we had together were very intense and revealed that there was a close entanglement between the problems he encountered at work and the sloppy way he dealt with relationships in his private life. In these talks my efforts were aimed at discussing his relationships with people, including me, as directly and openly as possible. This was intended to provide clarity and understanding, which would help him at his work. However, as the passage of time revealed, he was neither open nor direct in his talks with me. For instance, he said at one point that he had ended a relationship and then a while later he told me the opposite.

When I realized this, I felt a great sense of indignation, but also shame immediately afterwards. I was inclined to condemn him because he did not deal with our conversations as I had intended. I imposed a pattern onto him and thereby left him insufficient room for his own reality. I worked with the best intentions, but I apparently had no eye for what really was going on. I felt: you want to say something but I do not let you.

I then suggested to him that we would take a time out. I could use that to think about another sequel.

I eventually stopped coaching this manager and I recommended him to look for someone else. Our relationship was too heavily burdened to continue together. But I have learned from this experience to take myself less as a standard in this type of coaching situation, and to give more space to the specific way people want to deal with their problems.

Although this sub-section deals with the deficiency of rationality, I hope the above cases also reveal that rationality in principle serves a good purpose. The Brewer for instance had his eye on the quality of management, and the Coach on clarity and understanding of personal behaviour. We talked therefore on (p. 99) of "the achievement of the escape from the *il-y-a* which cannot easily be valued too high", to which escape representational thinking makes a contribution. "This appearance of representations is considered by Levinas as the apex of the hypostasis: the separation between the subject and the surrounding being are being radicalized in it" (p. 99). Rationality manages to keep the primeval *il-y-a* at bay through knowledge, insight and planning. Therefore it is possible to believe sincerely, in all these cases, that the acquisition of knowledge and ordering of the world, and that sincere faith and good will presupposed, are motives in the actions of reason. Indeed, it may be precisely because of that benevolent background that another, less sympathetic, aspect of representation becomes silhouetted so sharply: that is to say its illusory nature, or the tendency to act as *une force qui va*. Levinas formulated this as follows: "reason is single. And in this sense knowledge in the world never meets something really different. That is the deep truth of idealism" (p. 99). The ambivalence of the sincere faith in rationality over against the oppression into which that can bring one, is reflected in the next case.

Personal Effectiveness Training

I regularly receive requests to give a personal effectiveness training to managers at the level of the Board of Executives (C level personnel). To perform such tasks, I often ask a fellow trainer to join me. Between ourselves we then determine who will act as chief trainer, either my colleague or me.

Not long ago, such a training was held. It involved a group of eight people in executive positions who wanted to reflect on the effectiveness of their own actions. For this occasion I had asked an older colleague to co-lead the sessions. We agreed that, because of his experience, he would take the role of chief trainer and I would have the role of co-trainer.

I had some hesitations at this division of roles. For myself, I enjoy a fast training tempo and a maximum learning effect, while this colleague is inclined to long stories and focussing on a safe emotional atmosphere. But – I thought – precisely the combination of our different approaches could work out fruitfully, which made me decide for this set-up in our course. I estimated that in my role as co-trainer I could overcome the danger of a too slow tempo by providing the necessary acceleration myself.

Part of the training was a session in which each of the participants, in his or her turn, took their place on an empty chair in the circle of participants and put an issue with which he or she struggled in her/his work before the others. The others could then ask questions and subsequently propose suggestions for the handling of the issue. One of the participants did not have such an issue, but nevertheless she obediently came to sit down on the chair in the middle. When it appeared that there was nothing to discuss, with the consent of my colleague, I let the unquestioning lady go back to her own place in the circle. But I felt this was not enough. I thought she still had something to learn from it. Why did she take that place, if she had no question? It was our responsibility to analyze this further. I suggested to my colleague that he would draw a transaction model on the blackboard and would explain it, after which, using the model, I would, clarify the behaviour of the student more precisely. My colleague agreed with this action, but not wholeheartedly. It became a piece of joint bungling. My colleague felt visibly uncomfortable and his explanation was far from clear. My analysis did not come through with the group, and the student for whom it was all started had learned nothing.

Afterwards my colleague addressed me about this unfortunate incident. He pointed out to me that I had wanted too much and had lost from sight the safety of the situaton. I felt at that moment a deep embarrassment about my attitude and my performance. I had implicated my colleague in the stream of my own needs, while I knew he could not or would not work like that. Additionally, my colleague might have been right as regards the content. Maybe I really neglected the safety of the participants, in the name of ambitious learning effects that were so obvious for me, and because of that I was not professional enough. On the other hand, his tempo was very slow indeed and his goals modest, so professionally speaking my actions do not necessarily have to be judged negatively.

It is clear anyway that, prior to such cooperation, I should be more explicit about my method, in such a way that I would not inadvertently drag someone into the stream of my own ideas and ambitions about effective learning.

Resistance to Rationality

According to Levinas, man experiences a feeling of freedom, coupled with large pretensions with regard to his possibilities of ordering the world, in the exercise of rationality. But these pretensions are called to a halt wherever the representational I realizes that he has to deal with an Other. "But if freedom situates me effrontedly before the non-me in myself and outside of myself, (. . .) before the Other it retreats" (TI: 87). The Other is the only one who can pierce the illusion of my self-created universe. In proposition 4 (p. 128) on the translation of this event to organizations is was stated that, on the side of the organizer, this resistance of the organization-Other – given that organizations have a pretension of reasonableness and sound order – appears as incomprehensible and unreasonable. This is addressed in the next case, in which the organizer seems to have logic undeniably at his side.

Tilting the Organization

I was working at one time in a medium sized consultancy practice with 40 partners and an executive board, consisting of two executives/partners. I myself was one of the common partners, charged with assistance to the executive board.

An important internal issue within the organization was whether we had organized ourselves in a sound way.

Originally – well before my time – the company had been fully structured along lines of functional specification. Then there were groups of specialists, for example in the areas of finance, personnel or automation. But in practice, customers often appeared to want more comprehensive services. This meant that the organization also had to organize itself along lines of customer groups and market groups, in which the various functional specialists could work together in serving the customer. This development had led to a matrix structure in which the functional and customer/market orientations were combined. That structure existed for some 5 years already.

Gradually, the board became convinced that more needed to be done. In order to optimize the service for the customer the matrix should be tilted: the customer/market orientation should become dominant, at the expense of the functional orientation. Partners had to be primarily responsible for customer/market groups and no longer for functional specializations.

When I came to the organization several attempts had already been undertaken to overturn the organization. Those attempts were unsuccessful but the management was convinced of the importance of the tilting and wanted to try it again. I was involved in this new endeavour.

I was rather confident about the proposed action. In the first place because, like the executive board, I believed that there were very good arguments for a stronger customer/market orientation. Secondly, because we were well prepared for the change. We had a good picture of possible resistance and we thought we knew the ways to overcome it.

But it turned out differently. I realized that it failed when I saw the subscription list on which the partners could indicate the customer/market group for which they wanted to work. At the closing of the registration term, this list was only one third completed. For me this was a sobering and also an embarrassing moment. Apparently, the world is more complex than it appears in my picture of it.

A crisis committee was formed to attempt to prevent the disaster. The committee consisted of the board, myself and three partners. "Why don't we manage?" was our topic. One of the directors gave an overview of the situation. He asked us to help find causes for the failure of the tilting and to look for possible solutions. But even the discussion of those questions did not get off the ground. The partners were able to keep the discussion abstract. They said that the matrix structure was unclear and that it was difficult stuff. At no time did the objections become specific. I tried to intervene and asked them what really bothered them. From the corridors I understood that there was much uncertainty and doubt about personal competencies. But I felt that I was pushed away, I did not get through. I realized then for the second time: this may very well be a good plan, but it does not work; the world is more complex than my plan assumes.

I learned from this not to believe too easily in this kind of complete plans. I started to approach employees differently. Not: this is the way it should be done, but rather: look, this is a first idea for change, is this helpful for you? By working like that, as it were, you draw people into processes of change in a natural way. No longer then is the content paramount, but rather the steps you put together.

This story recalls p. 121 where we discussed Collinson as follows: "[H]e objects against a common approach to people in organizations, which seizes upon their rationality and autonomy. Opposing that approach he states (2003: 529) that there should be more attention given to the insecurity that people experience in organizations that can have an existential, psychological, social and economic character. He believes that "[b]y exploring the workplace construction of selves (. . .) a greater appreciation of subjectivity and its insecurities can enhance our understanding of the ways that organizational power relations are reproduced, rationalized, resisted and, just occasionally, even transformed" (2003: 535). This quote was in support of my contention that the Other, from whom the resistance comes, should in the context of organizations be understood as the person to whom organizational rationality is not self-evident. This statement was consistent with Levinas' views on the *il-y-a* and on the various stages of hypostasis that he distinguishes: "The two factors combined – first the discrepancy between the hypostasis-stage of organizations and the stage in which people find themselves, and secondly the veiled *il-y-a* that sticks to organizations – can, with employees who are sensitive to that, arouse repugnance and disgust against organizing and organization. This can manifest itself as a refusal to be organized, as job-refusal, melancholy or less articulate resistance" (p. 121). The latter seems to be reflected especially in the above case. This mechanism may help explain why more autonomy and empowerment, however rational they may sound, do not have the same attractiveness for many organization employees as they have for organizers.

The resistance against rationality is associated with an absolute difference between me and the Other, by Levinas. The absolute nature of that difference originates, as stated on p. 103, from the conceptualisation of the face as an independent source of meaning. It derives its meaning for us from nothing else but its presence. All attempts of rationality to insert that absoluteness into a rational whole, are no less than an insult to that absolutely different Other. That insult is an injury that "looks at me and accuses me in the face of the Other – whose very epiphany is brought about by this offense suffered, by this status of being stranger, widow and orphan" (TI: 244). So, Levinas situates the resistance primarily in the harrowing injury of who has been beaten and excluded. At organizational level, the figure of Bartleby from Melville's story and, to some extent, Ruud from the case *The Identity card Department* correspond to this portrait of the Other and his resistance.

But the appearance of the Other may be less poignant and yet produce the same effects. This was shown in the *Tilting* case and it will be shown in the next case in which there is question of taken for granted conceptions of rationality, and of a breaking through those conceptions by a resistance that shows rather a mature self-awareness than injury. It is not unlikely, however that this dignity has been dearly won, during a long process, and from many experiences of exclusion and humiliation.

Implementation of a New Pension Application

I worked for a period as a consultant in South Africa. This was several years after the end of the apartheid regime, and the social field of forces at that time was, as it still is now, largely determined by the aspiration of the South African government to black empowerment. This aspiration is aimed at the coming about of an economically well-rooted, black middle class, to be achieved by promoting black ownership of companies and putting blacks in high positions. For this goal measures are employed, which reward doing business with black-owned companies and which penalize opposite actions.

In this field of forces, I was approached by a (white) application provider who had problems with the implementation of an application at his (black) customer, a pension administration company. The application provider was angry and frustrated about the course of events. He told me that the implementation was under way already for 2 years and could have been completed already if only the customer would be more cooperative. But it was hard to work with this customer: the pension company wanted a new and flashy system, but did not seem to be interested in the efficiency gains that could be obtained with it. In addition, the company did not meet the agreements about commitment from its side. This led to constant irritations and misunderstandings between the provider and the customer, and the project threatened to run down completely. The request to me was to more precisely investigate matters through an independent audit. For that purpose I would have to interview both parties critically, and then make an analysis of the situation.

This seemed to me to be a nice assignment, because it was clear that continuing on the chosen path was not an option anymore. To be honest, I thought that the application supplier's position was largely right. He had a sound and professional approach to the project. He had a view on how to proceed and where efficiency gains could be won (if need with forced dismissals) and he had good engineers around to implement it. I saw it as part of my task to highlight the soundness of that approach to the project.

I started discussions with both parties. In preparation for my interview with the director of the pension company, I suggested a list of critical questions that also touched the breach of agreements on the part of his company.

I started the interview, based on my questionnaire, in a quite robust way. But rather quickly the director reacted and said: "Before we start our conversation, I want to do a step backwards. I want to make clear that there are major cultural differences between us and the application supplier and that therefore the implementation is not going well." He said the lack of interest in efficiency gains was not a deficiency, but a conscious choice. And that downsizing of the workforce was not a goal, but that it could also be reversed: to aim at keeping as many people as possible in employment.

I experienced this as a direct confrontation with a completely different mindset. I was surprised for a moment, taken aback by the intervention of the director. It felt like I was whistled back. But at the same time, perhaps because of the elegant and credible way the director took me one step back, I had the feeling that I learned something: efficiency is not everything. I then went through my questionnaire, but in a different way and tone than I first intended.

In my report of the conversation I have given an important place to cultural differences. Partly based on that report, the original efficiency objectives have been reduced. A black project manager has been put on the project to manage cultural differences.

Rationality Shame

Where the obvious validity of one's own rationality is being broken through by the appearance of the Other, I speak of rationality shame. This can be described as the breaking through of the autonomy, as the feeling of being brought up for discussion. Related to the situation in organizations it was stated (see p. 125) that, the more sincere the belief in rational order and organization, so the more painful is the experience of being whistled back. This is reflected in the case *Professional Nursing Training*.

Professional Nursing Training

Some years back I worked at a college as head of the Professional Nursing Training. I led a team of 13 teachers, most of whom were a lot older than me.

This age difference was no coincidence. The leadership of the college believed, at the time of my appointment, that the nursing training could use an impulse. The team of teachers had become a bit lethargic and was not very committed, and with me the leadership hoped to have found the young team leader to give it a boost. From my immediate superior, an energetic interim manager, I received the explicit mandate to improve the team's performance.

I liked the sound of that idea. The assignment offered me the chance to work in an innovating way and to create opportunities for employees to develop themselves further. At the same time I understood that in my actions I would have to use various proven management techniques to keep things on the right track. I wrote down clear agreements about the services they would provide with each of the team members, and through evaluation-interviews I followed exactly to what extent they met the agreements.

This approach aroused quite some resistance with the teachers. They had always been accustomed to a large degree of freedom, if not non-commitment, and that was over now. The fiercest resistance came from Marian, a teacher of whom it was quite clear that she did not meet the new requirements. She had little knowledge, only dealt with her own favourite topics and caused many complaints from students and fellow teachers. It seemed clear to me that I had to intervene here and I was encouraged to do so by my immediate superior, who said that such people should look for some other job.

I started conversations with Marian in which I confronted her with her behaviour. The aim was to prepare her for either a behavioural change for the better, or her departure from the organization. These talks were dispersed over a year.

After one of those talks I felt rather happy. I had the impression that Marian had understood my message and understood the seriousness of the situation. But the next day she spoke to me and said: "I found it very unpleasant yesterday. When I got home I realized that you force me into a track that I do not want. You're awful hard on me." She surprised me. Hard was the last thing I wanted to be, but I felt she was right: I had overturned her. But I allowed myself this thought for only a split second. My defensiveness then took over and I started to talk about my heavy task and her lack of responsibility. The conversation ended very unpleasantly.

I've never seen Marian afterwards. She had reported sick already earlier that year and I would soon switch to another job. But the question keeps haunting me. On the occasion of my farewell from the college I realized that in my interventions I had done things that were not good. I therefore didn't want a grand farewell. Instead I have held a short talk, supported by a remote controlled toy car that I bought for the occasion. The thing steered into the room on my command, but only let itself be turned in angles of 90°, which meant it collided with everything and everyone. It symbolized my performance at the college: I had tried to steer using remote control, while I should have sat in the car with someone next to me. Therefore today I listen more to what comes out of people themselves.

In the above case the painfulness of the confrontation stands out clearly. And so does the very natural tendency to forget the experience of shame as soon as possible, which may explain why case presenters often have to struggle so hard to dig out those experiences.

What also appears from *Professional Nursing Training* is that rationality shame is not itself rational. The organizer has plotted a deliberate course of action and thought well about implementation. But even then, perhaps precisely then, the above described, in fact existential kind of embarrassment, may strike. That is what we saw already in other cases, such as *The Identity Card Department* and *Standardization of a Brewer's Company*. It also is at work in the next case.

Migration of a Software System

I work at a large bank and I am charged with the running of a key application. This regards a so-called third line task, which means it is about the continuity of the application's functioning, especially in the long term. Most of my work consists in directing migration projects in which the current application version is replaced by the next version. A migration path includes many sub-projects, such as purchasing new hardware, its installation and testing of the new version. For the performance of some of these activities I can appeal to the Network Support Division of the bank, especially when it comes to installing the Operating System.

A year ago we had the transition from version 5 to version 6. I got offered assistance from Sander from the Network Support Division. He was an enthusiastic force and I was well pleased with him, partially since he offered to arrange things that, strictly speaking, were outside his obligations. I discussed with him my schedule for the migration process and we appointed deadlines for the parts that he would conduct.

The first part was the ordering of the hardware. Sander would place the order. When, right before the scheduled delivery date, I had not heard anything about the order, I asked him how matters stood. It appeared he had not yet ordered anything. I was annoyed, but he assured me that it would come swiftly. A week after the scheduled date hardware was supplied indeed, but it was not what we needed. Sander had placed the wrong order. I was now really angry. I talked to him and expressed my anger at such carelessness which threatened to endanger my project. He explained how it had come to happen like that, and assured me that for the rest all would proceed well. One way or another this had a disarming effect on me. Here stood a willing, enthusiastic worker before me and I felt embarrassment at such violent anger on my part.

The second part of his job for me was reserving a place for the server of the new software and providing a power supply. Both are core tasks of the network staff. But when the – this time correct – hardware was delivered, neither a server location, nor a power supply appeared to be arranged. The previously encountered pattern repeated itself. I was furious. I told Sander that he had failed again and that is was impossible to operate this way. He responded again with an explanation of the course of events, and assured me he would deal with the rest correctly. And again I felt ashamed of my hot-tempered violence.

Afterwards I have thought a lot about this course of events. New migration routes presented themselves and I was sure that I did not want to be "supported" in them by Sander. But simultaneously, I felt pity and that it was almost impossible to dismiss him: he wants to do a lot and to do it all in the best of ways. I had to make clear to the head of the Network Support Division that I now wanted to work with somebody else. And to do so not behind Sander's back, but yet in a way that I would not hurt him unnecessarily. How should I do this? I have talked extensively with my colleague about it and the result was an e-mail to the head Network Support, with a CC to Sander.

About the situation described above we can relate what happened by relation to the story of Bartleby: rationally speaking, there is not much going on. There are agreements between two parties in an employment relationship. One of the two parties does not meet his obligations, so the other can, within his powers, take measures. There is nothing unreasonable in that, and eventually that is what happens indeed, but only after the "normal" relationships have been broken through for a moment, and after as Bernasconi (2002: 240) says: "I lose my sense of *mine* in the face of the other." "(...)Levinas understands it to mean 'a subjectivity incapable of shutting itself up' (ibid.: 243). Here applies what Levinas says in *Het menselijk gelaat* (1978: 94; translation NvdV): "To be in a face to face relationship with somebody else – that means that I can not kill him. This is also the situation of being in a conversation."

Here there is a peculiar kind of impotence. That weakness is not so much physical in nature. Waldenfels (2002: 71) says in response to this phenomenon: "We can certainly contradict what the other says because the other is not a dogmatic authority, but we can not contradict the call and demand of the other's face which precedes any initiative we may take." In one way or another, in the confrontation with the other, the common mechanism of rationality – which acts by constantly relating other people and other things to what I control already – fails. To answer the question how the Face can hack into this fabric of relationships we suggested on p. 103: "Because the face, as call, breaks the laws to which knowing is bound usually. These laws prescribe that knowing is always a matter of referring: to horizons, backgrounds, or other knowledge in terms of which new knowledge can be formulated. Resulting in an endless game of mutual referrals. The face, on the contrary, as far as it calls upon us, expresses *itself* (TI: 51). It derives its meaning for us from nothing else than from its presence. In this sense it is absolute, detached, an independent source of meaning." This phenomenon occurs also in the next case.

Competency Profiles

From the start in my capacity as HR director of a construction company, I have tried to bring in the human dimension in its full width into the relationship between managers and their employees. My point was that a broad, open dialogue should be the norm. This was specifically reflected in the abolition of the assessment forms which were in use in the company. Instead now, assessments became dialogues in which basically everything can be discussed in an open way. From that the outcome is a conversation report.

Over time I experienced a problem in these dialogues. An orientation, or a focus, is missing which meant that chance had too much of a role in the possible outcomes of the discussions. What could I do? Should I start working with a checklist?

I decided on the establishment of a competency system. We developed competency profiles that can indicate what the company expects from its employees, but which simultaneously can help employees to grow and match those profiles.

By now I have serious doubts about the competency system. People may grow, but I am to be the one who indicates the direction?

My doubts were triggered by a conversation with a project manager. This man had been out of the running for months from a burnout. Through therapy and rest, he had slowly climbed out from the abyss and now he felt recovered enough to resume work. The conversation I had with him was the first initiative to that.

The conversation went well, we discussed various issues relating to the resumption of work, and the project manager showed fresh enthusiasm and said that he felt even better than before. Until I brought up the competency profiles issue at the end of the conversation. The man then seemed at once to be back to square one. He told me: I can not comply, with this transparency I can not be sufficiently human anymore.

This confrontation shocked me. I was wondering have I done well with those competency profiles?

In the rest of the conversation we managed to work it out. The regime of the competency profiles would also apply to this project manager, but in a more relaxed way. Additionally I resolved to think about good alternatives.

In this case it would have been just and reasonable if the director had thought with regard to the response of the project manager: "Oh dear, this man is not ready yet, he should have a further 3 months of rest to fully recover." That is the way to incorporate the Other into your own expectations and frames of reference. But that was not what went through the director's head. He thought: "Am I doing well (with those competency profiles)?", and was prompted to reflect on other directives.

A New Beginning

With regard to the opportunities for change arising from the confrontation with the Other, it was said on p. 107 said that the impact of the Other can, however briefly, shake up all representation. That creates room truly for new contents of thought and thus for change. Levinas himself says: "The relationship with the Other puts me into question, empties me of myself and empties me without end, showing me ever more resources" (Levinas 1998c: 94).

Restructuring of a Municipal Service

About 6 months ago I started as director of the Municipal Service for Building and Housing. Soon after I started I got the feeling that the Service was not balanced organizationally. There was nothing wrong with the commitment of the staff, but the internal organization was not right. The structure was not transparent, there were too many positions and too many people.

During the first period I looked around a lot. I wanted to determine how exactly things worked in practice and to verify whether my first impressions were correct. The feeling of my first impressions remained and my conviction grew that something drastic had to happen with this Service.

After about 2 months I have raised this issue at a Service MT-meeting with Ronald and Marc, my two assistant-directors. I told them that I was amazed at many things that I had found in the Service and that for my part in a number of areas things would have to change fundamentally. That seemed a bit exaggerated to them, change could also be implemented step by step. But yet they advised me to write down my thoughts. I did this. I set out all my observations, ending with the conclusion that I would like to have some things differently organized, and complete with a blueprint for an improved structure of the Service. I mailed the whole report to my fellow MT-members, asking them to respond.

There was no response. Two, three weeks passed and all remained quiet. Meanwhile also, I had raised the issue in the consultation with my fellow directors of the other Municipal Services. They agreed with my analysis and gave me the advice to actually transform the Service. Preferably by talking to the employees and convincing them, but if nothing would come out of that, by simply imposing it. I began to consider that the latter might prove to be needed. Indeed, I still did not hear any response from my assistant-directors. They mainly were busy with the affairs of their own departments, I stood alone when it came to the Service as a whole. Besides there was something else. By superior order it had just been determined that my Service had to let go about twenty people. The need for intervention pushed on and I was the one who had to realize it.

The tension that accompanied these thoughts was released at the next Service MT-meeting. Ronald complained about a modest improvement project that had just started and about the confusion that it entailed for his people. I immediately responded emotionally: "I really stand completely alone. You screen off yourself nicely within your departments and leave me with a rickety internal structure and a savings target!" Ronald in turn got emotional: "But indeed you completely go your own way. You send us schemes but that is not the same as entering the conversation. It feels like you have no faith in us. What do you do to yourself? We need to cooperate more." Marc joined with that approach.

This comment struck me as a painful reprimand. Ronald was right. I had not gone in depth. I had not wondered why they did as they did. It appeared that they had felt threatened by my blueprint, not only out of concern for their position in the organization, but also out of attachment to the professional values that had shaped the current structure.

Apart from shame, because of the way Ronald and Marc responded, I felt also relief: "I do not have to do it alone. I don't have to push through anything, because there is openness." We decided then to a 2-day retreat of the Service MT to intensively exchange views with each other on the usefulness and necessity of restructuring the Service. Thereby one thing was clear: we had to do it together.

One result of the retreat was the decision to reorganize the Service. But now according to a design which was much more balanced than I ever could have imagined alone. We are currently reaping the benefits.

Not in all cases was there such a tangible change result, as the result of a shameful confrontation. In some cases the result was expressed in terms of (intentions to) other modes of action by the organizer which could increase chances of successful change. This applies for instance to *Credit Card System, Professional Nursing Training*, and *Tilting the Organization*. In other cases the outcome of the confrontation was most of all the additional reflection on problems of organization and organizing. This was very evident in the case *The Identity Card Department* of which I present the end once again.

> I still do not know how I feel about this. The cooperation with the call center turned out to be a happy choice soon after the start. All employees were satisfied, even Ruud offered compliments. But that did not really help me in my puzzle. What was going on here? If Ruud had frankly said: "I don't do that", a good talking-to would have been given to him. You therefore perhaps could call it cowardice that he did not say that, but that's not what it feels like. With him it comes from very deep down. It is: up to here and no further, I just can not. It was a kind of defencelessness that meant I could not be angry anymore.
>
> I indeed would like to ask Ruud some questions. Why do you work so hard and at the same time back out from everything? I would like to discuss it with him. If the world was made up of only Ruuds, would not that be a big problem?

I am inclined to consider such reflection, also viewed from the perspective of the organizational cases, as a positive effect of the confrontation with the Other. It makes organizers more creative and sensitive to what more there is to the organization than strategy, structure and processes. Chances for change in the organization will only benefit from this insight.

Evaluation of the Performed Translation

The goal for this chapter was to translate Levinas' train of thought as we discussed it in Chapter 4 into the context of organizations. I referred to that train of Levinas's thought as "the second narrative of *Totalité et Infini*" and it includes the elements of the deficiency of rationality, radical resistance, rationality shame and possibilities for change. The question was how, in the context of organizing and managing, that narrative can be meaningfully understood.

With that intention, in Section 1 we investigated the organization studies literature. The conclusion was that some elements of Levinas' line of thought were reflected indeed, some other elements partially so and some others not at all. By joining together what we found in the literature and supplementing it with my own proposals for translation, a scheme could be constructed which outlines – as in a sketch – what Levinas' story in organizational practice could look like. Simultaneously we concluded that that scheme *in its entirety* was not to be found within the organizational literature.

Section 2 then undertook the translation effort in an entirely different way. Namely by, starting from quotations from Levinas and from the said a scheme of propositions, then collecting stories through interviews with organizers that could confirm the scheme. This yielded a dozen of cases, each one of which in its own way shows what the second narrative might look like, and this in its entirety. In this way it is shown, in my view, that Levinas' ideas can be related to the practice of management and organization through the presented scheme. Thus, the display of those ideas as contained in the scheme of propositions, may be conceived as their possible translation into the world of organizations.

Chapter 6
Conclusion

Introduction

This chapter contains some concluding thoughts. In the first section I shall argue that the contribution that Levinas can make to organization studies and to thinking about organizational change is located in the new language he provides. This new language offers opportunities for new thinking, and enables us to better understand problems and barriers that are marked by a somewhat enigmatic character. Subsequently in the second section I will discuss three remarkable aspects of this new language: the coincidence of critical knowledge and ethics, the urge to concretization and the ambivalence toward rationality. The third section performs the comparison which was announced already in Chapter 3 in presenting the two alternatives for representational thinking. Levinas' new language is compared with the language which organization studies scholars derive on the one hand from postmodernism and on the other hand from the work of Heidegger and Wittgenstein. Finally I conclude with an assessment of the chances of acceptance of Levinas' new language within organization studies.

New Language

The conclusion we reached in the previous chapter, in which we extensively discussed the translation of Levinas into management studies, can be interpreted in two ways. The fact that the crucial, second narrative of Levinas resonates only partially in the organization studies literature, and nowhere in its entirety, can be explained as the confirmation of a kind of unworldliness of Levinas: his thoughts are interesting, but those sciences that deal with social reality cannot confirm them.

However, that same lack of resonance can also be interpreted positively, namely and in itself as an addition to the management literature. The cases selected indicate that the second narrative indeed occurs in a recognizable way in organizational reality: it just happens. But for some reason, that happening has not yet consistently been the subject of discussion in management literature. The second narrative therefore brings up for discussion something which has not previously been thematized,

N. Van der Ven, *The Shame of Reason in Organizational Change*, Issues in Business Ethics 32, DOI 10.1007/978-90-481-9373-8_6, © Springer Science+Business Media B.V. 2011

and can thus be considered as an enlargement of organization studies. I support this second view.

To be able to introduce something new for discussion, language should be available in which the new can be expressed and thus becomes conceivable. Levinas'contribution to organization studies, in this positive view, is that he generated the language in which the second narrative may be formulated. My presentation of Levinas can be regarded as an effort to introduce that language into management science. The intended effect, as with all new language, is that phenomena which heretofore were invisible become visible, and disturbances that until now were incomprehensible become understandable.

Levinas has developed this new language in the course of argument on Western philosophy. His thinking can be regarded as a lifelong and sustained attempt – using different methods – to hold up to the light phenomena which were disregarded by that philosophy. More exactly, one specific disregarded phenomenon: the encounter with the Other and its impact, for which at different stages of his philosophical life Levinas sought different formulations. Richard Bernstein (2002: 252) says in this regard: "The metaphor that best captures the movement of Levinas' thinking is the one Derrida uses when he compares it to the crashing of a wave on a beach: always the 'same' wave returning and repeating its movement with deeper insistence. Regardless of what theme or motif we follow – the meaning of ethics, responsibility, the alterity of the other (*autrui*), subjectivity, substitution – there is a profound sense that the 'same' wave is crashing."

The Contents of the New Language

Through this book only a part of the new language that Levinas introduced has been brought into organization studies. It is the language Levinas uses in his work up to the time of *Totalité et Infini* and that is contained largely in what I have called "the second narrative" of that book. In *Autrement qu'être* he developed his ideas further, leading to the enrichment of Levinas' idiosyncratic vocabulary with some new concepts. I have left out of the scope of this book that later development.

For a good picture of the role Levinas' new language covered in this book, I will briefly review the second narrative again. This is the line of thought that starts from what Levinas calls the dogmatic bias of imperialist representation. In this formulation representation stands for human rationality; the use of human reason for objectifying cognition and thinking. Levinas refers to representation as imperialist because of its inherent property to consider itself as the origin of the world. From this illusory perspective, phenomena in the world – things and people – appear as constituted by human consciousness and as manipulable in representation. The dogmatic bias stems from that illusion: representation, *une force qui va*, is the boss in its own world, it is autonomous. It deals with resistance from outside as something which has to be adapted to its own reference frames, homogenized, encapsulated. It accepts no uniqueness and knows no critical authority from outside. But this self-sufficiency is simultaneously a self-*in*sufficiency. For the closed structure of representation and rationality manifests itself also as oppression, totality and lone-liness. "reason, being unique, cannot speak to another reason" (TI: 207). Levinas interprets this oppression as a return of the *il-y-a*, the frightening meaninglessness of formless being. The subject has just, through the hypostasis and representation, detached itself from it, but in a veiled way it returns into representation. On this basis we could speak about the deficiency of rationality, which is manifested as deception and exclusion.

To break this closure a force is needed which does not allow itself to be incorpo-rated. For Levinas that is the face of the Other in need. It can, if only for a moment, arrest the rushing rationality and question it. For that reason Levinas (1996: 54, 1998c: 19) calls the Face an absolute resistance, a resistance that cannot be encap-sulated by representation. The autonomy is broken and gives way to heteronomy. In this situation the I cannot escape but recognize the radical uniqueness of the Other. Van Riessen (1991: 19; translation NvdV) says about Levinas' descriptions: "They connect to the awareness that the other is unique." Here indeed we learn something, the Other is the truly critical instance that teaches me something new and can correct the deception for a moment.

For the I, the confrontation with the Other feels like a shock, a painful event. The Other calls me and my freedom to order, he whistles me back and makes me ashamed of my homogenizing rationality. Simultaneously, this confrontation is a new beginning. The I acquires new knowledge, and from the shock it derives the energy to represent and order the world once again, but now in a qualitatively enriched way.

Levinas designates this confrontation also in terms of responsibility. I am called to order and indicted. Namely: for having caused sadness in the eyes of the Other. Indeed, it is me who, through the exclusion generated by the imperialist representa-tion, is responsible for that sorrow. In the same way that the power of incorporating cognition is arrested by the unique significance that is embodied in the Other, so representational thinking will be disarmed face-to-face with the emerged responsi-bility. I cannot explain away the sorrow, the strength of the face is such that I can only acknowledge being guilty before it. I have no longer any defence in the face of defenceless resistance. The Other makes me responsible and restless. In this respect Van Riessen (1991: 19; translation NvdV) says, that Levinas' texts are an explana-tion of the realization "that there is no limit to the responsibility for the other, that it is not possible to rationalize this responsibility." Explaining it away is no longer an option.

The translation of this new language of Levinas to organization studies produced the following line of thought. Organizations can be regarded as the embodiment of rational, representational thinking, and organizers (managers, management consul-tants, trainers) as its representatives. Such embodiment entails a certain blindness to the illusory character inherent to representation, and implies a kind of imperialism which, in accordance with the nature of representation, wants to encapsulate resis-tance. The Other in the organization resists that blindness and imperialism, and it is possible that the organizer–in confrontation with the Other–is struck by the sor-row and the pain which are shown by the organization-Other. Where this occurs, the order for the organizer is turned upside down for a moment, and shame can strike with regard to one's own imperialist acting. That shame creates an opportunity for reflection and generates energy for new, more inclusive forms of organizing.

Remarkable Aspects of the New Language

For a closer inspection, I will highlight three remarkable aspects of the new language: the convergence of ethics and critique, the focus on the concrete, and the ambivalence toward rationality. For these three aspects I shall below indicate what is remarkable about them. With regard to the first two aspects, I will at the same time show how they emerge in organization studies when Levinas' language is used there.

Ethics and Critical Cognition Coincide in the Other

A special aspect of Levinas' language is that it enables descriptions in which the above effects of the encounter with the Other occur simultaneously. In one and the same movement I am shocked by the Other, questioned and made responsible. This encourages reflection and hence innovation and change. This connection emerges for instance when I present Van Riessen's (1991) quotes of the first section in their original context:

> Levinas' reflection (. . .) shows itself as a new interpretation of the relationship to the other, with attention to elements that generally receive little attention in philosophy. His texts are an explanation of the realization that there is no limit to the responsibility for the other, that it is not possible to rationalize this responsibility. They connect to the awareness that the other is unique . . . . (1991: 19)

What we could present above as on the one hand, an epistemological issue (awareness of the specific nature of the other), and on the other hand an ethical issue (the responsibility for the other) are now brought together as simultaneous aspects of the relationship with the other.

The connection of these two aspects is new in that it is unusual. That this connection of philosophy of knowledge and ethics within management studies is not common, is indicated by, among others, Parker and Baets. Jones (2003a: 227) says with regard to Parker: "Parker draws attention to the way that recent debates in organization studies have tended to focus on ontological and epistemological grounds, and in doing so attention has fallen away from questions of axiology, questions of position, ethics and politics." Baets outlines the need for a management perspective through which new comprehensibility may arise. His starting point is a quadrant of four complementary aspects on which attention should be focused simultaneously: faithfulness, truth, justice and functional appropriateness. For the aspects of truth and functional appropriateness there is enough attention. "A real understanding of man and his or her emotions, which somewhat paradoxically we could call 'a man of flesh and blood', we'll get only if we can merge these approaches with the 'authentic' and the 'just'" (Baets 2004: 51; translation NvdV).

This is exactly what happens in the language of Levinas, who regards the phenomena of deception (as an issue of truth) and exclusion (as an issue of justice) as ultimately not belonging to different categories, but as leading back to one and the same phenomenon: the disregard of the Other. Wyschogrod (2002: 190) says with regard to that: "Totality is for Levinas a freighted term that includes epistemological, historical and political meanings." Thus, the Other in this new language is, in one stroke, the source of ontology (the explanation of being) and of ethics (ideas about the good actions).

Indeed it is possible indeed to regard the Other primarily as an ethical category. From that perspective one can say that primacy is assigned to ethics in Levinas' language. If, however, we want to call the intervention of the Other an ethical event in the new language, we must realize that many of the usual notions associated with ethics do not apply here. In particular I refer on the one hand to the rationalization and universalization that are sought frequently in ethics, and on the other hand to its comfort-seeking objective. As regards rationalization, Van Riessen (1991: 19) already indicated that it is in conflict with Levinas' theme of the responsibility with which the Other saddles me, given the limitless responsibility for the Other. Critchley (2002: 12) states that

> (...) Levinas does not posit, *a priori*, a conception of ethics that then instantiates itself (or does not) in certain concrete experiences. Rather, the ethical is an adjective that describes, *a posteriori* as it were, a certain event or being in relation to the other irreducible to comprehension.

Therefore, based on Levinas' work, he concludes (2002: 22) that "ethics is entirely my affair, not the affair of some hypothetical, impersonal or universal I running through a sequence of possible imperatives. Ethics is not a spectator sport. Rather it is my experience of a demand that both I cannot fully meet and cannot avoid." And Bernasconi (2002: 237) warns that "[u]nlike much contemporary writing on ethics, Levinas does not assume or even expect rationality and morality to be in agreement."

Even further away if possible from Levinas' conception of ethics is the idea that ethics can bring peace to the mind. For the business and organizational ethics Robert Solomon expresses this view by suggesting "that business ethics should have the goal of making actors 'comfortable' when they face ethical problems" (quoted in Jones 2003a: 238; see also Jones, Parker, and Ten Bos 2005). If there is one thing Levinas wants to make clear, it is that the Other gives us unrest. According to Levinas, the kind of ethics that wants to channel injustices and tensions through rules and legislation is also needed, but the longer the unrest can be endured which leads up to them, the better the quality of the regulations will be.

Looking for the Concrete

As we have seen Levinas is driven in his philosophical search by an overwhelming desire for "real" meaning, a true transcendence. Conversely, you can say that he is frightened by a fundamental experience of meaninglessness from which he wishes to escape. He has striven hard to describe that experience, indicated as the experience of the *il-y-a*, an experience of deep meaninglessness.

He did this, as we may observe, at two levels: that of the primordial *il-y-a* – the indifferent, endlessly babbling being; and that of the veiled *il-y-a*, that adheres to the abstract, pale, universal products of representation.

To combat the loss of meaning that he finds at the second level, Levinas tries to connect with Husserl. What attracts him to Husserl are the latter's tireless attempts to counter the shortage of meaning of nineteenth century naturalism, one of the guises of representationalism that has dominated the West for centuries. Husserl labels the knowledge produced by naturalism as abstract. By that he means to say that the facts and objects that are identified by naturalism lack significance, because of the fact that in defining the world and things, naturalists renounce, already from the outset, the meaning that the world and things have for man. Men are merely interested in the existence of objects and facts, and thus reduce them to their measurable aspects. Husserl's efforts are aimed at finding again the concrete, and by this he means: the meaning which must have been present before objectification and abstraction. Critchley (2002) says in this respect: "This is what phenomenology calls the concrete: not the empirical givens of sense data, but the a priori structures that give meaning to those seeming givens." (Ibid.: 7)

Levinas takes over this focus from Husserl on originally given meanings that get lost in the process of objectifying cognition, i.e. representation. Following from Husserl, Levinas calls that loss of meaning abstraction, and he labels the object of his quest, that is original meaning, as the concrete. But, deviating from Husserl, Levinas does not look for those original meanings in the subject. Rather, along with Heidegger he seeks them, in the first instance, in the environment of man, in the horizons of being. Concretization in this approach then consists of identifying the meanings that lie in the social, historical and action contexts in which man finds himself. For Levinas the progress of Heidegger's ontology, compared to that of Husserl, lies in his attention to those everyday aspects of human existence.

But soon Levinas observes that this concretization does not go far enough for him. The meanings found in the horizons of being are not truly transcendent, by which Levinas means to say that they should come entirely from outside the subject. On the contrary, the ego remains, in the words of De Boer (1997: 8) "the perspectivist point from which the world of experience is "totalized" (Sartre). In his analysis of the world of tools, Heidegger demonstrates that all object-implements refer to each other and, in their totality, to their handler", that is to man. Learning, conceived as receiving meaning from something truly new and exterior, does not happen here. Looking for further concretization, Levinas arrives at the encounter with the Other. Here, according to him, there is question of an experience of meaning that escapes from our representation completely. The Other signifies just himself, and offers resistance to the encapsulation by representational thinking in a network of references. Van Riessen (1991) says in this respect:

> Contrary to Heidegger, for whom the empirical data remain 'ontic', and thus secondary with regard to the ontological approach, i.e. the explanation of being, Levinas gives priority to concrete empirical situations. Precisely in the method of concretization Levinas discovers the possibility to express the 'royal road' of ethics (TI:29): the ethics of the metaphysical transcendence is the relationship to the most concrete. Ontology can only become elucidation of existence if it presupposes this relationship to the other. (Ibid.: 150; translation NvdV)

To the degree that Levinas wants to be more concrete in his descriptions, you could say he is forced more and more towards the meaning which lies in the Encounter and which is essentially ethical in nature. Bernasconi (2002: 242) puts it this way: "In other words, the formal ontological analysis becomes ethical by virtue of the passage to concreteness." Obviously, for the meaning of the word "ethical" what is said about it in the previous section should be kept in mind. There are, primarily, no associations with rationalization and regulation.

This fits with what was mentioned above: the new language makes visible phenomena which until then were not visible. About the concretization on which that new language is focused, in a comparable way it can be said that it makes meanings visible which until then had disappeared from sight, because of abstraction and objectification. In line with this idea, the introduction of the new language into organizational studies was simultaneously a movement of continuing concretization in Chapter 5.

In order to achieve a full translation, the concepts of Levinas had to be linked to real life incidents. Levinas' second narrative could only be found in its entirety in the world of organizing and organizations as we took a position further away from contemplation and literature, and closer to the lived life. In the interests of completing the translation, we have had to move from organization studies literature, which most of the time focuses on theory and generalization, to stories about encounters between people in order to show the meanings that pop up there.

In bringing about this move to the micro level, a number of management writers have been very helpful. These are the authors who, in their own way, have observed too that for arriving at truly new meanings, that is, for development of knowledge and innovation that deserve that name, generalization and universalization constitute main obstacles. Gustavsen et al. (2001c) are such authors, appearing for example from the following quote:

> While words like improvement and development can be seen as the continuously better and more forceful implementation of 'given ideas'- total quality management, business process re-engineering, lean production, to mention but some of the major catch-words of the 1990s – innovation turns the attention more strongly towards the new, the break, the product or process which has not existed before. Attention has turned more towards the ability to do something unique rather than implement something 'given'. There was a need to keep this shift in mind and keep an eye open for experiences that could highlight the unique in innovation. (2001b: 235)

And then they conclude "Thus, as researchers, we must turn from a concern with regularities and representations of past events to unique, 'once-occurrent events of being'" (p. 239).

Mostly based on personal experience and research, some other authors note that successful innovations and changes in many cases originate at the micro level, so as a result of the interaction between two or more individuals. Thus Fosstenløkken, Løwendahl and Revang (2003) report, following their investigation of Knowledge Development Processes (KDPs), that they started at the level of strategic management: "[A]s we investigated KDPs in further detail, we found that we had to turn to the micro level of individual professionals and how they perceive the way KDPs take place in their firms in order to understand how these processes can be supported and enhanced" (p. 875). In the same vein Wood (2002) believes, referring to Dougherty, that

> [k]nowledge is also constituted in the far 'thicker' intricacies of the day-to-day activities and behaviour of practitioners themselves. Dougherty, in a study of organizational renewal through product innovation, shows how articulating visceral knowledge is a practical skill that calls for new roles and responsibilities from researchers and a fundamentally new contract between research and practice beyond the current instrumental view. On her model, if theories are to be useful they have to speak to everyday realities. (Ibid.: 155)

According to Jacques (1999) there is much to learn for managers "in that they do not understand the micro-processes through which value is produced in their organization" (p. 214).

Also, authors who aim mainly at improvement of human relations, emancipation and democratization in organizational change, choose the micro level as a useful starting point for observation. Alvesson and Willmott (1992) believe that "[a] slackening interest in grand critique facilitates an expansion of interest in the critical analysis of ordinary, everyday power relations and struggles" (Ibid.: 446). Borgerson (2003) stresses the importance of taking the actual interaction between people of flesh and blood as a point of departure for renewal: "[D]ifferences experienced in embodied interaction are said to make novelty, or the emergence of the undetermined, possible" (Ibid.: 1361). Reason (2003) lets this idea result into a grand vista, derived from Harman: "Throughout history, the really fundamental changes in societies have come about not from dictates of governments and the results of battles but through vast numbers of people changing their minds – sometimes only a little bit" (Ibid.: 283). This resembles the perspective sketched by Weick and Quinn (2004): "Careful attention to small short moments often brings the realization that, in fact, these moments are microcosms of larger, recurrent, fundamental processes" (Ibid.: 665).

In all the above quotations behind the generalizations and abstractions, the aspiration to retrieve prior meanings is apparent; that is a pursuit of concretization. And the quoted authors all look for that at the micro level of human interaction. That aspiration shows parallels with the efforts of Levinas, up to this point. The new language, that in Levinas results from his attention for the concrete, also focuses largely on the micro level. The specific feature of Levinas' approach – what he can add to the above approaches – is that he links shame and responsibility to the unique meaning that arises from the encounter with the Other. The ultimate concrete for Levinas resides in the intensity of those sensations. Responsibility, energy, meaning and innovation originate there at one and the same moment.

Ambivalence Toward Rationality

In the foregoing it has been mentioned several times that Levinas in his search was driven largely by the problem of the deficiency of rationality. The objectification and universalisation provided by reason are unavoidably accompanied by loss of meaning and a tendency to rigidity and dogmatism. The impulse which triggers new forms of rationality, coming from the encounter with the Other, gets betrayed by that rationality time and time again.

But that does not mean that Levinas does not appreciate representation and rationality. It should have become clear that Levinas considers representational thought as a major force. On the one hand, this may appear from his description of representation as the pinnacle of the hypostasis, the process of genesis of the subject. The illusion that is inherent to representation is simultaneously the force that enables people to free themselves from their surrounding, anonymous being, and to maintain themselves as separate beings. In this respect Groot (2003), in response to the analyses that Nietzsche made of representational thinking, says: "But this tragedy of thinking is also its merit. Indeed, the inescapable illusion is simultaneously the condition for survival amid a hostile world" (2003: 33; translation NvdV).

On the other hand Levinas considers it of utmost importance that the impulse, given by the encounter with the Other, encourages reflection. The impact should not be limited to just the restlessness resulting from the confrontation. The responsibility raised there calls for realization, and there is no other way for that to happen than within the domestic, organizational or societal frameworks in which the encounter occurred. These frameworks should be taken into consideration, because the elaboration of the impulse should not adversely affect third parties. But this new, more inclusive organization of relationships requires thinking, calculation, sound assessment of interests, in short the rationality that is representational thinking.

The importance which Levinas attaches to this social elaboration of the impulse is reflected in the high esteem he shows for institutions that partly originate in that impulse, such as jurisdiction, democracy and serious science. These all inevitably proceed in a generalizing way and therefore each of them is exposed to the risks of dogmatism, deception and exclusion, but one simply can not do without representational thinking. Levinas' position in this regard is similar to that of Gilian Rose when she says (quoted in Hull 1999) "The demonstration that Fascism and representation are inseparable does not lead to the conclusion, current in post-modern aesthetics, philosophy and political theory, that representation is or should be superseded. (. . .) [T]he subject of representation does not need to be superseded: the danger of its experience needs to be exposed" (Ibid.: 410, 411).

So with regard to representationalism, Levinas' position is essentially ambivalent. Representation always reaches back to originally meaningful events: the disputation of my property or my imperialist dogma by the Other. But simultaneously she continually gives rise to new illusions and dogmas, and thus betrays the original impulse. This ambivalence at the societal level is an important theme for Levinas, particularly in his book *Autrement qu'être*, which – largely – I have left out of consideration. There he focuses on the importance of the societal elaboration of the unrest brought about by the Face, or in his terms: of the ontological development of the metaphysical relationship. That focus compels him to pay in that book a lot of attention to the ongoing betrayal of the original impulse, a betrayal which is inherent to the rationality needed for building a society.

The New Language Compared to Two Alternatives

In Chapter 2 the exposition of Levinas' ideas about representation took place in the context of the finding that the usual rationality in management studies, in the form of representationalism, causes problems. In Chapter 3, prior to the presentation of Levinas, I described two organization studies currents that each in its own way look for an alternative to representationalism. One of them does so through an orientation towards the postmodernism of Foucault and Derrida, the other through a direct orientation towards Heidegger and Wittgenstein. I presented these currents in order to give an impression of how people in management science seek answers to the problems that representation poses by consulting philosophy; and also in order to be able to compare Levinas' answer with other answers. This comparison between the answer of Levinas and the two mentioned currents is the subject of this section.

The Addition with Regard to the Orientation Towards Postmodernism

The organization studies orientation towards the postmodernist thought of Foucault and Derrida has in the above been described on the basis of Chia's book *Organizational Analysis as Deconstructive Practice* (1996) which deals with that subject. In my evaluation of the postmodernist answer, I expressed my great appreciation for Chia's project, but also my doubts about its feasibility.

Now, after the presentation of Levinas' philosophy, I can express my evaluation in different terms, derived from that philosophy. My appreciation for Chia's project comes from the finding that, similar to Levinas, he is intrigued by the loss of meaning that occurs in our naming and knowing the world. That loss of meaning is situated by him in the use representationalism makes of a being-realistic ontology, which can be equated to the thing-ontology in Levinas. Chia notes that that loss of meaning manifests itself in faulty knowledge and in absolute claims of truth, with deception and exclusion as its effects. He wants to catch that loss of meaning when it occurs, and he shows that the insights of postmodernism can help in reaching that goal. His book can be read as a suggestion to systematically apply postmodernist deconstruction within organization studies in order to counter the loss of meaning.

My doubts about Chia's project focus on how one can track down the loss of meaning within organizations. He is right to direct the attention toward micro-practices for that. "We saw in Chapter 5 that acceptance of the postmodern critique of organizations implies the necessity to refocus on the micro-practices of organizing and to view organizations as relatively stabilized effects of such micro-practices instead of objective entities in their own right" (1996: 192). The reason is that the pursuit of more comprehensive statements, generalization and objecti-fication by definition entails loss of meaning. Because that meaning is ultimately located in "ongoing inter-actions of complex linguistic and social micro-practices that are inextricably associated with the taxonomic urge to order our life experi-ences" (1996: 208). This reflects the importance I above also attributed to micro situations.

However, the problem is that Chia seems to opt for an approach to these situ-ations from the perspective of an academic observer. Thus, according to Levinas, he cuts himself off from the opportunity of a direct encounter with what is the ulti-mate source of any meaning: the concrete other, in this case the organization-other. Because, I believe, that encounter can only occur from an attitude of participatory involvement in organizational situations. Chia suggests that this is not necessary. He acknowledges the temptations of thing-thinking and the pitfalls of representa-tion that can appear in organization studies analysis, but he believes it is possible to generate a kind of immunity against those phenomena. Namely, by focusing on pro-cesses and the emergence of entities, while apparently in the belief that with regard to static reality the real transcendence could be found there.

Levinas makes clear that *all* thought, even if it is aware of its being conditioned, is exposed to the treachery of representational thinking. This thinking continually creates – inherently to its nature – illusions, and tends to see the world as mate-rial on which it can apply its definitions. "Re-presentation deals with beings as if they were entirely self-supporting, as if they were substances. It has the power to disinterest itself – be it only for an instant, the instant of representation – from the condition of these beings. It triumphs over the vertigo of the infinite conditioning that true thought, and thought that is true, opens up in these beings. Without travers-ing the infinite series of the past to which my today nonetheless refers, I embrace this day, in all of its reality, and derive my very being from these fleeting moments" (DE: 112).

And for Levinas there is no reason why a deconstructionist organizational thinker would escape from that effect of representation.[1] The distinction between the verb-oriented and the object-oriented thinking is according to Levinas not fundamental,

---

[1] Also Derrida himself, with whom the concept of deconstruction is usually associated, has always considered the methodization of deconstruction as impossible (Richmond 1995: 180). Weiskopf and Willmott (1999: 567) point out in their discussion of Chia's position, that postmodernist constructions are as untenable as modernist constructions.

and both are subject to the imperialist tendencies of representationalism. The genuine transcendence – and therewith both the source of all meaning, and also the indication of loss of meaning – is to be found only in the direct encounter with the Other. The autonomous, lonesome organizational scientist or research school that deconstructs and reconstructs meanings to my mind is far removed from it. I find a confirmation of this idea, e contrario, in a passage of Kaulingfreks, Ten Bos and Letiche (2004: 3; translation NvdV) on the development in the Netherlands of Critical Management Studies. In apparent contradistinction to the situation from which Chia operates, they observe: "Remarkably, this philosophical interest for organizations has generally developed outside the academic world. We have particularly in mind here consultants who, in addition to their work with people in organizations, kept alive a philosophical-scientific interest." That is to say, at least in the Netherlands, approaches that are oriented toward philosophy and that show conceptual congeniality with Chia's approach flourish, from practical situations.

From the idea that the (work-related) encounter with the organization-Other is fundamental, flow the two concerns that I have expressed in my evaluation of the orientation towards postmodernism as represented by Chia in the course of Chapter 3. The first objection concerned the question of whether the possibilities to systematically counter the illusions generated by our thinking are not too easily taken for granted. Can you organize your own being criticized? Or does this idea testify of a new form of autonomy-thinking, which can easily lapse into sterile intellectuality?

With Levinas, I am inclined to think that the corrupting effect of representation in thought keeps manifesting itself, even though, after the Heideggerian turn, there is more awareness of the conditioned nature of that thinking. The truly critical instance which can break through that pattern is the Other, whom we come across in a compelling way. Thus we can derive from Levinas' thinking an indication of the direction in which overcoming these problems should be sought: research situations in which the organizational scientist is involved in a participatory way, so as to get the chance to encounter the Other.[2] These encounters give him a view on the source of meaning, before, inevitably, loss of meaning strikes again.

This focus of Levinas may as well give us an indication where to seek an answer to the second objection, that of the negative nature of deconstruction. We found, with Chia, that the postmodernist intellectual quest, this continually harking back, is an excruciatingly laborious undertaking that naturally begs the question from where you get the energy to carry it out. How do you maintain that unrest? This, in fact practical, question also occupies Levinas, when it comes to representation, which for him is synonymous with all thinking, modern or postmodern: "Where do I get this energy from?" Levinas believes that more is needed than the motive mentioned by Foucault: the desire to transform oneself. De Boer says, (1976: 39): "Of itself, human freedom is uninhibited. To know is to exercise freedom's power. Why, then,

---

[2]On p. 134 (footnote), I indicated that in this book I do not deal with the question whether certain conditions are required for the confrontation to occur. But it is clear that in the absence of interaction that occurrence certainly can not take place.

should this power be hampered by objectivity, why should it let itself be arrested by inconvenient truths? (. . .) This breach in natural dogmatism would be impossible without the presence of the Other's face, before whom arbitrariness shies back and is ashamed." Thus, Levinas' answer points in the same direction as the previous indication. The required energy and inspiration is found where you meet, in a binding way, the organization-Other and can be surprised.

The confrontation of the orientation towards postmodernism with Levinas' insights therefore leads me to conclude that such an orientation needs a supplement in the form of participatory research in organizations. There the opportunities are better for encountering – in the guise of the organization-Other– the surprising, critical instance, which both can counter the illusions of the intellect and can provide the inspiration for the continuous deconstruction of meanings.

The Addition with Regard to the Orientation Towards Heidegger and Wittgenstein

Philosophical insights at an earlier stage already encouraged organization studies scholars to be involved in participatory research. Heidegger and Wittgenstein attributed importance for the cognitive process to the fact that all our thinking is conditioned by our acting and social existence, and this has contributed to the emergence of greater attention to the relationship between knowledge and action. We described in Chapter 3 the current within organization studies that elaborates this insight and which includes Winograd and Flores, Gustavsen and Shotter.

According to these authors, the added value of this approach to organizations is located in the possibility of combating any loss of meaning associated with objectification by viewing objectification continuously against the background of the existential situation that gives rise to it: simultaneously, it was indicated that by this approach, the production of illusions through representational thinking is not eliminated. Also in the eyes of Weick and Gustavsen constant alertness remains necessary to hasty generalizations and ideological blindness. But that takes energy and therefore in the evaluation I ended up with the same comment as with regard to post-modernism – from where do you get the energy?

Levinas acknowledges this problem, as we have seen, and stresses that the required energy comes from the Other who breaks through the representation and can call us to order. Now, precisely participatory research wants to start from practical situations in which researchers are actively involved. So, one actively seeks the other, and this suggests that the condition is met that Levinas posed to critical knowledge: to be confronted with nay-sayers, with co-workers who resist the carefully thought-out plans and concepts, that is with the organization-Other.

It is doubtful however whether the Other functions in this way in the participatory research of organizations. My doubt is motivated by the observation in my evaluation of this orientation towards Heidegger and Wittgenstein, that there the problem of exclusion is not discussed in a satisfactory way. A weakness is the presumed functioning of the social world: communication and willingness to communicate are taken for granted. This research school seems not to know about exclusion, neither about the organization-Other as he emerged from my translation of Levinas to organizations. It seems this school is not familiar with the problem of basic incompatibility, let alone to have a response to it. This lack produces poor organization studies, because communication problems in organizations are on a large scale. According to my translation of Levinas to organizations, a better understanding of what is going on in organizations cannot do without involving this fundamental experience. Awareness of the existence of the organization-Other enables us to let loose the simplistic notion of self-evident, pre-given communication and to face, in a realistic way, the loss of meaning caused by exclusion. What is lacking in participatory research with regard to this issue is the thematizing of resistance which goes beyond being a repairable misunderstanding, an awareness of the existence of fundamental otherness of people and of incompatibility.

Levinas has designated this defect (see p. 93) as a deficit in the philosophy of Heidegger which was a source of inspiration for the mentioned group of authors. It is true that Heidegger sees people as centres of meaning, each a class of its own, and therewith recognizes differences between people. But that is not the transcendent otherness that Levinas has in mind and which substantially encroaches upon people. De Boer (1997: 11) says, in the wake of Levinas, the following about the other in Heidegger:

> [F]or Heidegger, as for Scheler, there is an original, underivable relation to the other. *(In this regard they are different from Husserl, but)* [w]hat Husserl and Heidegger have in common is that the other is exclusively considered as co-subject, as co-inhabitant of the world. He is a fellow knower and fellow worker, but not a partner.

This (existential-)phenomenological starting point has the important consequence that the existence of the other is not determinative for my own being. The being of the world-constituting subject is not influenced by the other; the subject is determined only by his contributing to a shared world. As in Descartes, the starting point of philosophy remains a monadic, solitary ego. Hence Levinas characterizes the phenomenological theory of the Other as the "return to oneself."

The only one who can stop this focus on the self and the Same and can provide thematizing of the exclusion, and thus better organization studies, is the organization-Other. What, then, is so different to the Other of Levinas? De Boer (1997: 12) says: "The other is not only someone I meet; he calls me to responsibility and accuses me. The height from which he speaks, therefore, is at the same time the dimension of Transcendence." At one and the same time he brings up for discussion the freedom of my knowing and the self-evidence of my communication and throws me out of the saddle. Here occurs something really new. Through the meaning he represents, he provides the energy required to resist the tendency to dogma and generalization which are inherent in understanding. In a single movement that meaning breaks through the simplistic idea that communication is a given. This enables a detecting of the loss of meaning which is associated with the exclusion and rejection of communication and which makes organizations so immobile.

Both within philosophy and within management studies, one might wonder whether there is space for the new language of Levinas. With respect to philosophy one could say that in the West it has functioned for centuries as the pre-eminent rational project. Levinas himself considers the Western philosophical tradition since Parmenides as oriented towards a truth which is single and stable. For its discovery that tradition relies heavily on reason, which encourages categorization and generalization. If now Levinas' aspiration precisely aims at concretization and at combating the loss of meaning that occurs with generalization, and if he is so ambivalent towards rationality, does he thus not place himself outside philosophy?

The same question can be asked with respect to organization studies and management which also like to present themselves as rational disciplines: does Levinas' language stand a chance of being accepted? Ten Bos (1999) pointed out to what degree organization studies is governed by the same objective as that of philosophy. "[P]hilosophizing and organizing are activities with more similarities than differences. They are part of the same culture (...). What Descartes did – thinking the world away, not being hungry and curious about it – has subsequently been done by many people in organizations. And often with the same goal: to arrive at unshakable certainty. Such certainty comes within reach only if you put aside your curiosity. Ultimately you can not take everything into account. Therefore a manager for example focuses only on the figures, omitting everything else, including the human life that is hidden behind those figures" (Ibid.: 17, 18; translation NvdV).

Levinas and Philosophy

Despite philosophy, Levinas managed to insert himself and his program in the discourse of philosophy in one way or another. From a very early point in his philosophical career it was his declared purpose, in his thinking, to express the experience of a genuine transcendence which goes beyond the transcendence of representation. With this he had in mind nothing else but absolute unpredictability and otherness. As said above, he thus moved into a trajectory diametrically opposite to the mainstream of Western philosophy which focuses on certainty and stable truth.

Until the eighteenth century, this certainty consisted in the belief in a stable knowable external world, and when that faith collapsed under the influence of Kant's "Copernican Revolution" there was little change, according to Levinas. In the words of Bernasconi (2002):

> In so far as whatever appears to consciousness is a function of the structures of subjectivity, as in Kant's schematism, there are no radical surprises in store for the subject (p. 236).

Even after Kant the striving for unshakable principles kept controlling philosophy. So, Levinas' movement was against the current.

But that is certainly not to say he stood alone in his criticism of the Western tradition. Since Nietzsche especially, the pretensions of Western philosophy have been seriously questioned by a growing number of philosophers. Levinas, for his pursuit of concretization, could align himself with Husserl and Heidegger. Simultaneously his orientation toward a radical newness forced him to go further than they did: this true unpredictability was not found in Husserl and not even in Heidegger, despite the latter's attention to the topic of death. Rudolf Bernet (2002) says in this respect:

> Levinas accuses both of them of developing an understanding of temporality that does not take sufficient account of novelty, unpredictability and impossibility. For Husserl, the event in which a new present suddenly emerges is understood as the fulfilment of a preceding anticipatory intention, which means that the new is never truly new. At first sight, the same objection could not be made to Heidegger, who carefully distinguishes *Vorlaufen* from anticipation and who specifies that the death to which this *Vorlaufen* is related belongs to the order of the impossible. To which Levinas replies that, for Heidegger, death is still the *possibility* of an impossibility, not the <u>impossibility</u> of every possibility. (Bernet 2002: 87)

But Levinas' criticism of the rationalist tradition did not prevent him from attaching simultaneously a high value to objectifying thinking and knowing, the goals at which rationalism aims. That explains why, going against the main current of the philosophical tradition, he wished to express the above mentioned focus on transcendence in the very language of that tradition. His goal was to put at least the associated issues on the agenda in philosophical circles. Given the dissemination of his work at this time, he to some extent succeeded in his efforts.

Levinas and Organization Studies

In the first instance Levinas' ideas are as strange for organization studies as they were for philosophy. But, despite philosophy, if it appeared to be possible to raise issues like radical resistance, responsibility for the Other and radical innovation within philosophy, why should that, despite organization studies, be impossible within organization studies? This may be even easier to carry out as Levinas' ultimate source of meaning is the proximity of people. As we saw already, and though this proximity can actually be dismissed by organization studies, this is much harder than to dismiss it with philosophy. It is not by pure chance that the translation of Levinas' language to organizations can only be completed by turning to empirical case studies.

It may be true that Levinas' language does not describe the reality of organizers at the top of organizations in a recognizable way. Their reality is primarily that of control, and more precisely remote control, which makes intensive use of the language of representation. In general, they are more screened off from direct encounters with their employees than middle and lower managers are. Ten Bos (1999) points out that in this, whether or not cherished, isolation lies the main parallel with philosophers. "The solitary severity of philosophers is not unknown to many people in organizations. "It's lonely at the top" is sung by many a CEO. The most important decisions you take in deep solitude, far removed from the big world and with great severity." (p. 18; translation NvdV)

On the other hand in some cases, and also among senior organizers, there is an awareness of the limits of the efforts of traditional control. People are regularly aware of the glass ceiling that hangs over efforts to change and of the need to think in a new way about change and renewal. One realizes that the language of remote control, the language of representation, no longer suffices in all cases, and especially not in knowledge-intensive environments. "The free ride is ending now", says Jacques (1996: 179), "In knowledge intensive environments, competitive advantage will go to the organization that can successfully 'partner' with 'Home Incorporated'."

Hosking (2004) puts it as follows:

> Key to this is a shift away from language as representation to language (in the broadest possible sense of the word) as a process of coordinated actions (...) These coordinations are relational unities: an act makes no contribution to reality construction processes unless it is supplemented in some way. (p. 263)

The future lies therefore in successful interaction, whereby the latter should not be viewed as the taken-for-granted given that the Heidegger- and Wittgenstein-oriented approaches to organization studies think interaction is. The success of coordinated actions will depend on the non-obvious consent of those to whom the organizer addresses himself – i.e. the employees.

Boonstra (2004a: 11) notes the growing recognition that, especially in knowledge-intensive environments, the balance-seeking Planned Change and Organizational Development do not suffice any longer, because these approaches do not do justice to the complexity of reality. In this regard he points to, among other things, the globalization and developments in communication technologies as complicating factors. Levinas' new language enables us to indicate yet another, entirely different complicating factor, which in case of neglect may create mysterious problems.

That factor is the *il-y-a*-experience of employees in organizations, which means also in organizations that the experience of meaning and sense, let alone of shared meaning and sense, are no pre-given facts. But precisely the assumption of a pre-given meaning, so characteristic of organizations as the embodiment of representation, has always been an important support for organizers in their structuring work. Not to be able any longer to rely on the self-evident presence of sense, let alone a communally shared sense, is a disruptive factor of importance.

As long as its weight is not acknowledged in change processes, it remains likely that you will be unpleasantly surprised. Especially if, as Boonstra indicates, under the influence of globalization and increasing environmental complexity, a trend already manifests itself towards greater decentralization and self-management of employees. This trend increases the weight of the critical success factor "man", with his interactions and with his (lack of) experience of sense.

Managers who are prepared to reflect seriously on the blockages they encounter, will inevitably have to devote more attention to the consequent interactions on factory floor level. Jacques (1999) says in this respect:

> Strategically linking HRM with organizational goals is leading these managers back to the long-buried question of value in that they do not understand the micro-processes through which value is produced in their organization. (p. 214)

But beyond that, in line with Levinas' thinking, they will be confronted by the organization-Other, with his sometimes cryptic and absolute resistance: "Those who will become influential will be those most able to face contradiction without imagining it can be resolved". (Jacques 1999: 213)

To the degree that within organization studies awareness grows that employees are the key to success, Levinas' language will become more important. It will then become a matter of seriously dealing with "the worries and fears, hopes and loyalties, commitments and self-images of participants". (Townley, Cooper, and Oakes 2003: 1067).

An inhibiting factor for the acceptance of Levinas' new language is that it leads to a breaching of the imperialism of representational and organizational thinking. Because exactly that factor: the representational thinking which in organizations wishes to expand at full power, is like the *force qui va* that Levinas sees embarrassed by the appearance of the organization-Other. And that embarrassment for one's own thinking, the rationality shame, cannot but be experienced as painful by organizers. The momentum is interrupted, impotence appears, and reflection and even a form of passivity emerge. Deuten and Rip (2000) express the fear that this may raise with organizers: "Their becoming reflexive might actually destroy their effectivity. So their illusion of agency should be kept intact?" (p. 90).

In this context "agency" can be read as an equivalent of the autonomous representational thinking that creates its own world, like in a game. For an organizer to acknowledge the radical resistance and the inherent call of the organization-Other is a massive concession. Ten Bos (2004b) asks not without reason, after observing that the confrontation with infinity makes us uneasy, the question: "how much disorganization do we wish to allow in an organized world?" (p. 6; translation NvdV).

Because of the appreciation he retains for rationality and representational thinking, the work of Levinas, may be regarded simultaneously as an encouragement to organize and organizations. Indeed, the impulse from the encounter with the Other calls for a structuring of reality which cannot do without reason. Levinas' new language can thus help us to give a nuanced response, for example to Ten Bos' question cited above: because that language makes a distinction between two types of infinity and unrest. On the one hand there is the endless meaningless *il-y-a* and the disquiet it causes. This must be confronted, and representation and organization – the latter being a manifestation of representation – make a highly valued contribution to that contest.

But there is also the infinity of the Face which causes disquiet. Levinas says such unrest should be admitted and endured for as long as possible, because in that discomfort originate the breaking the dogma of representation, the improving of relationships and change. The necessity to think rationally and resist rationality simultaneously is reflected in the following quotation from Jacques (1999) "What are the possibilities for engagement and resistance within, not in opposition to, managerial initiatives for process improvement?" (p. 211).

It may well be that the openness and passivity of which Levinas speaks will for some time continue to sound too strange within the context of organizations. But for as long as organizers and organization studies scholars continue to seriously raise questions about opportunities for organizational change – then so long people who genuinely intend to understand what is happening in organizations and acknowledge the enigmatic nature of the resistance they sometimes incur, may find Levinas' language helpful and supportive of reflection.

Then it might transpire that while his language is especially "new" for philosophy and organization studies, in other respects it is as old as the world: people, for example within families, on factory floors, in schools and nursing homes, have always known who the Other is. And in that moment we can perhaps finally agree for organization studies that "[T]he core challenge may perhaps be seen as finding the new in the trivial" (Gustavsen et al. 2001b: 272).

Afterword

It is now almost 5 years since the Dutch edition of this book appeared under the title *Shame and Change*. The question arises as to whether the book has led anywhere. Did it inspire further developments?

Of course I can not answer that question for other people, but for myself I can. The most valuable development based on the book for me is the practice of the workshops *Thinking for someone else*.

In these workshops the key question is: what happens when one person thinks for another? Through this question and using the personal stories of participants the workshops examine what happens when one person thinks for another person, when that other person does not like that and unexpectedly looks sad and falls silent. The thinker, then, may suddenly be ashamed of himself, he feels as having made an intrusion into the other's domain.

It sometimes happens that after participants in the workshop have intensively discussed the phenomenon of "thinkshame", they notice: "After all, it's something very small, isn't it?"

They are right, because we had talked for 2 h about confrontations which lasted just a split second, between not more than two people, and often with some trivial cause. The reason for this narrow focus of the workshop is that the transgression that thinking for another person may cause, is most acutely perceptible at such moments. When the thinker reads from the face of his interlocutor: I may have the best of intentions but now I am going too far – exactly then thinkshame may strike most intrusively.

Because of the perceived vehemence of the thinkshame, the small suddenly becomes very powerful. What happens in this moment is also very important from a philosophical point of view: thinking – even the well-meant, euphoric thinking – apparently causes harm. And thinking doesn't realize this by itself, but apparently needs some external force to become aware of that. The autonomy we cherish so much doesn't manage to carry on without moments of heteronomy.

Thus the workshops offer real-life illustrations of what from a philosophical perspective I think to be the greatest concrete merit of Levinas' work: it breaks through the almost taken for granted dominance of the "autonomy-thinking" that, in the

N. Van der Ven, *The Shame of Reason in Organizational Change*, Issues in Business Ethics 32, DOI 10.1007/978-90-481-9373-8, © Springer Science+Business Media B.V. 2011

last resort, cannot but take the I for its startingpoint. And that therefore is in fact appallingly lonely.

How deeply the autonomy tradition has become entrenched in our thinking often appears when – philosophically or not – we speak about the other. It is quite common then to lead back your experience of that other person to what, as a subject, you do to him. As a subject you are open to the other, or you should be open to him. You as a subject give meaning to what the other says, or should give it meaning. The subject must do it all, eventually.

By contrast, Levinas insists that the Other happens to you, if only for a split second. The Other surprises you, the face is something truly external and other, something one cannot invent. And the enjoyable thing about the workshops is that they often lead to statements from participants in which they wish to emphasize that for that critical moment, while they themselves were *not the actors*, something external (the other) just completely and unpredictably broke in.

Precisely because of the contrary and unlikely nature of Levinas' message, the credibility of my own and Levinas' argument was already a theme when I wrote the book. It makes a good story – but is it reflected in reality? That was an important question for me. Hence the cases in the book based on interviews which could serve as confirming evidence.

At this moment I am even more reassured. Because many workshops I have seen since the book first appeared confirm that the true exteriority that Levinas is talking about is a lived existential experience.

And at the same time, a very trivial one.

Acknowledgements I would like to conclude this Afterword with a word of gratitude to the people who helped to realize this translation. David Bevan, Neil Olivier, Campbell Jones and Mollie Painter Moreland, without your sustained confidence and focused efforts this book would not have appeared. Thank you so much!

Zaandam, The Netherlands
February 2011

Naud Van der Ven

Abbreviations Used for the Works of Levinas

DE   Discovering Existence with Husserl
EE   Existence and Existents
I   The Theory of Intuition in Husserl's Phenomenology
OB   Otherwise Than Being
TI   Totality and Infinity
TO   Time and the Other

Consulted Works

Abrahamson, E. 1996. Technical and aesthetic fashion. In *Translating organizational change*, eds. B. Czarniawska and G. Sevón. Berlin: Walter de Gruyter.

Albrow, M. 1997. *Do organizations have feelings?* London: Routledge.

Alvesson, M., and H. Willmott. 1992. On the idea of emancipation in management and organization studies. *Academy of Management Review* 17 (3): 432–464.

Argyris, C. 1957. *Personality and organization*. New York, NY: Harper Brothers.

Argyris, C. 1982. *Reasoning, learning and action: Individual and organizational*. San Francisco, CA: Jossey-Bass.

Argyris, C. 2003. A life full of learning. *Organization Studies* 24 (7): 1178–1192.

Armenakis, A., and A. Bedeian. 1999. Organizational change – A review of theory and research in the 1990s. *Journal of Management* 25 (3): 293–315.

Armstrong, H. 2000. The learning organization: Changed means to an unchanged end. *Organization* 7 (2): 355–361.

Baets, W. 2004. *Wie orde zaait zal chaos oogsten*. Assen: Koninklijke Van Gorcum.

Barnett, R. 2000. Working knowledge. In *Research and knowledge at work: Perspectives, case-studies and innovative strategies*, eds. J. Garrick and C. Rhodes. London: Routledge.

Bashein, M., M. Marcus, and P. Riley. 1994. Business process reengineering: Preconditions for success and failure. *Information Systems Management* 9 (2): 24–31.

Bauman, Z. 1976. *Towards a critical sociology*. London: Routledge & Kegan Paul.

Bauman, Z. 1989. *Modernity and the holocaust*. Cambridge: Polity Press.

Bauman, Z. 1993. *Postmodern ethics*. Oxford: Blackwell.

Bauman, Z. 1998. *De moderne tijd en de holocaust*. Amsterdam: Boom. Originally: (1989) *Modernity and the holocaust*.

Beer, M., R. Eisenstat, and B. Spector. 1990. *The critical path to corporate renewal*. Boston, MA: Harvard Business School Press.

Beiser, F. 1998. The context and problematic for post-Kantian philosophy. In *A companion to continental philosophy*, eds. S. Critchley and W. Schroeder. Oxford: Blackwell.

Berger, P., and Th. Luckmann. 1966. *The social construction of reality*. New York, NY: Doubleday.

Berglund, J., and A. Werr. 2000. The invincible character of management consulting rhetoric: How one blends incommensurates while keeping them apart. *Organization* 7 (4): 633–655.

Bernasconi, R. 2002. What is the question to which 'substitution' is the answer? In *The Cambridge companion to Levinas*, eds. S. Critchley and R. Bernasconi. Cambridge: Cambridge University Press.

Bernet, R. 2002. Levinas's critique of Husserl. In *The Cambridge companion to Levinas*, eds. S. Critchley and R. Bernasconi. Cambridge: Cambridge University Press.

Bernstein, R. 2002. Evil and the temptation of theodicy. In *The Cambridge companion to Levinas*, eds. S. Critchley and R. Bernasconi. Cambridge: Cambridge University Press.

Blaug, R. 1999. The tyranny of the visible: Problems in the evaluation of anti-institutional radicalism. *Organization* 6 (1): 33–56.

Bohm, D. 1992. *Wholeness and the implicate order.* London: Ark Paperbacks.

Böhm, S., and C. Jones. 2003. Images of organization. *Ephemera* 3 (3): 162–165.

Bolle, E. 2002. Heidegger en existentieel management. *Filosofie in Bedrijf* 14 (4): 34–42.

Boomkens, R. 2003. Identiteit en cultuur. In *Kernthema's van de filosofie,* eds. M. van Hees, E. de Jonge, and L. Nauta. Amsterdam: Boom.

Boonstra, J. 2000. *Lopen over water: Over dynamiek van organiseren, vernieuwen en leren.* Inaugurale rede, 10 februari 2000 aan de Universiteit van Amsterdam.

Boonstra, J. 2004a. Introduction. In *Dynamics of organizational change and learning,* ed. J. Boonstra. Chichester: Wiley.

Boonstra, J. (ed.). 2004b. *Dynamics of organizational change and learning.* Chichester: Wiley.

Borgerson, J. 2003 on Griffin, D. 2002. The Emergence of leadership: Linking self-organization and ethics. *Organization Studies* 24 (8): 1359–1363.

Braverman, H. 1974. *Labour and monopoly capital.* New York, NY: Monthly Review Press.

Brown, J., and P. Duguid. 1991. Organizational learning and communiteis-of-practice: Toward a unified view of working, learning, and innovation. *Organizational Science* 2: 40–57.

Burrell, G. (ed.) 2000. Special issue on discourse, epistemology and organization. *Organization* 7 (3): 371–544.

Calás, M., and L. Smircich. 1992. Using the "F" word: Feminist theory and the social consequences of organizational research. In *Gendering organizational analysis,* eds. A. Mill and P. Tancred. Newbury Park, CA: Sage.

Calori, R. 2002. Organizational development and the ontology of creative dialectical evolution. *Organization* 9 (1): 127–150.

Caluwé, L. de, and H. Vermaak. 1999. *Leren veranderen: een handboek voor de veranderkundige.* Alphen aan den Rijn: Samson.

Caluwé, L. de, and H. Vermaak. 2004. Thinking about change in different colours. In *Dynamics of organizational change and learning,* ed. J. Boonstra. Chichester: Wiley.

Case, P. 1995. Representations of talk at work: Performatives and "Performability". *Management Learning* 26 (2): 423–443.

Chia, R. 1996. *Organizational analysis as deconstructive practice.* Berlin: Walter de Gruyter.

Collinson, D. 2003. Identities and insecurities: Selves at work. *Organization* 10 (3): 527–547.

Cools, C., J. Kers, and M. Van der Ven. 1992. De relevantie van aandeelhouderwaarde als ondernemingsdoelstelling. In *Handboek Financiële Leiding en Organisatie,* eds. P. Duffhues, J. Groeneveld, and J. Oonincx. Alphen aan den Rijn: Samson.

Cooper, R. 1989. Modernism, post modernism and organizational analysis 3: The contribution of Jacques Derrida. *Organization Studies* 10 (4): 479–502.

Cooper, R. 1992. Formal organization as representation: Remote control, displacement and abbreviation. In *Rethinking organization,* ed. M. Reed. London: Sage.

Cooper, R. 1993. Technologies of representation. In *Tracing the semiotic boundaries of politics,* ed. P. Ahonen. Berlin: Mouton de Gruyter.

Cooper, R., and J. Law. 1995. Organization: Distal and proximal views. In *Research in the sociology of organizations,* ed. S. Bacharach. Greenwich, CT: JAI.

Covey, S. 1997. *De zeven eigenschappen van effectief leiderschap.* Amsterdam: Contact.

Critchley, S. 2002. Introduction. In *The Cambridge companion to Levinas,* eds. S. Critchley and R. Bernasconi. Cambridge: Cambridge University Press.

Critchley, S. 2003. *Continentale filosofie.* Utrecht: Het Spectrum.

Czarniawska, B. 1997. *Narrating the organization: Dramas of institutional identity.* Chicago, IL: University of Chicago Press.

Davies, P. 2002. Sincerity and the end of theodicy: Three remarks on Levinas and Kant. In *The Cambridge companion to Levinas,* eds. S. Critchley and R. Bernasconi. Cambridge: Cambridge University Press.

Dawe, A. 1978. Theories of social action. In *A history of sociological analysis,* eds. T. Bottomore and R. Nisbet. London: Heinemann.

Day, R. 2001. Ethics, affinity and the coming communities. *Philosophy & Social Criticism* 27 (1): 21–38.

De Boer, Th. 1976. *Tussen filosofie en profetie*. Baarn: Ambo.

De Boer, Th. 1989. *Van Brentano tot Levinas; Studies over de fenomenologie*. Meppel: Boom.

De Boer, Th. 1997. Levinas on substitution. In *The rationality of transcendence*, ed. Th. De Boer. Amsterdam: Gieben.

De Boer, Th. 1997. *The rationality of transcendence*. Amsterdam: Gieben.

Deuten, J., and A. Rip. 2000. Narrative infrastructure in product creation processes. *Organization* 7 (1): 69–93.

Dinten, W. van. 2002. *Met gevoel voor realiteit. Over herkennen van betekenis bij organiseren*. Wijk bij Duurstede: Sezen. Delft: Eburon.

Durkheim, E. 1969. *De sociologische methode*. Rotterdam: Universitaire Pers Rotterdam. Originally: (1895) *Les règles de la méthode sociologique*.

Duyndam, J., and M. Poorthuis. 2003. *Levinas*. Rotterdam: Lemniscaat.

Editorial Introduction to the Special Issue. 1999a. Amazing tales: Organization studies as science fiction. *Organization* 6 (2): 579–590.

Editorial Introduction to the Special Issue. 1999b. Human and inhuman resource management. *Organization* 6 (2): 181–198.

Editorial Introduction to the Special Issue. 2005. The iron cage in the information age: The legacy and relevance of Max Weber for organization studies. *Organization Studies* 26 (4): 493–499.

Fineman, S. 1996. Emotion and organization. In *Handbook of Organization Studies*, eds. S. Clegg, C. Hardy, and W. Nord. London: Sage.

Fosstenløkken, S., B. Løwendahl, and Ø. Revang. 2003. Knowledge development through client interaction: A comparative study. *Organization Studies* 24 (6): 859–879.

Foucault, M. 1983. The minimalist self. In *Michel Foucault: Politics, philosophy, culture*, ed. L. Kritzman. London: Routledge.

Fournier, V. 2002. Theory and practice. *Organization* 9 (1): 176–179.

Gagliardi, P. 1986. The creation and change of organizational cultures: A conceptual framework. *Organization Studies* 7: 117–134.

Garfinkel, H. 1967. *Studies in ethnomethodology*. Englewood-Cliffs, NJ: Prentice-Hall.

Gergen, K. 1992. Organization theory in the postmodern era. In *Rethinking organization*, ed. M. Reed. London: Sage.

Gergen, K. 2003. Beyond knowing in organizational inquiry. *Organization* 10 (3): 453–455.

Giddens, A. 1991. *Modernity and self-identity*. Cambridge: Polity.

Greenwood, R., and T. Lawrence. 2005. Editorial introduction to the special issue: The iron cage in the information age: The legacy and relevance of Max Weber for organization studies. *Organization Studies* 26 (4): 493–499.

Grit, K., and P. Meurs. 2004. Stilstaan; Over de gevaren van verandermanagement. In *Arbeid, tijd en flexibiliteit*, eds. A. Witteveen, T. Korver, and H. Achterhuis. Schiedam: Scriptum.

Groot, G. 2003. *Vier ongemakkelijke filosofen; Nietzsche, Cioran, Bataille, Derrida*. Amsterdam: SUN.

Gustavsen, B. 1998. Enterprise development 2000. In *Development coalitions in working lives; The 'Enterprise Development 2000' program in Norway*, ed. B. Gustavsen. Amsterdam: John Benjamins Publishing Company.

Gustavsen, B. 2001. Contemporary European developments. In *Creating connectedness. The role of social research in innovation policy*, eds. B. Gustavsen, H. Finne, and B. Oscarsson. Amsterdam: John Benjamins Publishing Company.

Gustavsen, B. 2003. Action research and the problem of the single case. *Concepts and transformations* 8 (1): 93–99.

Gustavsen, B., H. Finne, and B. Oscarsson. 2001a. Introduction. In *Creating connectedness. The role of social research in innovation policy*, eds. B. Gustavsen, H. Finne, and B. Oscarsson. Amsterdam: John Benjamins Publishing Company.

Gustavsen, B., H. Finne, and B. Oscarsson. 2001b. Innovation: Working together to achieve the unique. In *Creating connectedness. The role of social research in innovation policy*, eds. B. Gustavsen, H. Finne, and B. Oscarsson. Amsterdam: John Benjamins Publishing Company.

Gustavsen, B., H. Finne, and B. Oscarsson. (eds.). 2001c. *Creating connectedness. The role of social research in innovation policy.* Amsterdam: John Benjamins Publishing Company.

Guthrie, W. 1978. *The greek philosophers; From Thales to Aristotle.* London: Methuen.

Hampton, J. 2000. Rationality, practical. In *Concise Routledge encyclopedia of philosophy,* 742–743. London: Routledge.

Hassard, J. 1993. Postmodernism and organizational analysis: An overview. In *Postmodernism and organizations,* eds. J. Hassard and M. Parker. London: Sage.

Hassard, J., and M. Parker. 1993. *Postmodernism and organizations.* London: Sage.

Have, S. ten, and W. ten Have. 2003. *Het boek verandering.* Amsterdam: Nieuwezijds.

Hernes, T., and T. Bakken. 2003. Implications of self-reference: Niklas Luhmann's autopoiesis and organization theory. *Organization Studies* 24 (9): 1511–1535.

Hoogenboom, M., and R. Ossewaarde. 2005. From iron cage to pigeon house: The birth of reflexive authority. *Organization Studies* 26 (4): 601–619.

Horkheimer, M., and Th. Adorno. 1987. *Dialectiek van de Verlichting.* Nijmegen: SUN. Originally: (1947) *Dialektik der Aufklärung.*

Hosking, D.M. 2004. Change works: A critical construction. In *Dynamics of organizational change and learning,* ed. J. Boonstra. Chichester: Wiley.

Hull, R. 1999. Actor network and conduct: The discipline and practices of knowledge management. *Organization* 6 (3): 405–428.

Husserl, E. 1954. *Die Krisis der europäischen Wissenschaften.* Den Haag: Martinus Nijhoff.

Jacobs, D. 2003. Innovatie en irritatie. *Filosofie in Bedrijf* 15 (4): 53–58.

Jacques, R. 1996. *Manufacturing the employee.* London: Sage.

Jacques, R. 1999. Developing a tactical approach to engaging with 'Strategic' HRM. *Organization* 6 (2): 199–222.

Janssens, M., and C. Steyaert. 1999. The inhuman space of HRM: SSSSSSSSSSSSSSensing the subject. *Organization* 6 (2): 371–383.

Jones, C. 2003a. As if business ethics were possible, 'within such limits'.... *Organization* 10 (2): 223–248.

Jones, C. 2003b. Theory after the postmodern condition. *Organization* 10 (3): 503–525.

Jones, C., M. Parker, and R. Ten Bos. 2005. *For business ethics.* London: Routledge.

Jong, M.-J. de. 1997. *Grootmeesters van de sociologie.* Amsterdam: Boom.

Kanter, R.M., B. Stein, and T. Jick. 1992. *The challenge of organizational change: How companies experience it and leaders guide it.* New York, NY: Free Press.

Kaulingfreks, R. 1999. *Gunstige vooruitzichten. Filosofische reflecties over organisaties en management.* Kampen: Kok Agora.

Kaulingfreks, R., R. Ten Bos, and H. Letiche. 2004. Van de redactie: Critical management studies in Nederland. *Filosofie in Bedrijf* 16 (2–3): 1–3.

Knights, D., and G. Morgan. 1991. Corporate strategy, organizations, and subjectivity: A critique. *Organization Studies* 12: 514–536.

Knights, D., and H. Willmott. 1989. Power and subjectivity at work: From degradation to subjugation in social relations. *Sociology* 23 (4): 535–558.

Knights, D., and H. Willmott. 2000. *The reengineering revolution: Critical studies of corporate change.* London: Sage.

Koene, B. 2001. Sensemaking in organizations. *Management & Organisatie* Juli/Augustus 2001 (4): 88–96.

Kotter, J., and D. Cohen. 2002. *Het hart van de verandering.* Schoonhoven: Academic Service.

Landsberger, H. 1968. *Hawthorne revisited. Management and the worker, its critics, and developments in human relations in industry.* New York, NY: Cornell University.

Latour, B. 1988. The politics of explanation: An alternative. In *Knowledge and reflexivity: New frontiers in the sociology of knowledge,* eds. S. Woolgar and M. Ashmore. London: Sage.

Law, J. 1992. *Notes on the theory of the actor-network: Ordering, strategy and heterogeneity.* Unpublished manuscript from the Department of Social Anthropology of Keele University, cited in Chia (1996).

Lee, N., and J. Hassard. 1999. Organization unbound: Actor-network theory, research strategy and institutional flexibility. *Organization* 6 (3): 391–404.

Levinas, E. 1932. Martin Heidegger et l'ontologie. *Revue Philosophique de la France et de l'Étranger nr.* 116 (1932): 395–431.

Levinas, E. 1978. *Het menselijk gelaat*. Baarn: Ambo.

Levinas, E. 1982. *De Dieu qui vient à l'idée*. Parijs: Vrin.

Levinas, E. 1985. *Time and the other* (trans: Cohen, R.). Pittsburgh, PA: Duquesne University Press.

Levinas, E. 1987. *De totaliteit en het Oneindige*. Baarn: Ambo. *Essay over de exterioriteit* (trans: De Boer, T., and Bremmers, C.; annotated by De Boer, T.). Originally: (1961) *Totalité et Infini*.

Levinas, E. 1991. *Totality and infinity. An essay on exteriority* (trans: Lingis, A.). Dordrecht: Kluwer.

Levinas, E. 1995. *The theory of intuition in Husserl's phenomenology*. Evanston, IL: Northwestern University Press.

Levinas, E. 1996. *Basic philosophical writings* (collected by Peperzak, A., Critchley, S., and Bernasconi, R.). Bloomington, IN: Indiana University Press.

Levinas, E. 1998a. *De l'existence à l'existant*. Oorspronkelijk: (1947). Parijs: J. Vrin. In *Engelse vertaling: (2001) existence and existents*, ed. vertaald door Alphonso Lingis. Pittsburgh, PA: Duquesne University Press.

Levinas, E. 1998b. *Discovering existence with Husserl*. Evanston, IL: Northwestern University Press.

Levinas, E. 1998c. *Collected philosophical papers* (trans: Lingis, A.). Pittsburgh, PA: Duquesne University Press.

Levinas, E. 1998d. *Otherwise than being or beyond essence* (trans: Lingis, A.). Pittsburgh, PA: Duquesne University Press.

Levinas, E. 2003. *On escape*. Stanford, CA: Stanford University Press. Originally: (1935). *De l'évasion*.

Linstead, S. 2002. Organization as reply: Henri Bergson and casual organization theory. *Organization* 9 (1): 95–111.

Linstead, S., and R. Grafton-Small. 1992. On reading organizational culture. *Organization Studies* 13: 331–355.

Luijk, F. van. 2003. *Hoe krijg ik ze zover?* Amsterdam: Uitgeverij Nieuwezijds.

Lynd, H. 1958. *On shame and the search for identity*. London: Routledge & Kegan Paul.

Maanen, J. Van. 1995. Style as theory. *Organization Science* 6 (1): 133–143.

Maas, A. 2004. OS: elkaar uit de weg gaan als nieuwe communicatiestrategie? *Filosofie in Bedrijf* 16 (2,3): 108–117.

Mann, Th. 2003. *Schopenhauer en Nietzsche*. Soesterberg: Aspect.

March, J. 1971/1988. *Decisions and organizations*. Oxford: Blackwell.

Mayo, E. 1933. *The human problems of an industrial civilization*. London: Routledge.

Melville, H. 1969. Bartleby, the scrivener: A story of wallstreet. In *Great short works of Herman Melville*. New York, NY: Harper and Row.

Miner, J. 1984. The validity and usefulness of theories in an emerging organizational science. *Academy of Management Review* 1984 (9): 296–306.

Mintzberg, H. 1973. *The nature of managerial work*. New York, NY: Harper & Row.

Mintzberg, H. 2004. *Managers, not MBA's*. New York, NY: Prentice Hall.

Munro, R. 2000. Organized worlds: Explorations in technology and organization with Robert Cooper. *Work, Employment & Society* 14 (2): 404–406. Review of Chia, R. (1998).

Nauta, R. 2003. Schaamte – een psychologische verkenning. *Speling* 55 (3): 16–22.

Nispen, J. van. 1996. Edmund Husserl. *Kritisch denkerslexicon* 20: 1–19.

O'Connor, E. 1999. Minding the workers: The meaning of 'Human' and 'Human Relations' in Elton Mayo. *Organization* 6 (2): 223–246.

Orlikowski, W. 1996. Improvising organizational transformation overtime: A situated change perspective. *Information System Research* 7 (1): 63–92.

Osborne, D., and T. Gaebler. 1993. *Reinventing government*. New York, NY: Plume.

Pålshaugen, Ø. 1998. *The end of organization theory*. Amsterdam/Philadelphia: John Benjamins Publishing Company.

Parker, M. 1993. Life after Jean-François. In *Postmodernism and organizations*, eds. J. Hassard and M. Parker. London: Sage.

Parker, M. 1997. Dividing organizations and multiplying identities. In *Ideas of difference*, eds. K. Hetherington and R. Munro. Oxford: Blackwell.

Parker, M. 2003. Introduction: Ethics, politics and organizing. *Organization* 10 (2): 187–203.

Parker, M., M. Higgins, G. Lightfoot, and W. Smith (eds.) 1999. Special issue: Amazing tales: Organization studies as science fiction. *Organization* 6 (4): 579–692.

Peperzak, A. 1978. Inleiding en verklarende noten. In *Het menselijk gelaat*, ed. E. Levinas. Baarn: Ambo.

Peperzak, A. 1997. *Beyond the philosophy of Emmanuel Levinas*. Evanston, IL: Northwestern University Press.

Peters, T. 1988. *Thriving on chaos; Handbook for a management revolution*. London: Macmillan.

Peters, T., and R. Waterman. 1982. *Search of excellence; Lessons from America's best-run companies*. New York, NY: Harper & Row.

Pettigrew, A. 1987. Context and action in the transformation of the firm. *Journal of Management Studies* 24 (6): 649–670.

Pettigrew, A. 1988. *The management of strategic change*. Oxford: Blackwell.

Pettigrew, A., R. Woodman, and K. Cameron. 2001. Studying organizational change and development: Challenges for future research. *Academy of Management Journal* 44 (4): 697–713.

Pfeffer, J. 1993. Barriers to the advance of organizational science: Paradigm development as a dependent variable. *Academy of Management Review* 18 (4): 599–620.

Poirié, F. 1987. *Emmanuel Lévinas. Qui êtes-vous?* Lyon: La Manufacture.

Putnam, H. 2002. Levinas and judaism. In *The Cambridge companion to Levinas*, eds. S. Critchley and R. Bernasconi. Cambridge: Cambridge University Press.

Räisänen, C., and A. Linde. 2004. Technologizing discourse to standardize projects in multi-project organizations: Hegemony by consensus? *Organization* 11 (1): 101–121.

Reason, P. 2003. Action research and the single case. *Concepts and Transformations* 8 (3): 281–294.

Reason, P., and W. Torbert. 2001. The action turn. Toward a transformational social science. *Concepts and Transformations* 6 (1): 1–37.

Rhodes, C. 2000. Reading and writing organizational lives. *Organization* 7 (1): 7–29.

Richmond, S. 1995. Deconstruction. Entry. In *The Oxford companion to philosophy*, ed. T. Honderich. Oxford: Oxford University Press.

Roberts, J. 2003. The manufacture of corporate social responsibility: Constructing corporate sensibility. *Organization* 10 (2): 249–265.

Rorty, R. 1996. *Solidariteit of objectiviteit. Drie filosofische essays*. Meppel: Boom.

Safranski, R. 1995. *Heidegger en zijn tijd*. Amsterdam: Atlas. (trans: Wildschut, M.). Originally: (1994): *Ein Meister aus Deutschland. Heidegger und seine Zeit*.

Scarbrough, H. 2002. BPR: RIP? *Organization* 9 (1): 179–181.

Schneider, S. 1999. Human and inhuman resource management: Sense and nonsense. *Organization* 6 (2): 277–284.

Scott, W.R. 1981. *Organizations; Rational, natural, and open systems*. Englewood Cliffs, NJ: Prentice-Hall.

Scott-Morgan, P., E. Hoving, H. Smit, and A. van der Slot. 2001. *Het einde van de veranderingsmythe*. Amsterdam: Pearson Education.

Senge, P. e. a. 2000. *De dans der Verandering*. Schoonhoven: Academic Service.

Shotter, J. 1998. An organization's internal public sphere: Its nature and its supplementation. In *The end of organization theory*, ed. Ø. Pålshaugen. Amsterdam/Philadelphia: John Benjamins Publishing Company.

Shotter, J. 2000. Wittgenstein and his philosophy of beginnings and beginnings and beginnings. *Concepts and Transformation* 5 (3): 349–362. Amsterdam/Philadelphia: John Benjamins Publishing Company.

Shotter, J. 2004. Expressing and legitimating 'actionable knowledge' from within 'the moment of acting'. *Concepts and Transformations* 9 (2): 205–229.

Shotter, J., and J. Lannamann. 2002. The situation of social constructionism; Its 'imprisonment' within the ritual of theory-criticism-and-debate. *Theory and Psychology* 12 (5): 577–609.

Sichtman, S. 2005. *Het eerste Nationaal Onderzoek Verandermanagement.* Amsterdam: InterMaat.

Smith, D. 2001. Organizations and humiliation: Looking beyond Elias. *Organization* 8 (3): 537–560.

Spoelstra, S. 2004. In de naam van kritiek. *Filosofie in Bedrijf* 16 (2, 3): 4–15.

Steyaert, C., and M. Janssens. 1999. Human and inhuman resource management: Saving the subject of HRM. *Organization* 6 (2): 181–198.

Steyaert, C., and M. Janssens (eds.) 1999. Special issue on HRM. *Organization* 6 (2): 179–383.

Sturdy, A. 2003. Knowing the unknowable? A discussion of methodological and theoretical issues in emotion research and organizational studies. *Organization* 10 (1): 81–105.

Sturdy, A., and Ch. Grey. 2003. Beneath and beyond organizational change management: Exploring alternatives. *Organization* 10 (4): 651–662.

Taylor, C. 1995. *Philosophical arguments.* Cambridge, MA: Harvard University Press.

Ten Bos, R. 1997. Business ethics and Bauman ethics. *Organization Studies* 18 (6): 997–1014.

Ten Bos, R. 1999. Kruimels voor Lazarus. In *Managementwijzer: Filosofie en management*, 16–20. Noordwijk: De Baak Management Centrum VNO.

Ten Bos, R. 2000. *Fashion and Utopia in management thinking.* Tilburg: Proefschrift Katholieke Universiteit Brabant.

Ten Bos, R. 2002. Leuteraars of niet? In *Het Financieele Dagblad*, 20. 31 Aug 2002.

Ten Bos, R. 2004a. Arbeid: Spasme of geste. In *Arbeid, tijd en flexibiliteit*, eds. A. Witteveen, T. Korver, and H. Achterhuis. Schiedam: Scriptum.

Ten Bos, R. 2004b. Spookrijders: Een reflectie over de onschuld van desorganisatie. *Filosofie in Bedrijf* 16 (1): 3–20.

Ten Bos, R., and R. Kaulingfreks. 2001. *De hygiënemachine.* Kampen: Agora.

Ten Bos, R., and C. Rhodes. 2003. The game of exemplarity: Subjectivity, work and the impossible politics of purity. *Scandinavian Journal of Management* 19: 403–423.

Ten Bos, R., and H. Willmott. 2001. Towards a post-dualistic business ethics: Interweaving reason and emotion in working life. *Journal of Management Studies* 38 (6): 769–793.

Toulmin, S. 1990. *Cosmopolis; The hidden agenda of modernity.* New York, NY: The Free Press.

Toulmin, S. 2001. *Terug naar de rede.* Kampen: Agora.

Toulmin, S., and B. Gustavsen. 1996. *Beyond theory; Changing organizations through participation.* Amsterdam: John Benjamins Publishing Company.

Townley, B. 1993. Foucault, power/knowledge, and its relevance for human resource management. *Academy of Management Review* 18: 518–545.

Townley, B., D. Cooper, and L. Oakes. 2003. Performance measures and the rationalization of organizations. *Organization Studies* 24 (7): 1045–1071.

Tsoukas, H. 1996. The firm as a distributed knowledge system: A constructonist approach. *Strategic Management Journal* 17: 11–26.

Van de Ven, A., and M. Poole. 1995. Explaining development and change in organizations. *Academy of Management Review* 20 (3): 510–540.

Van der Ven, N. 2001. Bauman, Levinas en de bedrijfsethiek. *Filosofie in Bedrijf* 13 (4): 26–37.

Van Riessen, R. 1991. *Erotiek en dood met het oog op transcendentie in de filosofie van Levinas.* Kampen: Kok Agora.

Van Riessen, R. 1995. Ethiek zonder grond: de representatiecrisis bij Lyotard en Levinas. In *Als woorden niets meer zeggen. . .De crisis rond woord en beeld in de huidige cultuur*, eds. I. Bulhof and R. van Riessen. Kampen: Kok Agora.

Veghel, H. van. 2003. Schaamte, schroom en eerbied in relatie tot het heilige. *Speling* 55 (3): 9–14.

Vetlesen, A. 1994. *Perception, empathy and judgment. An inquiry into the preconditions of moral performance*. University Park (PE.): Pennsylvania State University Press.

Visker, R. 2005. *Vreemd gaan en vreemd blijven*. Amsterdam: SUN.

Waldenfels, B. 2002. Levinas and the face of the other. In *The Cambridge companion to Levinas*, eds. S. Critchley and R. Bernasconi. Cambridge: Cambridge University Press.

Weick, K. 1989. Theory construction as disciplined imagination. *Academy of Management Review* 14 (4): 516–531.

Weick, K. 2003. Theory and practice in the real world. In *The Oxford handbook of organization theory*, eds. H. Tsoukas and C. Knudsen, 453–475. Oxford: Oxford University Press.

Weick, K.E. 2004. Mundane poetics: Searching for wisdom in organization studies. *Organization Studies* 25 (4): 653–668.

Weick, K., and R. Quinn. 2004. Organizational change and development. In *Dynamics of organizational change and learning*, ed. J. Boonstra. Chichester: Wiley.

Weiskopf, R., and H. Willmott. 1999. The organization of thought. *Organization* 6 (3): 559–571.

Willmott, H. 1993. Strength is ignorance; Slavery is freedom: Managing culture in modern organizations. *Journal of Management Studies* 30 (4): 515–552.

Winograd, T., and F. Flores. 1986. *Understanding computers and cognition*. Norwood, NJ: Ablex Publishing Corporation.

Witteveen, A. 2004. Van de redactie. *Filosofie in Bedrijf* 16 (4): 2.

Wittgenstein, L. 1961. *Tractatus logico-philosophicus*. London: Routledge.

Wood, M. 2002. Mind the gap? A processual reconsideration of organizational knowledge. *Organization* 9 (1): 151–171.

Wyschogrod, E. 2002. Language and alterity in the thought of Levinas. In *The Cambridge companion to Levinas*, eds. S. Critchley and R. Bernasconi. Cambridge: Cambridge University Press.

Index